TEACHER'S GUIDE

GRADE 9

READING AND WRITING Sourcebook

Authors

Robert Pavlik

Richard G. Ramsey

Great Source Education Group

a Houghton Mifflin Company
Wilmington, Massachusetts
www.greatsource.com

Authors

Dr. Richard G. Ramsey is currently a national educational consultant for many schools throughout the country and serves as president of Ramsey's Communications. He has been a teacher and a principal for grades 1–12 for 23 years. Dr. Ramsey has also served on the Curriculum Frameworks Committee for the State of Florida. A lifelong teacher and educator and former principal, he is now a nationally known speaker on improving student achievement and motivating students.

Dr. Robert Pavlik taught high school English and reading for seven years. His university assignments in Colorado and Wisconsin have included teaching secondary/content area reading, chairing a reading/language arts department, and directing a reading/learning center. He is an author of several books and articles and serves as director of the School Design and Development Center at Marquette University.

CONSULTANT Catherine McNary of Proviso West High School in Illinois is a reading specialist who works with teachers of struggling readers. She has been an invaluable consultant during the development of the *Sourcebook* series. She is currently pursuing a doctorate in reading.

Great Source® is a registered trademark of Houghton Mifflin Company.

Printed in the United States of America.

International Standard Book Number: 0-669-47138-0

1 2 3 4 5 6 7 8 9 10   06 05 04 03 02 01 00

Readers and Reviewers

Marsha Besch
Literacy/Secondary Curr. Coordinator ISD #196
Rosemount, Minnesota

Tim McGee
Worland High School
Worland, Wyoming

Mary Grace
Marshall Middle School
Janesville, Wisconsin

Shelly L. Fabozzi
Holmes Middle School
Colorado Springs, Colorado

Jim Burke
Burlingame High School
San Francisco, California

Phyllis Y. Keiley-Tyler
Education Consultant
Seattle, Washington

Jenny Sroka
Learning Enterprise High School
Milwaukee, Wisconsin

Glenda Swirtz
Flint Southwestern Academy
Flint, Michigan

Jeff Wallack
Learning Enterprise High School
Milwaukee, Wisconsin

Jay Amberg
Glenbrook South High School
Glenview, Illinois

Sherry Nielsen
Curriculum and Instruction
Saint Cloud, Minnesota

Deborah Schroeder
Harlan Community Academy
Chicago, Illinois

Richard Stear
Central Office
Rochester, New York

Hilary Zunin
Napa High School
Napa, California

William Weber
Libertyville High School
Libertyville, Illinois

Beverly Washington
Fenger High School
Chicago, Illinois

Lyla Fox
Loy Norrix High School
Kalamazoo, Michigan

Eileen Davis
Banneker Academic High School
Washington, D.C.

Christine Heerlein
Rockwood Summit High School
Fenton, Missouri

Barbara Ellen Pitts
Detroit, Michigan

Kimberly Edgeworth
Palm Beach Lakes High School
West Palm Beach, Florida

Jeffrey Hicks
Whitford Middle School
Beaverton, Oregon

Mark Tavernier
Norfolk, Virginia

Gina La Manna
Southeast Raleigh High School
Raleigh, North Carolina

Jennifer Sharpe-Salter
Southern Nash Sr. High School
Bailey, North Carolina

Elizabeth Dyhouse
Longfellow Middle School
Flint, Michigan

Rose Chatman
Dayton Public Schools
Dayton, Ohio

Gereldine Conaway
Mumford High School
Detroit, Michigan

Barb Evans
Lorain City Schools
Lorain, Ohio

Deborah Gonzalez
Puget Sound Education School District
Burien, Washington

Rosita Graham
Winter Halter Elementary School
Detroit, Michigan

Elaine Hanson
Mounds View School District
Saint Paul, Minnesota

Barbara Heget
Milwaukee, Wisconsin

Patrick Horigan
Milwaukee, Wisconsin

Rose Hunter
Whittier Middle School
Flint, Michigan

Ray Kress
Wilson Middle School
Newark, Ohio

Evelyn McDuffie
Beaubien Middle School
Detroit, Michigan

Robin Milanovich
Jefferson High School
Edgewater, Colorado

Dr. Howard Moon
Kenosha School District
Kenosha, Wisconsin

Jeanette Nassif
Central High School
Flint, Michigan

Dr. Joe Papenfuss
Racine Unified School District
Racine, Wisconsin

Lori Pfeiffer
West Bend School District
West Bend, Wisconsin

Evelyn Price
Milwaukee, Wisconsin

Karen Rano
Educational Consultant
River Forest, Illinois

Karen Ray
Darwin Elementary School
Chicago, Illinois

Renetha Rumph
Flint Southwestern High School
Flint, Michigan

Sarike Simpson
Racine, Wisconsin

Branka Skukan
Chopin School
Chicago, Illinois

Stephanie Thurick
Minneapolis Public Schools
Minneapolis, Minnesota

Gloria Tibbets
Curriculum Institute
Flint, Michigan

Anita Wellman
Northwestern High School
Detroit, Michigan

Barb Whaley
Akron City Schools
Akron, Ohio

Ray Wolpow
Western Washington University
Bellingham, Washington

Robin Gleason
Wilson Elementary School
Wauwatosa, Wisconsin

Kay Briske
Janesville School District
Janesville, Wisconsin

Table of Contents

Table of Contents

Lesson Resources

PUPIL'S EDITION SKILLS AND STRATEGIES

The chart below identifies the strategies for each part of each pupil's edition lesson.

Selection	I. Prereading	II. Response Notes	Comprehension	III. Prewriting
1. The Good Daughter (essay)	quickwrite	question	directed reading	narrowing a topic
2. **Bridges** (autobiography)	think-pair-and-share	mark and highlight	directed reading	group discussion
3. **Pilots' Reflections** (nonfiction)	skimming	question	retelling	main idea and details
4. **Adventures of the U-202** (nonfiction)	K-W-L	question/clarify	prediction	topic sentence and details
5. **you're being so good, so kind** (fiction)	walk-through	question	double-entry journal	character cluster
6. **Maud Martha and New York** (fiction)	read-aloud	react and connect/ visualize	directed reading	draw a place
7. **Legal Alien** (poem) **Immigrants** (poem)	picture walk	react and connect	double-entry journal	brainstorm/web
8. **A Simple Proposition** (fiction)	anticipation guide	clarify	plot chart	group discussion
9. **The Cyclops' Cave** (myth)	preview	clarify	predict/story frame	storyboard
10. **Hercules** (myth)	think-pair-and-share	mark and highlight	graphic organizer/ directed reading	clustering
11. **The Richer, the Poorer** (story)	compare/contrast chart	predict/question	directed reading	organize details
12. **The Richer, the Poorer**, continued	anticipation guide	react and connect	double-entry journal	theme and details
13. **Animals Unite!** (fiction)	prediction guide	clarify/question	directed reading	graphic organizer
14. **The Fast** (autobiography)	quickwrite	clarify/react and connect	story frame/ directed reading	group discussion
15. **A Sea of Dunes** (nonfiction)	picture walk	question	graphic organizer	main idea and details
16. **The Widows of the Reserves** (nonfiction)	think-pair-and-share	mark and highlight	directed reading	compare and contrast
17. **Ramiro** (autobiography)	walk-through	react and connect	directed reading	narrowing a topic
18. **Ramiro**, continued	preview	predict/visualize	reciprocal reading	graphic organizer
19. **Refusing Service** (autobiography)	anticipation guide	question	story frame	fact and opinion
20. **Time to Look and Listen** (essay)	skimming	react and connect	graphic organizer	supporting an opinion
21. **A Soldier's Letter Home** (letter)	K-W-L	mark and highlight/ question	directed reading	clustering
22. **Good-bye** (autobiography)	picture walk	predict/clarify	predict	brainstorm
23. **Harrison Bergeron** (story)	word web	visualize/react and connect	double-entry journal	main idea and details
24. **The Kid Nobody Could Handle** (story)	think-pair-and-share	question/predict	reciprocal reading	story map

IV. Writing	Grammar/Usage	V. Assessment
paragraph	capitalizing sentences and end punctuation	understanding
personal experience paragraph	sentence fragments	meaning
letter	greetings and closings of letters	ease
summary	capitalizing names	enjoyment
descriptive paragraph	run-on sentences	depth
descriptive paragraph	comma splices	style
poem	capitalizing proper nouns	meaning
review	capitalizing place names	understanding
story	using consistent verb tense	enjoyment
descriptive paragraph	subject-verb agreement	ease
compare and contrast paragraph	using commas in a series and in compound sentences	style
expository paragraph	using commas to set off adverbs and parenthetical expressions	depth
descriptive paragraph	comparative adjectives and irregular comparisons	understanding
journal entry	apostrophes in contractions	meaning
summary	capitalizing names of places, languages, groups	ease
article	commas with two adjectives and transitional words	depth
autobiographical paragraph	commas in dates and with appositives	style
character description	commas with introductory words and quotations	depth
opinion paragraph	capitalizing initial word in sentence and quotation	meaning
article of opinion	apostrophes with possessives	understanding
letter	subject-verb agreement	depth
journal entry	confusing word pairs	style
3-paragraph essay	punctuating and italicizing titles of works	enjoyment
story episode	end punctuation	ease

TEACHER'S GUIDE SKILLS AND STRATEGIES

The chart below identifies the strategies for each part of each teacher's edition lesson.

Selection	Vocab	Prereading	Comprehension
1. **The Good Daughter** (essay)	prefixes	a) quickwrite b) picture walk	a) directed reading b) graphic organizer
2. **Bridges** (autobiography)	context clues	a) think-pair-and-share b) quickwrite	a) directed reading b) graphic organizer
3. **Pilots' Reflections** (nonfiction)	prefixes	a) skim b) preview	retelling
4. **Adventures of the U-202** (nonfiction)	suffixes	a) K-W-L b) quickwrite	a) predicting b) graphic organizer
5. **you're being so good, so kind** (fiction)	negative prefixes	a) walk-through b) quickwrite	a) double-entry journal b) reciprocal reading
6. **Maud Martha and New York** (fiction)	context clues	a) read-aloud b) picture walk	a) directed reading b) double-entry journal
7. **Legal Alien, Immigrants** (poems)	context clues	a) picture-walk b) quickwrite	a) double-entry journal b) graphic organizer
8. **A Simple Proposition** (fiction)	prefixes	a) anticipation guide b) picture walk	a) plot chart b) directed reading
9. **The Cyclops' Cave** (myth)	prefixes	a) preview b) picture walk	a) predictions b) story frame
10. **Hercules** (myth)	Greek and Latin roots	a) think-pair-and-share b) K-W-L	a) character organizer b) reciprocal reading
11. **The Richer, the Poorer** (story)	synonyms	a) compare and contrast b) read-aloud	a) directed reading b) double-entry journal
12. **The Richer, the Poorer**, continued	antonyms	a) anticipation guide b) K-W-L	a) double-entry journal b) retelling
13. **Animals Unite!** (fiction)	homographs	a) prediction guide b) read-aloud	directed reading
14. **The Fast** (autobiography)	homophones	quickwrite	a) story frame b) reciprocal reading
15. **A Sea of Dunes** (nonfiction)	prefixes	picture walk	a) graphic organizer b) directed reading
16. **The Widows of the Reserves** (nonfiction)	suffixes	a) think-pair-and-share b) prediction	directed reading
17. **Ramiro** (autobiography)	prefixes	walk-through	a) directed reading b) sequence chart
18. **Ramiro** continued	suffixes	a) preview card b) retelling	a) reciprocal reading b) sequence organizer
19. **Refusing Service** (autobiography)	Latin and Greek word parts	anticipation guide	a) story frame b) directed reading
20. **Time to Look and Listen** (essay)	Greek prefixes and suffixes	a) skimming b) read-aloud	graphic organizers
21. **A Soldier's Letter Home** (letter)	roots	K-W-L	a) directed reading b) double-entry journal
22. **Good-bye** (autobiography)	Latin roots	a) picture walk b) anticipation guide	a) predictions b) graphic organizer
23. **Harrison Bergeron** (story)	prefixes	a) word web b) picture walk	a) double-entry journal b) retelling
24. **The Kid Nobody Could Handle** (story)	suffixes	a) think-pair-and-share b) quickwrite	a) reciprocal reading b) double-entry journal

Questions	Literary Skill	Prewriting	Assessment
a) comprehension b) critical thinking	point of view	narrowing a topic	multiple-choice test
a) comprehension b) critical thinking	theme	group discussion	multiple-choice test
a) comprehension b) critical thinking	tone	a) main idea and details b) group discussion	multiple-choice test
a) comprehension b) critical thinking	style	a) topic sentence and details b) storyboard	multiple-choice test
a) comprehension b) critical thinking	theme	a) character cluster b) topic sentences	multiple-choice test
a) comprehension b) critical thinking	a) imagery b) style	a) draw a place b) web	multiple-choice test
a) comprehension b) critical thinking	free verse	brainstorm	multiple-choice test
a) comprehension b) critical thinking	plot line	a) group discussion b) topic sentences	multiple-choice test
a) comprehension b) critical thinking	plot	a) storyboard b) Venn diagram	multiple-choice test
a) comprehension b) critical thinking	characterization	a) clustering b) group discussion	multiple-choice test
a) comprehension b) critical thinking	irony	a) organize details b) Venn diagram	multiple-choice test
a) comprehension b) critical thinking	character development	a) theme and details b) sequencing	multiple-choice test
a) comprehension b) critical thinking	satire	a) graphic organizer b) word web	multiple-choice test
a) comprehension b) critical thinking	autobiography	a) group discussion b) character cluster	multiple-choice test
a) comprehension b) critical thinking	metaphor	a) main idea b) gathering details	multiple-choice test
a) comprehension b) critical thinking	tone	a) compare and contrast b) Venn diagram	multiple-choice test
a) comprehension b) critical thinking	flashback	a) narrowing a topic b) story star	multiple-choice test
a) comprehension b) critical thinking	personification	a) graphic organizer b) story frame	multiple-choice test
a) comprehension b) critical thinking	chronological order	a) fact and opinion b) opinion statement	multiple-choice test
a) comprehension b) critical thinking	tone	a) supporting an opinion b) narrowing a topic	multiple-choice test
a) comprehension b) critical thinking	chronological order	a) clustering b) topic sentences	multiple-choice test
a) comprehension b) critical thinking	inference	a) brainstorming b) graphic organizer	multiple-choice test
a) comprehension b) critical thinking	a) simile b) irony	main idea and details	multiple-choice test
a) comprehension b) critical thinking	characterization	a) story map b) quickwrite	multiple-choice test

CORRELATION TO *WRITERS INC* ©2001

Like the *Writers INC* handbook, the *Sourcebook* will appeal to teachers who believe that writing is a way of learning or a means of discovery and exploration. Students pursue ideas and interpretations in the *Sourcebook*. They jot notes, create organizers, plan and brainstorm compositions, and write drafts of their work. The *Sourcebook* is one way students clarify in their minds what they have read and how they respond to it. And, in the end, students learn how to write different kinds of compositions—a paragraph, a description, a letter, a character sketch, a persuasive paragraph, or review.

Students are also invited to revise their compositions in a feature called Writers' Checklist. These features, found in Part IV Writing, highlight two or three critical questions and explain some aspect of grammar, usage, and mechanics. These features are brief mini-lessons. They invite students to look back at their writing and apply some aspect of grammar, usage, or mechanics to it.

In the *Sourcebooks*, both the kinds of writing and the mini-lessons on grammar, usage, and mechanics afford the best opportunities to use the *Writers INC* handbook as a reference. To make this convenient, both the writing activities and the mini-lessons are correlated below to the ©2001 *Writers INC* handbook.

Selection Title	Writing Activity/ Writers INC Reference (pages)	Writers' Mini-Lesson/ Writers INC Reference (pages)
1. The Good Daughter	paragraph 95–104	capitalization 475–477 ending sentences with punctuation 455, 467 complete thoughts 83–85
2. Bridges	personal experience paragraph 98, 147–153	sentence fragments 83
3. Pilots' Reflections	letter 158–159	greetings and closings of letters 298–299 commas in letters 457–461.3 capitalization in letters 475–477
4. Adventures of the U-202	summary 403–404	capitalization 475–477
5. you're being so good, so kind	descriptive paragraph 156–157	run-on sentences 84
6. Maud Martha and New York	descriptive paragraph 156–157	comma splices 84
7. Legal Alien *and* Immigrants	poems 179–184	capitalization 475–477
8. A Simple Proposition	review 222–223	capitalization 475–477
9. The Cyclops' Cave	short story 168–172	verb tenses 507–512
10. Hercules	character description 105–114	subject-verb agreement 526–527
11. The Richer, the Poorer	compare and contrast paragraph 202–204	commas 457–461.3
12. The Richer, the Poorer, cont.	expository paragraph 140, 241	commas 457–461.3
13. Animals Unite!	descriptive paragraph 156–157	adjectives 513
14. The Fast	journal entry 144–146	apostrophes 472–473

Selection Title	Writing Activity/ Writers INC Reference (pages)	Writers' Mini-Lesson/ Writers INC Reference (pages)
15. A Sea of Dunes	summary 403–404	capitalization of ethnic groups and languages 475, 476.5
		capitalization of specific places 475
16. The Widows of the Reserves	article 105–113	commas 457–461.3
17. Ramiro	autobiographical paragraph 152–153	commas in dates and places 460.1–460.2 commas around explanatory phrases 458.1
18. Ramiro, cont.	character description 156–157	commas to set off introductory phrases 458.4 commas to set off quotations 460.3
19. Refusing Service	opinion paragraph 215–220	capitalization 475–477
20. Time to Look and Listen	opinion article 215–220	apostrophes for possession 472.3–472.4
21. A Soldier's Letter Home	letter 215–220	subject-verb agreement 526–527
22. Good-bye	journal entry 143–154	their, there, they're 499 it's, its 496
23. Harrison Bergeron	three-paragraph essay 227–232	titles 468.1, 470.2
24. The Kid Nobody Could Handle	story episode 167–172	end punctuation 455.1, 467

OVERVIEW

The *Sourcebook* is directed to struggling readers. These students seldom receive adequate help, partly because they need so much. They need to be motivated. They need quality literature that they can actually read. They need good instruction in strategies that will help them learn how to transform a mass of words and lines into a comprehensible text. They need help with getting ready to write; with grammar, usage, and mechanics; and with writing different kinds of texts themselves—letters, journal entries, summaries, and so forth.

A Comprehensive Approach

Because of the multitude and enormity of their needs, struggling readers all too often are subjected to a barrage of different remedies. It is all too easy simply to say "This doesn't work" and turn to yet another text or strategy. The *Sourcebook* takes a holistic approach, not a piecemeal one. Through a five-part lesson plan, each *Sourcebook* lesson walks the student through the steps needed to read actively and to write well about literature.

The five-part lesson plan is:

I. **BEFORE YOU READ** (prereading)

II. **READ** (active reading and responding to literature)

III. **GATHER YOUR THOUGHTS** (prewriting)

IV. **WRITE** (writing, revising, grammar, usage, and mechanics)

V. **WRAP-UP** (reflecting and self-assessment)

Through a comprehensive, structured approach, students can see the whole process of reading and writing. By following a consistent pattern, students can internalize the steps in the process, and they can move forward and experience success along the way, on a number of different fronts at once. See also the book and lesson organization on pages 18–22.

A Strategy-Intensive Approach

The *Sourcebook* also is a strategy-intensive approach. Each *Sourcebook* builds students' repertoire of reading strategies in at least three areas.

1. To build motivation and background, prereading strategies are used to get students ready to read and to help them see the prior knowledge they already bring to their reading experiences.

2. To build active readers, each *Sourcebook* begins with an overview of interactive reading strategies (called response strategies), explicitly showing students six ways to mark up texts. Then, at least one of these strategies is used in each lesson.

3. To build comprehension, each *Sourcebook* uses six to nine different comprehension strategies, such as prediction, reciprocal reading, retelling, and using graphic organizers. By embedding these strategies in the literature, the *Sourcebook* shows students exactly which strategies to use and when to use them, building the habits of good readers.

A Literature-Based Approach

Above all, the *Sourcebook* takes a literature-based approach. It presents 24 selections of quality literature of various genres by a wide range of authors. Some selections focus on literature; others are cross-curricular in emphasis, taking up a subject from history or geography; and others focus on issues of importance and relevance to today's students.

An Interactive Approach

The *Sourcebook* is, in addition, an interactive tool. It is intended to be a journal for students, where they can write out their ideas about texts, plan and write out compositions, and record their progress throughout the year. Students should "own" their *Sourcebooks*, carrying them, reading in them, marking in them, and writing in them. They should become a record of their progress and accomplishments.

Lesson Planning

A **Sourcebook** lesson can be taught in approximately 10 class periods, whether that is over two, three, or even four weeks.

DAY 1 Build background and discuss unit theme. Introduce selection.

DAY 2 Read introduction. Start prereading activity.

DAY 3 Continue prereading activity. Discuss activity.

DAY 4 Introduce selection. Discuss response strategy and example. Read.

DAY 5 Finish reading and do comprehension activities in selection.

DAY 6 Start prewriting activities.

DAY 7 Continue with prewriting activities.

DAY 8 Begin writing activity.

DAY 9 Talk about mini-lesson and revise writing.

DAY 10 Reflect on selection and what was learned.

Assessment

The **Sourcebook** includes a multiple-choice test for assessment, as well as a more holistic self-assessment in the pupil's book in Part V. Either of these are useful gauges of student progress. Teachers would, of course, like to demonstrate the progress their students have made—the number of grade levels students have progressed throughout the year. In point of fact, that progress is enormously difficult to demonstrate with any degree of reliability. The best measure of student progress will most likely be a student's marked-up **Sourcebook** and the greater confidence and fluency with which students will be reading by the end of the year.

WHO IS THIS BOOK FOR?

Struggling Learners

Frequently high schools have classes specifically designed for students who consistently rank in the lower 50 percent of the class. Instead of the usual focus on literary masterworks, these classes focus on improving reading and writing skills and often are labeled with anonymous-sounding names such as English I, Applied Communication, or Fundamentals of Reading and Writing. The *Sourcebook* was designed with such courses in mind. It offers a comprehensive program of student-appropriate literature, strategy building, writing, and revising. Quite often teachers in these classes pull an exercise from one text on the shelf, a reading from another, and a blackline master activity from still another. The materials are a patchwork, with the teachers making the best of the meager offerings available.

Each *Sourcebook* has a comprehensive network of skills (see pages 6–9) that brings together the appropriate literature, reading strategies for that literature, and prewriting, writing, and revising activities. Students who work through even two or three entire selections will benefit greatly by seeing the whole picture of reading actively and writing about the text. They will also benefit from the sense of accomplishment that comes through completion of a whole task and that results in creative, original work of their own—perhaps some of the first they have accomplished.

Reading Classes

Students who clearly are reading two or more levels below grade often are put into "special reading" courses. Quite often these classes feature a great number of blackline masters on discrete skills, such as "main idea and details," "analogies," and the like. Such classes are ideal for the *Sourcebook*. Instead of covering one discrete skill, each *Sourcebook* selection offers students reading strategies that they can use on any text, and it offers them high-quality literature. All too often students in reading classes are given "high-interest" materials. The materials have regulated vocabulary and short sentences and are on topics that range from natural disasters to biographies of rock divas. The *Sourcebook* focuses on high-quality literature that is also high interest because it addresses questions and issues of significance to students.

With the *Sourcebook*, a better choice exists. The literature was chosen specifically with struggling readers in mind. It offers compelling subjects, such as the Holocaust and prejudice, and offers a worthy challenge for students.

ESL Classes

Students for whom English is a second language can also benefit from the *Sourcebook*, even though the *Sourcebook* is not an ESL program. The literature selections in the *Sourcebook* vary in difficulty level. The level for each selection is given on the first page of the *Teacher's Guide* lesson. But the subjects of the literature—immigrants, being an outsider, understanding different cultures—are ones that will naturally appeal to ESL students.

In addition, summaries of each selection appear in Spanish in the *Teacher's Guide*, along with additional help with vocabulary and comprehension. So, while not explicitly for ESL students, the program offers good support for them and may be more appropriate than some of the other materials they are currently using.

Alternative Settings

Many school systems also have whole schools or classes that are called "alternative" for students who for a variety of reasons are not mainstreamed. The *Sourcebook* is appropriate for these students as well, if only because of its literature selections, which focus on themes of identity, prejudice, and separateness about which many alternative students will have a natural interest.

Summary

The *Sourcebook* cannot reach every struggling student. It is not a panacea. It will be helpful with struggling readers, especially those who are reading a grade level or two below their academic grade. The challenges struggling readers face, especially those reading more than two grades below their academic grade level, ought not be underestimated or minimized. Reading and writing deficits are hard, almost intractable problems for high school students and require a great amount of effort—on the part of the teacher and the student—to make any real improvement. The *Sourcebook* is one further tool in helping create better readers and writers.

FREQUENTLY ASKED QUESTIONS

Because the *Sourcebooks* were extensively reviewed by teachers, a number of commonly asked questions have surfaced already, and the answers to them might be helpful in using the program.

1. Why is it called a *Sourcebook*?

The word *Sourcebook* captures a number of connotations and associations that seemed just right. For one, it is published by Great Source Education Group. The word *source* also had the right connotation of "the place to go for a real, complete solution," as opposed to other products that help in only a limited area, such as "main idea" or "analogies." And, lastly, the term *Sourcebook* fits nicely alongside *Daybook*, another series also published by Great Source that targets better readers and writers who need help in fluency and critical reading, as opposed to this series, which targets struggling readers.

2. Can students write in the *Sourcebook*?

Absolutely. Only by physically marking the text will students become truly active readers. To interact with a text and truly read as an active reader, students *must* write in the *Sourcebook*. The immediacy of reading and responding right there on the page is integral to the whole idea of the *Sourcebook*. By writing in the text, students build a sense of ownership about their work that is impossible to match through worksheets handed out week after week. The *Sourcebook* also serves, in a sense, as the student's portfolio and can become one of the most tangible ways of demonstrating a student's progress throughout the year.

3. Can I photocopy these lessons?

No, you cannot. Each page of the pupil's book carries a notice that explicitly states "copying is prohibited." To copy them illegally infringes on the rights of the authors of the selections and the publishers of the book. Writers such as Dorothy West, Piri Thomas, Walter Dean Myers, and others have granted permission to use their work in the *Sourcebook*, but have not granted the right to copy it.

You can, however, copy the blackline masters in this *Teacher's Guide.* These pages are intended for teachers to photocopy and use in the classroom.

4. Can I skip around in the *Sourcebook*?

Teachers will naturally wish to adjust the *Sourcebook* to their curriculum. But a logical—that is, the optimum—order of the book is laid out in the table of contents. The difficulty of the literary selection, the kind and difficulty of writing assignments, the amount of scaffolding provided for a specific reading strategy—all are predicated on where they occur in the text. Easier assignments and selections, naturally, tend to cluster near the beginning of the *Sourcebook*; in the back half of the book, both the assignments and selections challenge students with more rigorous demands.

5. Where did the strategies used throughout the book come from?

Most of the reading strategies used are commonplace in elementary classrooms throughout the country. They are commonly described in the standard reading education textbooks, as well as at workshops, conferences, and in-services. What is unusual in the *Sourcebook* is the way these strategies have been applied to high school–appropriate literature.

6. Why did you label the strategies with names such as "stop and think" when it is really just directed reading or some other reading technique?

The pupil's edition of the *Sourcebook* uses student-friendly terms, such as "stop and think," "retell," or "stop and record." Throughout, an attempt was made to motivate students, not hammer them with pedagogical terms. Leaden-sounding names for reading strategies (for example, directed reading strategy or reciprocal reading) seemed counterproductive for students, even while being perfectly descriptive to teachers. The same logic explains why such student-friendly titles as "Before You Read" were used instead of "Prereading." In the *Teacher's Guide*, reference is frequently made to the more formal pedagogical term (directed reading) alongside the friendlier student term (stop and think).

7. **Has anyone told you that the *Sourcebook* doesn't follow the textbook definition of a number of strategies?**

Yes, absolutely. Teachers who reviewed the **Sourcebooks** were quick to mention that "textbook" definitions and application of strategies were not followed. One clear example is reciprocal reading. It is an intervention strategy where a reading partner or teacher works with a student to clarify, question, predict, and summarize; but the **Sourcebook** is a text, not a walking-and-breathing reading tutor. As a result, the questioning strategy of reciprocal reading is employed in the **Sourcebook**, with full knowledge that the technique cannot be perfectly replicated using a book. Yet the force of these strategies seemed too potent simply to discard, so, like any good teacher, the **Sourcebook** authors adapted a strategy to fit their particular needs.

8. **How were the selections chosen and what is their readability?**

The decision to use "real" or "quality" literature by well-known authors was, in fact, made by teachers. They selected the authors they wanted to use with their students. They insisted that the quality and force of the literature itself—not its readability—become the primary selection criteria for the literature. Especially when a selection would become the focal point of an extended lesson, the literature had to be primary. "If my students are going to spend several days on a lesson, the literature needs to be worth spending time and attention on it," one early reviewer said.

Plus, they insisted that their struggling readers be challenged. Among teachers of struggling readers, a consistent appeal was that the literature challenge their students, yet also give them lots of support. Challenge and support were the watchwords that guided the development of the **Sourcebook** program. Choosing high-quality literature was the first consideration; secondarily, the syntactical difficulty, sentence length, and vocabulary level were also considered.

9. **How can I know if my students can read this literature?**

Teachers have a number of ways to know how well their students can read the selections. For one, they can simply try out a lesson or two.

Second, teachers can also use a 20- or 30-word vocabulary pretest as a quick indicator. For each selection, select 20 words randomly from a selection. Ask students to circle the ones they know and underline the ones they don't know. If students know only one to five or six to nine words, then the selection will probably be frustrating for them. Spend some time preteaching the key vocabulary.

10. **What if my students need even more help than what's in the book?**

This *Teacher's Guide* has been designed as the next level of support. Extra activities and blackline masters on vocabulary, comprehension, prewriting, and assessment are included here so that they can be used at the teacher's discretion. Parts of each lesson could have been scaffolded for five to ten more pages, but at a certain point more worksheets and more explanation become counterproductive. Teachers advised the authors again and again to give students worthwhile literature and activities and let the students work at them. Students' work will not be perfect, but, with the right tools, students will make progress.

ORGANIZATION

Book Organization

Each **Sourcebook** has 24 selections organized into three general categories:

1. Contemporary Issues

2. Cross-curricular Subjects

3. Literature

The purpose of this organization is to provide selections that are relevant and purposeful in students' lives. By pairing two selections together, students can take the time to build extended background on a topic or idea (for example, identity, the Holocaust), building upon knowledge they learned in earlier selections. Each of the 12 units in the **Sourcebook** is introduced by an opener that helps teachers build background on the subject. Ways to teach and introduce each opener are included in the **Teacher's Guide**.

Lesson Organization

Each lesson in the **Sourcebook** has five parts:

I. Before You Read

- Each lesson begins with **I. Before You Read** to emphasize to students how important prereading is. The lesson starts with an introductory statement that draws students into the lesson, often by asking a provocative question or making a strong statement.

- The prereading step—the critical first step—builds background and helps students access prior knowledge. Among the prereading strategies (see page 6) included in Part I of this **Sourcebook** are:

- Think-Pair-and-Share

- K-W-L

- Anticipation Guide

- Preview or Walk-through

- Skimming

- Picture Walk

- Quickwrite

- Word Web

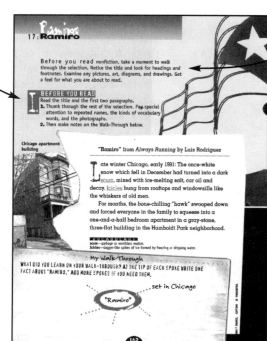

II. Read

- The reading step, called **II. Read,** begins with an invitation to read and suggestions for how to respond to the literature and mark up the text. An example is provided.

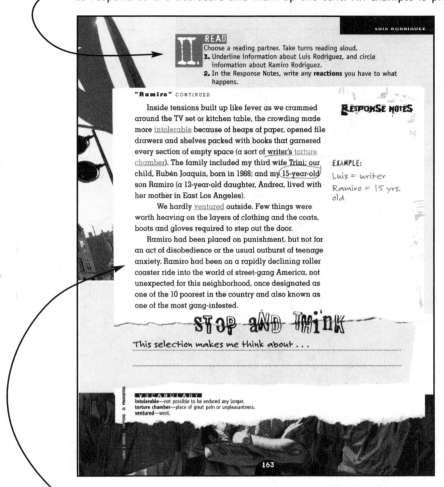

- The selection follows, with the difficult vocabulary highlighted throughout the selection and defined at the bottom of the page.

- Then, within the selection, a powerful comprehension strategy is embedded to help build in students the habits of good readers. Among the comprehension strategies included (see also page 50 in Part II of this **Sourcebook**) are these:

- Predict

- Stop and Think (directed reading)

- Stop and Clarify, Question, Predict (reciprocal reading)

- Storyboard (using graphic organizers)

- Double-entry Journal

- Retelling

- Story Frame

III. Gather Your Thoughts

- The prewriting step is called **III. Gather Your Thoughts**. It starts with the literature selection. Through two or three carefully sequenced activities, the prewriting step helps students go back into the literature in preparation for writing about it.

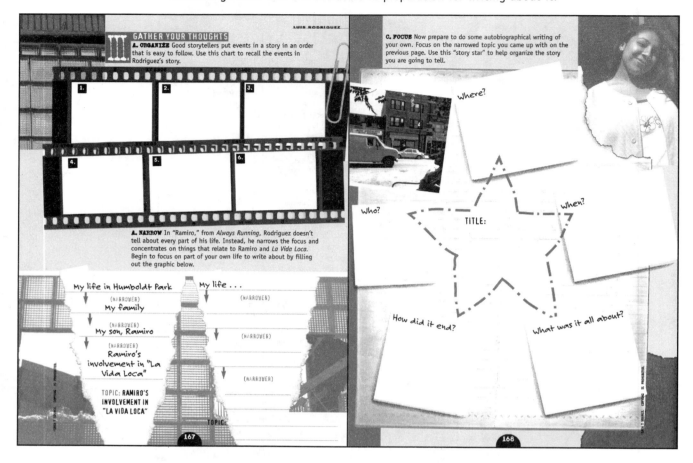

Among the more common prewriting activities are these:

- Character Map
- Main Idea and Supporting Details
- Brainstorming
- Building a Topic Sentence
- Forming an Opinion
- Supporting a Main Idea

IV. Write

- The writing step begins with step-by-step instructions for building a writing assignment. Taken together, these instructions form the writing rubric for students to use in building the assignment. Among the writing assignments students are asked to write are these:

- Paragraph with topic sentence and supporting details

- Narrative paragraph

- Expository paragraph

- Compare and contrast paragraph

- Paragraph of reflection

- Autobiographical paragraph

- Journal entry

- Story

- Character sketch

  See page 7 for a full list.

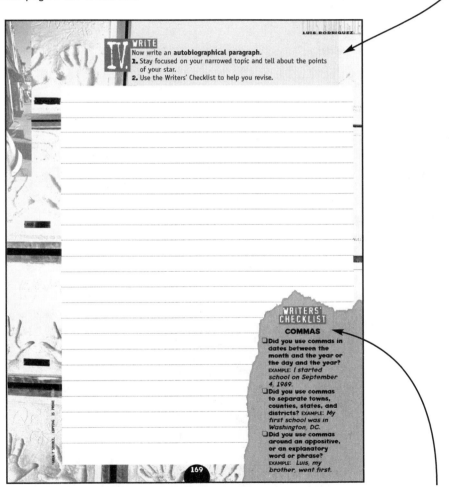

- Each **IV. Write** also includes a **Writers' Checklist**. Each one is a brief mini-lesson on a relevant aspect of grammar, usage, or mechanics. The intent of the **Writers' Checklist** is to ask of the students appropriate questions after they write, instilling the habit of going back to revise, edit, and proof their work. The **Writers' Checklist** also affords teachers the opportunity to teach relevant grammar, usage, and mechanics skills at a teachable moment.

V. Wrap-up

- The last step of each lesson is to reflect. Students are asked a question about their reading and writing experience from the **Readers' Checklist**. This "looking back" is intended to help students see what they learned in the lesson. They are intentionally asked more than simply, "Did you understand?"

- For good readers, reading is much, much more than "Did you get it?" Good readers read for pleasure, for information, for the pure enjoyment of reading artfully written material, for personal curiosity, for a desire to learn more, and countless other reasons. So that students will begin to see that reading is worthwhile to them, they need to believe the payoff is more than "Did you get it?" on a five-question multiple-choice test.

- The **Sourcebook** attempts with **V. Wrap-up** to help students ask the questions good readers ask of themselves when they read. It attempts to broaden the reasons for reading by asking students to consider six reasons for reading:

- Meaning

- Enjoyment

- Understanding

- Style

- Ease

- Depth

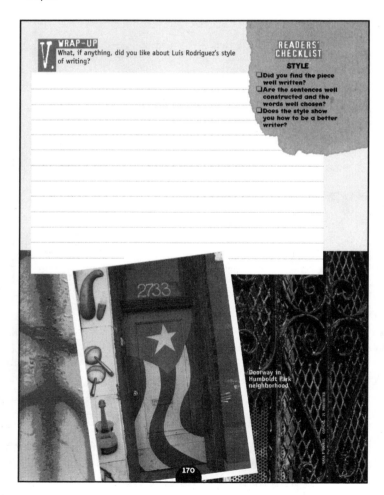

Organization

TEACHER'S LESSON PLANS

Each lesson plan for the teacher of the *Sourcebook* has eight pages:

PAGE 1 Overview and Background

- The chart at the beginning of each lesson plan gives an "at-a-glance" view of the skills and strategies, plus the difficulty level of the reading and five key vocabulary words.

- Background on the author and selection and a graphic are included.

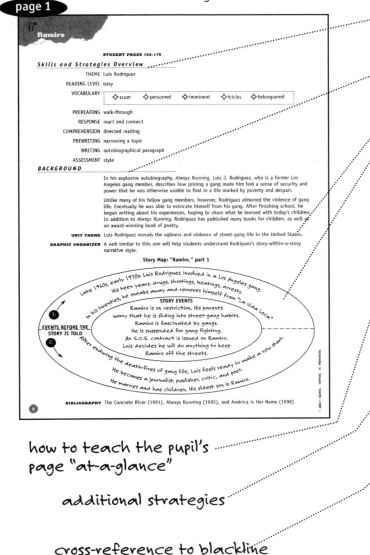

overview chart

additional background

tie-in to theme

model graphic organizer

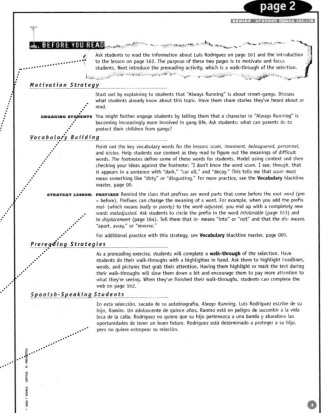

how to teach the pupil's page "at-a-glance"

additional strategies

cross-reference to blackline master

selection summary in Spanish

PAGE 2 Before You Read

- The first page of the teacher's plan begins with a motivation strategy and a suggestion for vocabulary building. Additional prereading strategies are suggested, along with a summary of the selection in Spanish.

Each lesson plan in the *Sourcebook Teacher's Guide* follows the pupil's lesson step-by-step.

PAGE 3 **Read**

- The response strategy gives students one way to interact with the text as they read.

- Additional comprehension strategies are suggested, along with a *Comprehension* blackline master found later in the lesson.

- The discussion questions cover both literal and interpretative levels of thinking.

- A literary skill is suggested for each selection, allowing teachers to build literary appreciation as they provide basic support with reading comprehension.

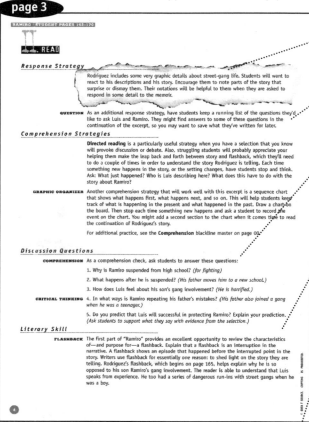

how to teach the pupil's page "at-a-glance"

interactive reading (or response) strategy

additional help with comprehension

discussion questions and literary skill

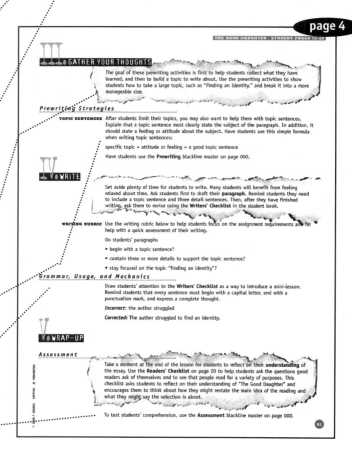

how to teach the pupil's page "at-a-glance"

additional prewriting strategies

mini-lesson on grammar, usage, and mechanics

two forms of assessment—Readers' Checklist and test

PAGE 4 **Gather Your Thoughts, Write, Wrap-up**

- The page begins with additional help with prewriting and references another blackline master that offers additional support.

- Next, the students write and are directed to the **Writers' Checklist** in the pupil's book, which gives the grammar, usage, and mechanics mini-lesson.

- The writing rubric gives teachers a way to evaluate students' writing.

- The lesson ends with reference to the **Readers' Checklist** in the pupil's book, encourages students to reflect on what they have read, and cross-references the **Assessment** blackline master.

Each lesson plan in the *Sourcebook Teacher's Guide* has four blackline masters for additional levels of support for key skill areas.

PAGE 5 Vocabulary

- Each **Vocabulary** blackline master helps students learn the meanings of five words from the literature selection and focuses on an important vocabulary strategy, such as understanding prefixes, root words, and word families.

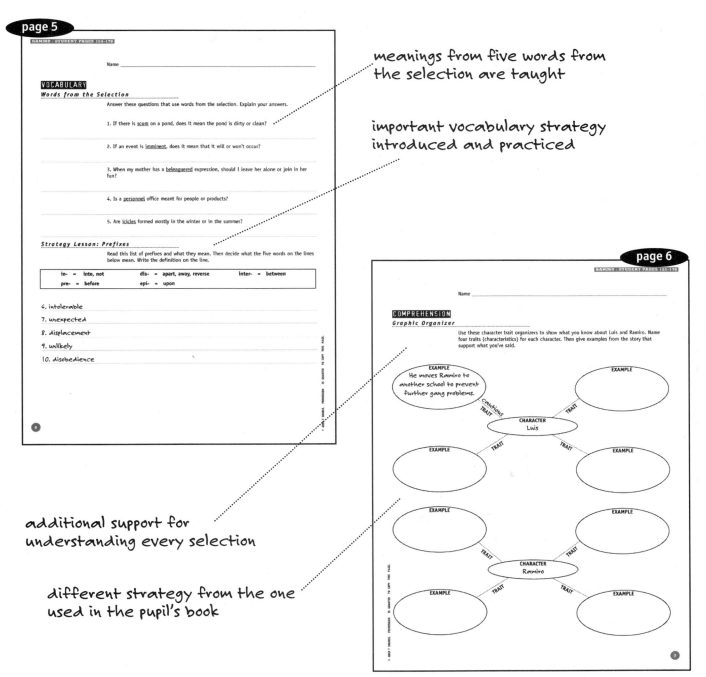

meanings from five words from the selection are taught

important vocabulary strategy introduced and practiced

additional support for understanding every selection

different strategy from the one used in the pupil's book

PAGE 6 Comprehension

- Each **Comprehension** blackline master affords teachers still another way to build students' understanding of the selection, using a different strategy from the one found in the *Sourcebook*.

PAGE 7 Prewriting

- Occasionally students will need even more scaffolding than appears in the pupil's lesson as they prepare for the writing assignment.

- The "extra step" in preparing to write is the focus of the **Prewriting** blackline master.

PAGE 8 Assessment

- Each lesson in the *Sourcebook* ends with the opportunity for students to reflect on their reading with the **Readers' Checklist**. This self-assessment is an informal inventory of what they learned from the reading.

- The **Assessment** blackline master gives a multiple-choice test on the selection and suggests a short-essay question for a more formal assessment.

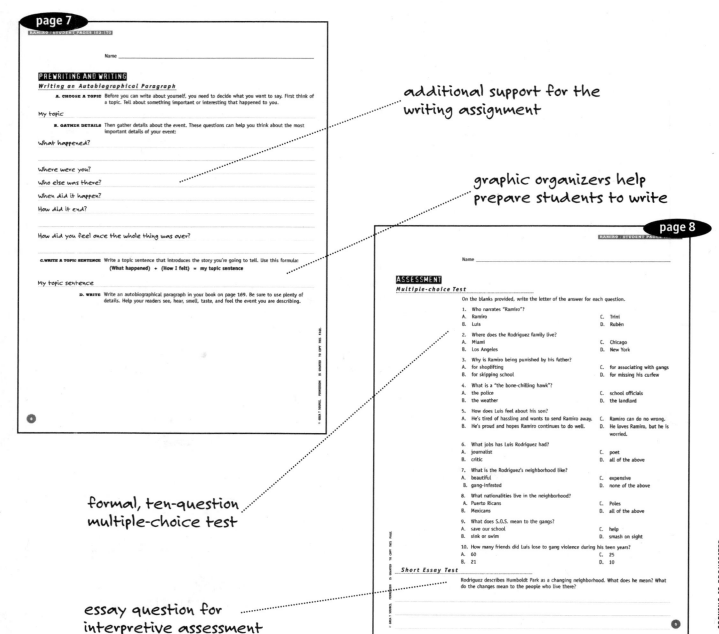

additional support for the writing assignment

graphic organizers help prepare students to write

formal, ten-question multiple-choice test

essay question for interpretive assessment

Teaching Struggling Readers

BY DR. RICHARD G. RAMSEY

What It Means to Teach

I enjoy being an educator. . . . We have the best job in the world, because we touch the future every day. We are in the business of making dreams come true for children. . . . And every day that I get up I'm excited about just going to work because now I know I have an opportunity to touch another life. . . . We have so many kids right now in our country coming to us from all walks of life, walking through our school doors every single day. When they walk through those doors, they're looking for one thing: they have open eyes, open minds, and open hearts seeking your validation. . . . The last thing children need to have done to them when they walk into your classroom is to be discouraged. They need hope, they need to be inspired by you every single day. . . .

The names of those who practice our profession read like a hall of fame for humanity: Booker T. Washington, Buddha, Confucius, Ralph Waldo Emerson, Leo Buscaglia, and many, many others. . . . Through and through the course of being a teacher, I've been called upon to be an actor, a nurse, a doctor, a coach, a finder of lost articles, a money lender, a taxicab driver, and also a keeper of the faith. I'm a paradox and I speak loudest when I listen the most to my students. I, as a teacher, am the most fortunate person who labors. A doctor is allowed to bring life into the world in one magic moment, but I, as a teacher, I am allowed to see that life is reborn each and every day with new questions, ideas, and friendship. I'm a warrior doing battle every single day against peer pressure, negativity, fear, conformity and prejudice. . . .

Elements of Teaching

ATTITUDE But there are three things I always say that a teacher has to have to be able to survive: The first thing you have to have is the proper attitude. . . . I say attitudes are contagious, is yours worth catching? . . . Our attitude plays a big role when we're dealing with children and I tell myself to come to school smiling every day, be happy. . . . Children are looking for you to be that positive example for them. . . . Every day we have two choices. . . . You can complain about your job every day and let children fail or you can begin to love what you do every single day and make sure that every child has the opportunity to be successful. . . .

Life is a challenge. We are challenged with diverse populations that we're not accustomed to working with. Life is a gift. Teach our children that you only go around one time and it's not a practice run. Respect the gift of life. Life is an adventure. . . . Life is also a saga . . . and teach our kids that there will be a better tomorrow if they just hold on and don't quit. Life is also a tragedy; unfortunately we are going to lose kids to homicide, drug abuse, and all kinds of dreadful diseases. And I say, hold on to those that we have because they are our future. Life is also a duty; you have a duty as a teacher to teach every child the way you would want somebody to teach yours, and if you do that, you've done your duty for that day. Life is also a game; be the best player so you can help children. Life is an opportunity; take advantage of it and make sure that the children understand that opportunities in life only come one time. Life is also a struggle; fight it with every ounce of energy that you have to do the best with children. Life is also a goal; set goals for yourself, set goals for the children. But more importantly, make sure that you work with them so they can achieve the goals they've set. Finally, life is a puzzle; but if all of us today take back what we have and work together as a team, we can solve that puzzle and make sure that children are successful in life. To teach is to heal, to teach is to love, to teach is to care, to teach is to set high expectations. You are a teacher. There are many kids waiting for you and looking in your eyes every day and saying, "I need your help, I need your motivation." But remember, you don't motivate with fear, you may get compliance, but you certainly won't get commitment.

CARE Good teaching, as I tell my teachers all the time, does not come from behind the desk, it comes from behind the heart. . . . And kids know whether you care about them, and kids can be successful because excellence can be obtained if you just care more than other people think is wise, risk more than others think is safe, dream more than others think is practical, and expect out of your students more than others think is possible. An unspoken belief can teach young minds what they should be. You as a teacher can make that difference. . . . Remember, good teachers explain, superior teachers demonstrate. The great teachers, they inspire their students every single day. And if a kid can be inspired by you, he's going to want to come to your class every day, he's going to give you his best or her best every single day. . . .

COMMITMENT I'm going to tell a little story to you called, "Three Letters of Teddy."

"Teddy's letter came today and now that I've read it, I will place it in my cedar chest with the other things that are important in my life. I, as a teacher, had not seen Teddy Starlin since he was a student in my fifth-grade class fifteen years ago. It was early in my career and I had only been teaching for two years. From the first day he stepped into my class, I disliked him. Teachers are not supposed to dislike any child, but I did and I showed my dislike to this young boy."

Any teacher would tell you it's more of a pleasure to teach a bright child. It's definitely more rewarding to one's ego with any teacher, with their credentials, a challenge working with a bright child and keeping them challenged and learning while they spend a major effort for those students who need help. Any teacher can do this, most teachers do, but she said she didn't, not that year. In fact, she concentrated on her best students and let the others follow along the best they could. Ashamed as she is to admit it, she took pleasure in using her red pen. And every time she came to Teddy's paper, the cross marks, and they were many, were always a little larger and a little redder than necessary. While she didn't actually ridicule the boy, her attitude, ladies and gentlemen, was obvious and quite apparent to the whole class for he quickly became the class goat, the outcast, the unlovable and the unloved child in that classroom. He didn't know why she didn't like him, nor did she know why she had such an intent dislike for this boy. All he wanted was somebody just to care about him, and she made no effort on his behalf. . . .

She knew that Teddy would never catch up in time to be promoted to the sixth-grade level. She said he would be a repeater. And to justify herself, she went to his folder from time to time. He had very low grades for the first four years but not failures. How he had made it, she said, she didn't know. But she closed her mind to all of the personal remarks in Teddy's folder. It said: first grade—Teddy shows promise by working attitude but has poor home situation. Second grade—Teddy could do better but his mother is terminally ill and he receives no help at home. Third grade—Teddy's a pleasant boy, helpful but too serious, slow learner. His mother, she passed away at the end of the year. Fourth grade—very slow but well behaved. His father shows no interest at all. She said, well, they passed him four times but he would certainly repeat the fifth grade, she said, it would do him good.

And then the last day before the holidays arrived, the little tree on the reading table supported paper and popcorn chains and many gifts were underneath the tree awaiting a big moment. Teachers always get several gifts at Christmas, she said, but hers that year were more elaborate than ever. Every child had brought her a gift and each unwrapping brought squeals of delight and the proud giver received profusive thank yous. His gift wasn't the last one she picked up; in fact, it was in the middle of the pile. Its wrapping was a brown paper bag and he had colored Christmas trees and red bells all over it and it was stuck together with masking tape. And it read "for Ms. Thompson, from Teddy, I love you." The group was completely silent, and for the first time she felt very embarrassed because all of the students stood there watching her unwrap that gift. And as she removed the last bit of masking tape, two items fell to her desk, a gaudy rhinestone bracelet with several stones missing and a small bottle of dime store cologne half empty. She heard the snickers and the whispers from the students and she wasn't even sure that she could hold her head up and look at Teddy, but she said, "Isn't this lovely." And she asked Teddy to come up to help her fasten the clasp. He smiled as he fixed the clasp on her arm and then there were finally a few hesitant oohs and ahs from the students. But as she dabbed the cologne behind her ears, all the little girls got up to get a dab behind theirs. She continued to open the gifts until she reached the bottom of the pile. They ate their refreshments and the bell rang. The children filed out and shouted, "See you next year, Merry Christmas," but Teddy, he waited at his desk. When they all had left, he walked toward her clutching his books and his gift to his chest with tears streaming down his face and he said to her, you smell just like my mom, her bracelet looks real pretty on you, too. I'm glad you like it. He left quickly. She got up and locked the door, sat at her desk, and wept resolvedly to make Teddy what she had deprived him of, to be a teacher who cared.

She stayed every afternoon with Teddy until the last day of school. Slowly but surely, he caught up with the rest of the class. Gradually, there was a definite upward curve in his grades. He didn't have to repeat the fifth grade; in fact, his average was among the highest in the class. Even though he was moving next year with his father, she wasn't worried because Teddy had reached a level that would serve him anywhere, because her teaching training had taught her that success deals success. She didn't hear from Teddy until seven years later when his first letter appeared in the mailbox. It said, "Dear Ms. Thompson, I want you to be the first to know that I'll be graduating second in my class next month, very truly yours, Teddy Starlin." She sent him a congratulatory card, wondering what he would do after graduation. Four years later she received another letter. It said, "Dear Ms. Thompson, I want you to be the first to know that I was just informed that I will be graduating first in my class. The university hasn't been easy; however, I liked it." She sent him silver monogrammed cufflinks and a card, so proud of him that she could burst. The final note came from him. It said, "Dear Ms. Thompson, I want you to be the first to know that as of today I am Theodore J. Starlin, M.D., how about that?" He said, "I'm going to be married in July, to be exact, and I want to ask you if you would come and do me a big favor, I would like you to come to my wedding and sit where my mom would have been if she was alive. I have no family now because my dad died last year. Ms. Thompson, you are all I have left, please come to my wedding, very truly yours, Teddy Starlin." She said, "I'm not sure what kind of gift one sends to a doctor on completion of medical school and state board; maybe I'll just wait and take a wedding gift," but she said, "my note cannot wait." It said, "Dear Ted, congratulations, you made it, you did it yourself. In spite of those like me and not because of us, this day has come for you. God bless you and I'll be at your wedding with bells on."

You have a lot of students like that in your classroom right now; all they need is a push. These kids are coming to us and they're looking for that special person to be there for them. . . .

RESPONSIBILITY We have a responsibility to touch the lives of children. But the question is: "Are we walking away from the children who need us, or are we coming to them and picking them up when they fall down? Children are not responsible for their parents, they are not responsible for where they live, they're only trying to make it with the conditions that they have. . . . Don't quit on children. Let them know they can be somebody. . . .

NOTE The article above is a transcript adapted from a lecture.

BY DR. ROBERT PAVLIK

REFLECTIONS • What was one of your most valuable learning experiences that involved reading and writing?

• What made the learning experience so valuable? So memorable?

Defining Expert Readers and Writers

Experts in various professions have extensive content knowledge and efficient skills:

> . . . experts have acquired extensive knowledge that affects what they notice and how they organize, represent, and interpret information in their environments. This, in turn, affects their abilities to remember, reason, and solve problems. (Bransford, Brown, and Cocking, 1999)

Novices, in contrast, lacking extensive content knowledge and efficient skills, tend to make confusing interpretations, record and retrieve information laboriously, and solve problems inaccurately.

The overall goal of the **Sourcebook** is to build expert readers and writers, learners who develop extensive content knowledge and efficient skills for using reading and writing to meet their needs within and beyond school. Expert readers and writers also develop their own "voices" for interacting within and among families, fellow learners, and community members. Far too many high school students, especially those at the lower end of the academic spectrum, lack extensive content knowledge or efficient skills. As a result, they can become confused, confusing, inefficient, and ineffective when attempting to use reading and writing to meet their needs. In addition, far too many high school students do not develop their own "voices."

REFLECTIONS • For which school subjects were you a novice or an expert reader? A novice or expert writer? How did you know?

• How would you describe your "voice" in high school? today?

• Which of your recent/current students would you describe as novice or expert readers? As novice or expert writers? How do you know?

• How would you describe the "voices" of your students?

Using Culturally Diverse Literature

Rapidly changing national demographics require us to reconsider what fiction and nonfiction literature we include in our curricula. In essence, to what extent do we study the literature from and about people who helped shape the United States, and to what extent do we study the literature from and about people who shape the United States today and are shaping the future of the United States?

The **Sourcebook** provides fiction and nonfiction selections that represent current demographics of high school students. Approximately 60 percent of the selections represent traditional ideas and values, while the remaining 40 percent represent the ideas and values of several other cultures. This range of culturally diverse literature provides optional selections for meeting students' needs to

• understand themselves.

• understand the worldviews and culture of the United States.

• understand others.

• understand the worldviews and cultures of other countries.

For students, this range of culturally diverse literature provides meaningful, authentic opportunities to read and write and to learn new and familiar vocabulary in a variety of contexts. In addition, the breadth and depth of the selections can inspire further student reading, student-teacher discussions, and student-student discussions.

REFLECTIONS • How culturally diverse was the fiction you studied as a high school student? The nonfiction?

• How valuable was the literature you studied in high school for the four needs cited above?

• What are the demographics of your students?

• What cultures and "voices" must your literature selections address?

Using an Interactive Instructional Approach

Current approaches for improving the reading and writing of high school students range . . .

• from telling students to "practice, practice, practice" their reading and writing. In essence, teachers tell students to read a lot to become better readers and write a lot to become better writers.

• to identifying a student's level of skill mastery for reading and writing and, then, organizing students into groups for appropriate reading and writing skills instruction.

• to inviting students to discover their own strategies through teacher-guided discussions.

• to creating stimulating environments and meaningful projects around significant themes that motivate students to build and refine their uses of reading, writing, speaking, listening, and viewing.

All of these approaches to instruction have proven effective in recent decades, especially with populations of similar students. However, increasing numbers of high school students represent diverse cultures, perform well below their potential, speak English only in school, and attend school irregularly.

Vygotsky's thinking (1978) inspires and informs much of our approach to instruction. We believe that today's high school students can become expert readers and writers despite the challenges confronting them. To do so, students need

• meaningful, authentic fiction and nonfiction.

• an approach to instruction that respects how they are trying to learn within their fragmented, often chaotic lives.

• teachers and materials that direct and guide them to form, state, and test strategies for reading with peers and adults.

Therefore, our overall instructional approach involves modeling what expert readers and writers do as they negotiate with fiction and nonfiction and, then, inviting students to adapt what they learn from the modeling to their own reading and writing strategies. In the process, students can build and refine their thinking with others in order to apply the strategies on their own as needed.

For example, the *Sourcebook* opens with a feature entitled **"Responding to Literature"** that directs and invites students to

• see examples of written responses to ideas in a short selection from an expert reader-writer.

• engage a strategy sheet for making similar responses.

• make similar responses to a short selection on their own.

We apply this overall instructional approach throughout the *Sourcebook*.

REFLECTIONS
- What instructional approaches did your teachers apply to improve your reading and writing?

- Which approaches did you as a high school student find valuable? Not valuable?

- As a teacher, what instructional approaches have you found effective and why? Ineffective and why?

Teaching Meaning-making Strategies

Research studies on expert readers and writers reveal two important insights:

- Expert readers and writers will use a variety of strategies automatically when they encounter new and difficult tasks—strategies that novice readers and writers would not use.

- A number of reading and writing strategies have been developed and can be taught (Paris, Wasik, and Turner, 1991; Dahl and Farnan, 1998).

Within our five-part lesson framework for each piece of fiction and nonfiction, students apply several meaning-making strategies to become expert readers and writers.

Part I. Before You Read

Struggling novice readers tend to avoid most types of reading in and outside of school. Even some expert readers often choose to spend only a few minutes each day reading in and outside of school, on either assigned or independent reading. The reasons why high school students choose not to read range from having poor reading skills to responding to peer pressure and even gender expectations.

The *Sourcebook* addresses these avoidance behaviors by presenting two prereading strategies per selection and guiding students to apply the strategies successfully. We assign specific strategies for each selection to get students doing something before they read, e.g., asking their opinions, engaging with a sample from the selection to read, or responding to a quick survey about their expectations. Our prereading strategies applied among the selections include these:

- Walking through a selection

- Using an anticipation guide

- Using K-W-L

- Using word webs

- Using a read-aloud

- Using a think-pair-and-share

- Previewing

- Skimming and scanning

Initially, engaging students in the prereading strategies motivates them to "get into" any selection. Eventually, students apply these prereading strategies to build background, activate prior knowledge, or raise questions that become part of the purpose for reading. With consistent practice, coaching, and guided reflection over the use of prereading strategies, students can build and refine their own lifetime prereading strategies.

Part II. Read

Novice readers usually do not choose to read with pencil in hand and mark up the text. Their reasons range from fearing to write in the text to not having a personal system of symbols for their responses, to fearing to make their "thinking tracks" public, to not having accurate language for describing the author's content and structure in annotations. Expert readers typically mark up a text, though not always. They will often mark up texts in which they find new or difficult information. They will rarely mark up texts in which they find familiar, easy-to-access or easy-to-remember information.

The *Sourcebook* addresses these varying comfort levels by presenting one or more interactive reading strategies per selection and guiding students to apply the strategies successfully. Our goal is to get students actually to write in their texts. The interactive reading strategies include these:

- Marking and highlighting

- Questioning

- Clarifying

- Visualizing

- Predicting

- Reading and connecting

The major purposes of these interactive reading strategies are to help students learn how and when to mark up texts and how to focus on specific content or structures of texts. Later, as their abilities develop for describing, labeling, commenting on, and reorganizing the information they read, students may find that these strategies slow down rather than accelerate their reading—a behavior indicating that they are becoming more expert readers.

Struggling novice readers often find themselves reading with no understanding or, even worse, reading with their eyes closed and imagining they are making sense of a piece of fiction or nonfiction. Expert readers develop new levels of understanding each time they read whole texts or parts of texts. They have learned where to pause and reread and how to apply any of several strategies to help understand what they read.

The comprehension strategies applied in the *Sourcebook* include these:

- Directed reading

- Predicting

- Using graphic organizers

- Using reciprocal reading questions

- Retelling

- Making double-entry journals

We assign one of these tried-and-true strategies to the appropriate types of fiction and nonfiction. Our goal is to model how expert readers come to understand a text. Ultimately, after students experiment with a variety of comprehension strategies, they will modify the strategies for their purposes until the strategies are no longer recognizable as they are developed in the *Sourcebook*—another indication of an expert reader in the making.

Part III. Gather Your Thoughts

Struggling novice writers usually do not choose to engage in any prewriting activities when they have a choice. Expert writers, while they vary widely in the breadth and depth of their prewriting strategies, view prewriting activities as the time when personally significant learning takes place. Prewriting activities provide the time and the means for engaging in critical and creative thinking.

Part III of the *Sourcebook* presents one or more prewriting strategies per selection. Students receive step-by-step guidance for applying each strategy successfully. The prereading strategies we apply among the selections include these:

- Discussing in pairs and small groups

- Clustering details
- Drawing a place
- Brainstorming
- Quickwriting
- Using anecdotes
- Comparing and contrasting
- Using a graphic organizer
- Using storyboards

Most of these prewriting activities involve two or more persons. Most thinking is social, according to Vygotsky; group interactions following various learning experiences, including reading and before writing, provide students with valuable opportunities to develop, refine, and internalize their purposes and plans for writing.

Part IV. Write

Struggling novice writers often think of completing a writing assignment as involving a two-step, one-time process—just sit down and write. They often postpone completing writing assignments, thinking that once they sit down and write, they can complete the assignment in one work session. Expert writers think of completing a writing assignment as involving several steps, e.g., narrowing the topic, planning, gathering data, drafting, revising one or more times, sharing and publishing; personalizing ways to complete each of the steps; and involving more than one work session.

The *Sourcebook* invites students to engage in several small writing tasks. Note the types of writing listed in the Table of Contents to the left of each selection title. The writing tasks become increasingly larger so that students come to view the writing process as a series of recursive, interlocking steps. When students present and reflect on their best writing samples, they come to understand how the writing process varies among types of writing and among students—another indication of an expert writer.

Part V. Wrap-up

Being able to answer such reflection questions as these indicates how well readers and writers understand the fiction and nonfiction selections they study:

1. UNDERSTANDING Did I understand? How do I know?

Is the message or point clear?

Can I restate what it was about?

2. EASE Was it easy to read?

Was I able to read it smoothly and without difficulty?

3. MEANING Did I learn something or take away something from it?

Did it affect me or make an impression?

4. STYLE Did I find it well written?

Was the writing well crafted, the sentences well constructed, the words well chosen?

Does it show me how to be a better writer?

5. DEPTH Did it make me think about things?

Did it set off thoughts beyond the surface topic?

What are the immediate implications for me? Others?

What are the long-term implications for me? Others?

6. ENJOYMENT   Did I like it?

Was the experience pleasurable?

Would I want to reread it or recommend it to someone?

Answering such questions as these honestly and consistently for a wide variety of texts and purposes indicates that a learner is becoming an expert reader.

REFLECTIONS   • What strategies do you find personally valuable?

   for prereading?

   for reading?

   for gathering your thoughts?

   for writing?

   for reflecting on your reading and writing?

• What are your roles when using the ***Sourcebook*** to build expert readers and writers? How might your roles change during this school year?

• How can you create the most significant learning experiences when your students use reading and writing?

REFERENCES   Bransford, J. D., A. L. Brown, and R. R. Cocking, eds. *How People Learn: Brain, Mind, Experience and School.* Washington, D.C.: National Academy Press, 1999.

Cawelti, G., ed. *Handbook of Research on Improving Student Achievement.* 2nd ed. Arlington, Va: Educational Research Service, 1999.

Graves, M., and B. Graves. *Scaffolding Reading Experiences: Designs for Student Success.* Norwood, Mass.: Christopher-Gordon Publishers, 1994.

BY CATHERINE MCNARY

The Situation in High School

In high school, strategic reading is an essential learning tool. Unlike grade school, in which the learning environment is child-centered and focused on learning to learn, the high school is departmentalized and focused on the learning of subject area content. Two primary learning mediums are used to disseminate information—classroom lecture and textbook reading. The high school student is expected to have sufficient vocabulary, background knowledge, metacognitive strategies, and motivation to translate textbook print into usable, applicable information.

For some students, the expectations are realistic. For many, they are not. (The 1998 NAEP assessment stated that 31 percent of fourth graders, 33 percent of eighth graders, and 40 percent of twelfth graders attained a proficient level of reading [Donahue, Voelkl, Campbell, & Mazzeo, 1999].) What happens with the 67 percent of students in eighth grade and the 60 percent of students in twelfth grade who are not proficient readers? What strategies and teaching methods have been proven to provide this group with the best possible instruction in reading so that they, like their more able peers, may keep pace with the high school curriculum?

In the literature, five traits have been identified that provide readers with the cognitive tools to learn from text: general cognitive capacity, reader strategies and metacognition, inferential and reasoning abilities, background knowledge, and basic reading skills (Van Den Broek & Kremer, 2000). Most high school students, even those reading two years below grade level, have adequate basic skills, and general cognitive capacity is beyond the purview of the high school. However, the remaining abilities are integral to an instructional program at the high school level and include these:

- reader strategies and metacognition,

- inferential and reasoning ability, and

- background knowledge.

Best Practices to Use with High-Risk Students

Dr. Norman Stahl has suggested ten recommendations for programs from research for teaching high-risk college students (Stahl, Simpson & Hayes, 1994). Dr. Stahl's list can be consolidated into four components that are relevant to high school reading programs and that match the five traits for success outlined by Taylor and others.

Best practices for a high school reading program should reflect instruction in these four components:

1. develop background knowledge

2. model metacognitive strategies and promote their independent usage

3. incorporate writing into the curriculum

4. develop vocabulary

Develop Background Knowledge

The importance of developing background knowledge has been emphasized by several researchers (Alvermann & Moore, 1996). Because reading is thought to be a construction of meaning in which the reader not only absorbs information from the text but also combines that information with his or her own prior knowledge, background is essential. The reader cannot interact with the text without prior understanding of the content. He or she would have no anchor upon which to build.

Teachers use several strategies to build background before reading. These include field trips, films, guest speakers, discussions, short articles, library research and projects, anticipation guides, K-W-L, brainstorming, quickwrites, DRTA, simulations, questionnaires, structured overviews, and advance organizers.

The *Sourcebook* is organized with a prereading activity at the beginning of each selection. These prereading activities include quickwrites, K-W-L, anticipation guides, previews, and other sound activities. Not only do these lessons serve as models for prereading strategies, they also provide strategic practice for students.

Other important prereading practices that go hand-in-hand with background building are setting purpose and previewing. Just as a reader must have background information to interact with text, a reader must also have a clear understanding of why he or she is reading a selection. Purpose can be set by teacher direction. Instead of suggesting, "Read Chapter Five for a quiz on Tuesday," the teacher should probably say, "Read Chapter Five to find three reasons why or how a problem was solved. Concentrate on the sequence of the solution." This small change gives a concrete purpose to the reading and helps students to focus on the main idea.

Previewing is another strategy that directs a student to discover the main idea of the text. Previewing activities include looking at titles, subheadings, chapter questions, photos, and captions. The information gathered acts as a director for how the student approaches the information.

These strategies are not new to teachers. The challenge is the number of times students must practice the strategy before it is internalized, until it can be done independently. The *Sourcebook* provides numerous opportunities for practicing each strategy. Repeated practice helps the student make the strategy automatic. The *Sourcebook* also provides the student with a written record of his or her strategy development. This record allows the student to monitor his or her own progress.

Model Metacognitive Strategies

It is clear from the literature that strategic readers comprehend print more efficiently (Paris, Wasik, & Turner, 1996) than those readers without strategies. Typically, the less-able reader has no plan for attacking print—he or she just reads every word, each with the same emphasis. He or she skips problematic words or passages or rereads them in exactly the same manner—with no strategies for monitoring the effectiveness of his or her comprehension. The goal of strategic reading instruction is to model a variety of strategies to students (both teacher and student generated), give students sufficient guided and independent practice to incorporate the strategies into his or her own portfolio, and to observe the student using these strategies in his or her own independent reading. This instruction will then allow students to monitor the effectiveness of their own reading—and adjust if the reading has not been sufficient.

For many high school readers, self-monitoring of comprehension is a new concept. Explicit instruction and practice are necessary for these students to develop self-monitoring techniques. Several strategies are available. While a student reads, he or she should mark up the text, underlining and highlighting information. In addition, note-taking of text during reading is also suggested. Students should be taught to write down the questions that come up while reading; write down issues that need clarification or that they wish to discuss; draw pictures of characters they need to visualize; note any parts or quotes within the selection that provoke a reaction; and graph any process or sequence that seems important. The *Sourcebook* is excellent for modeling and providing students with the opportunity to practice student-generated during-reading strategies.

In the space called "**Response Notes**," students record questions, clarifications, pictures, and graphic representations. Highlighting and underlining are also modeled. In addition, students can write in their books. Reading teachers are often at a disadvantage in teaching self-monitoring because students do not own the books and cannot write in the books they are reading. Consequently, these strategies are ignored or modified beyond recognition. With the *Sourcebook,* these activities can be practiced as they are meant to be—in the book. This is an opportunity for both teacher monitoring and self-monitoring of strategy acquisition.

Many of the during-reading strategies are teacher generated. These include K-W-L, DRTA, and study guides. Two of the teacher-generated strategies the *Sourcebook* encourages during reading are **stop and think** questions and the **double-entry journal. Stop and think** (directed reading) activities function like a within-text study guide. Text is broken, at a strategic place, with a question box. Students are expected to stop and answer the question and then continue reading.

The location of the **stop and think**, within text, is of great value. This proximity helps to keep students connected to text to evaluate both their response and the place in text that referenced it. The repeated usage of **stop and think** in the *Sourcebook* permits students the practice to make the connection from text to response, as well as to establish a habit of questioning to check for understanding while reading.

The **double-entry journal** also appears within text. The student is required to stop reading and respond to a quote. This strategy not only emphasizes the importance of closely attending to text but also brings the student's experience and prior knowledge into the reading process. The strategy is quite useful in helping students learn how to interpret text, especially when they later write about it.

Many activities are used to assess knowledge of a selection after reading. These include dramatizations, debates, tests, and group and individual projects. These culminating activities reflect the use of many strategies but are not a single strategy themselves. Any unit in the *Sourcebook* lends itself to the development of a culminating activity. For example, after reading "Pilots' Reflections," a culminating activity might be for groups in the class to choose an aspect about World War I on which to present. After-reading strategies that reflect the reader's process of organizing and applying his thoughts about the selection can be exemplified by content mapping, summarizing, discussion, and guided writing.

The *Sourcebook* uses the strategies of content mapping and summarizing, as well as journaling and webbing to encourage student reflection. The content mapping, which is text structure sensitive, is a particularly good way for students to "gather their thoughts" after reading. In this manner, graphic organizers are modeled and made available for practice.

One of the most powerful strategies for showing an understanding of main idea and subsequent detail is the ability to summarize. Summarization is not an easy task. Several activities that include mapping main idea and detail, both graphically and in prose, accompany summary writing activities in the *Sourcebook*. Graphic and prose organizers are explained in a step-by-step fashion. Repeated practice, paired with these several instructional models, is a valuable practice.

Incorporate Writing into the Curriculum

In reviewing the literature on writing, one statement summarizes the current thinking:

> We believe strongly that in our society, at this point in history, reading and writing, to be understood and appreciated fully, should be viewed together, learned together, and used together (Tierney & Shanahan, 1996).

Writing and reading complement each other. Each can be used as a strategy to strengthen the other. **Quickwrites** at the beginning of a selection can bring up background and focus purpose for reading. During reading, note-taking and questioning can increase metacognitive awareness and enhance comprehension. After reading, summarizing, journaling, and paragraph and theme writing can extend thought and enhance higher-order thinking.

The *Sourcebook* is an excellent resource for presenting reading and writing in tandem. Writing is integrated into before, during, and after reading instruction. Journal responses, paragraph and theme writing, summarization, quickwrites, and the graphic organizers are integrated seamlessly with the reading, creating a complete, fully integrated lesson.

Develop Vocabulary

Several researchers have shown that direct instruction in vocabulary does enhance comprehension (Beck & McKeown, 1996). It is known that effective vocabulary instruction connects prior knowledge to new words (Lenski, Wham, & Johns, 1999) and provides instructional strategies that promote the active processing of words (Beck & McKeown, 1996). Examples of strategies that do this are: list-group-label, concept mapping, semantic feature analysis, synonym clustering, semantic mapping, and word sorts. Each of these strategies is involved in mapping word relationships. For example, a synonym cluster begins with a word and attaches three synonyms to that word. Attached to those three synonyms are three more synonyms, and so on.

All the above strategies can be used independently with a word journal or a word box, in pairs or small groups with a word box or a word journal, or as a whole-class activity with a word box or a word wall. It is most effective if new vocabulary is highly visible and used.

The *Sourcebook* best enhances vocabulary instruction by making the student aware of the need for growth in vocabulary. Each selection has difficult vocabulary words highlighted in the text and defined at the bottom of the page. In addition, the *Teacher's Guide* includes practice on selected words from the lesson and introduces students to a vocabulary strategy.

Conclusion

The teaching of secondary reading is not an easy endeavor. Pressures by other teachers, students, and administrators are apparent daily. Not only is the reading teacher faced with the classroom challenges of students with diverse and serious issues but also with unrealistic expectations and goals from other teachers and administrators.

Because students in the classroom are diverse in their educational needs, the secondary reading teacher is constantly juggling curriculum and time to focus on the individual needs of his or her students. Each reading teacher is his or her own research assistant, constantly reviewing the literature for best practices and strategies, to motivate and engage the reluctant reader. He or she is forever combing the teacher store for materials that are relevant, strategic, and appropriate.

The *Sourcebooks* are a fine resource. Not only do they model strategies at the cutting edge of research, they are also made up of good-quality, highly motivating literature, both narrative and expository. Selections from authors such as Dorothy West, Edith Hamilton, Lensey Namioka, and Phyllis Ntantala reflect the populations of our classes and their multicultural nature.

Here is a quick guide to the main prereading, comprehension, and reflecting strategies used in the *Sourcebooks*. In order to help students internalize these strategies, the number and use of them was limited so that students could encounter them repeatedly throughout the book.

Overview

PREREADING STRATEGIES
Picture Walk

What It Is

A picture walk is a prereading activity in which students look at the images from a selection to get a sense of what the selection will be about. Other strategies may be more powerful, but a picture walk is a necessary strategy for all students to have in their repertoire. Once they become more skilled readers, they will most likely use it in conjunction with other prereading strategies—for example, skimming.

How to Introduce It

Have students page through the selection and look at the images.

Ask them questions such as the ones below to help them reflect on the images.

- How do the images make you feel?
- Based on the images, what do you think the selection will be about? Why?

Read the selection.

Encourage students to generate other questions of their own.

After reading, invite students to return to the images to discuss the accuracy of their predictions.

Example

The photo of . . .	tells me . . .
The photo of . . .	tells me . . .

Why It Works

Picture walks get students, especially visual learners, actively involved in the prereading process. Questions about the images spark students' interest, activate prior knowledge, and encourage prediction.

Comments and Cautions

As an extension to the activity, invite students to add a new image, either before reading (to illustrate their prediction) or after.

Picture walks work well with both fiction and nonfiction material. You can also use a modified version for selections involving graphic sources, such as maps and diagrams.

What It Is

K-W-L is a pre- and post-reading strategy designed to facilitate students' interest in and activate their prior knowledge of a topic before reading nonfiction material. The letters *K, W,* and *L* stand for "What I **K**now," What I **W**ant to Know," and "What I **L**earned."

Look at the example of a K-W-L chart from Lesson 4, "Adventures of the U-202."

Example

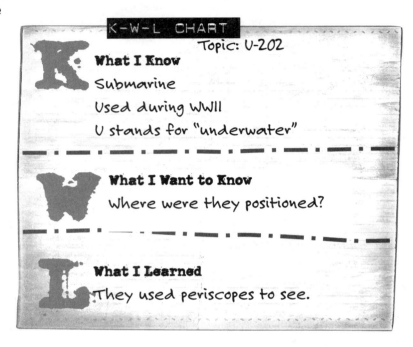

How to Introduce It

For students unfamiliar with the strategy, you might try to introduce K-W-L as a whole-class activity. Once students are familiar with the strategy, they can complete the charts on their own.

Ask students what they know about the topic. List their answers in the *K* column.

Discuss what students hope to learn about the topic from reading the selection. Write their questions in the *W* column.

Read the selection.

Return to the chart and list what students learned in the *L* column.

Why It Works

Brainstorming (the *K* part) activates prior knowledge. What sets K-W-L apart from other prereading strategies is that K-W-L also encourages students to ask questions (the *W* component), thereby setting meaningful purposes for their reading. Returning to the chart (the *L* component) brings closure to the activity and demonstrates the purposefulness of the task.

Comments and Cautions

Don't worry about the accuracy of the answers under the *K* column; this is a brainstorming activity; students can correct any errors later during the *L* part of the activity.

After brainstorming, have students categorize their lists into three or four general groups.

You might add a fourth column, "What I Still Need to Learn," for questions that aren't answered in the text or that arise after reading the material.

Anticipation Guide

What It Is

An anticipation guide is a series of statements to which students respond, first individually and then as a group, before reading a selection. For example, in Lesson 8, "A Simple Proposition," students are asked to agree or disagree with statements such as "Boys do better at mathematics than girls."

Example

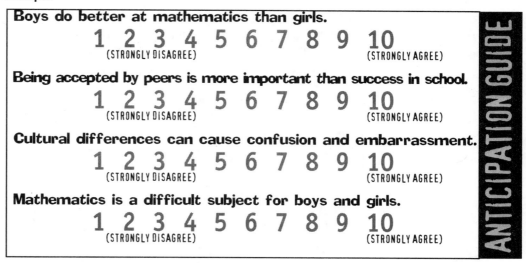

How to Introduce It

Have students read the statements. (When making your own guides, keep the number of statements to fewer than 10. More than that makes it difficult to discuss in detail.)

Discuss the students' responses. This is the point of an anticipation guide—to discuss. Build the prior knowledge of one student by adding to it the prior knowledge of other students, which can be done through discussion. The discussion of anticipation guide statements can also be a powerful motivator, because once students have answered the statements, they have a stake in seeing if they are "right."

Encourage students to make predictions about what the selection will be about based on the statements.

Then read the selection.

After reading the selection, have students return to their guides and re-evaluate their responses based on what they learned from the selection.

Why It Works

Anticipation guides are useful tools for eliciting predictions before reading both fiction and nonfiction. By encouraging students to think critically about a series of statements, anticipation guides raise expectations and create anticipation about the selection.

Comments and Cautions

This is a motivational activity. Try not to allow the class discussion to become divisive or judgmental; the teacher's role is that of a facilitator, encouraging students to examine and re-examine their responses. The bigger stake students have in an opinion, the more they will be motivated to read about the issue.

The focus of the guides should not be whether students' responses are "correct" or not but rather the discussion that ensues after completing the guides individually.

Anticipation guides work well in counteracting clichés and stereotypes, as in Lesson 8, "A Simple Proposition."

You can turn the entire anticipation guide process into a whole-group activity by having students respond with either "thumbs up" or "thumbs down."

Preview or Walk-through

What It Is

Previewing is a prereading strategy in which students read the title and first paragraph or two of a selection and then reflect on a few key questions. It asks the students to "sample" the selection before they begin reading and functions very much like the preview to a movie. Occasionally it is simply referred to as a *walk-through* and is a less formal variation of skimming and scanning.

How to Introduce It

Previewing can be done as an individual or group activity. You might introduce it to the group and in later lessons encourage students to work on their own.

Read aloud, or have students read to themselves, the first paragraph or two of a selection.

Have students respond to four or five questions about the selection. Their responses will be predictions based on their initial sampling of the piece. Questions might include these:

- What is the selection about?
- When does it take place?
- Who is in it?
- How will the selection end?

Read the rest of the selection.

Return to the questions and discuss the accuracy of students' predictions. Were they surprised at how the selection turned out based on their initial preview? Why or why not?

Example

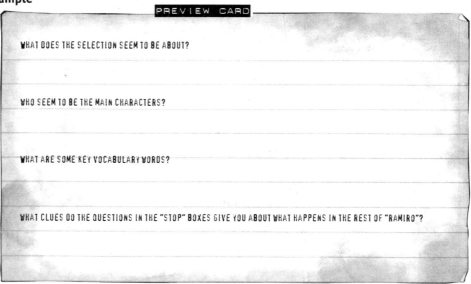

PREVIEW CARD

WHAT DOES THE SELECTION SEEM TO BE ABOUT?

WHO SEEM TO BE THE MAIN CHARACTERS?

WHAT ARE SOME KEY VOCABULARY WORDS?

WHAT CLUES DO THE QUESTIONS IN THE "STOP" BOXES GIVE YOU ABOUT WHAT HAPPENS IN THE REST OF "RAMIRO"?

Why It Works

Previews work because they provide a frame of reference in which to understand new material. Previews build context, particularly when students read about unfamiliar topics. Discussing the questions and predicting before reading helps students set purposes for reading and creates interest in the subject matter.

Comments and Cautions

Previews work best with more difficult reading selections, especially texts with difficult vocabulary. Previewing helps students to understand a context for a selection—what's the subject? Where's the story located? Who's involved?

Once students are familiar with previews, you might ask them to generate their own list of questions and have a partner respond to them.

Quickwrite

What It Is

A quickwrite is just what the name implies, a short, one- to ten-minute activity in which students write down their thoughts about a topic. Quickwriting is impromptu writing, without concern for spelling and grammatical conventions. It is intended to help students articulate some of the prior knowledge they have on a subject.

How to Introduce It

Provide students with a topic on which to focus.

Invite students to write about whatever comes to mind regarding the topic.

Encourage students to share their quickwrites in a small group. Discuss their similarities and differences.

Ask students to predict what they think the selection will be about based on their quickwrites.

Read the selection.

Discuss the connections between students' quickwrites and the selection.

Example

Why It Works

Quickwriting works as a prereading strategy on a number of levels. For one, the very process of writing without regard to writing conventions frees up students to write from a deeper level of understanding. Quickwriting encourages students to make connections between their own lives and the reading material, activates prior knowledge, and sparks interest. Quickwriting can also help correct misconceptions about a topic.

Comments and Cautions

As an extension to the activity, have students quickwrite again after reading the selection and compare their two quickwrites to see what they've learned from reading the material.

What It Is

Skimming is a prereading strategy in which students look over the entire selection to get a sense of what it will be about. It is one of the best prereading strategies and best known. Much of the time, however, students never learn how to skim effectively and what to look for.

How to Introduce It

Skimming is a useful tool, both for prereading and content area reading, but one that many students have difficulty mastering. Therefore, introduce skimming as a whole group activity; teacher modeling might work best for the initial activity. Skimming involves these activities:

Examining the table of contents

Reading the first and last paragraph

Checking the selection's length and reading difficulty

Reading any captions

Looking over illustrations

Noting section headings, diagrams, and other graphic sources

Example

SKIMMING

✔ How long ago was World War I?

✔ How did countries use planes during the war?

✔ What did W. S. Douglas do when he saw an enemy plane?

To help students master the technique of skimming, provide them with a series of questions to answer about the selection, as in the example above. Questions such as these provide a clear purpose for skimming and help students focus their attention on the key parts of the selection.

Why It Works

Skimming is an excellent tool for setting purposes and activating prior knowledge before reading nonfiction material. Like a picture walk, skimming draws students into a selection.

Comments and Cautions

Skimming works best when students have a clear purpose for going through a selection. Direct students, for example, to underline one to two words in each line of the first and last paragraph, or to circle names or words that appear a number of times.

Teach a clear method for skimming and try not to assume students will know what it means.

Think-Pair-and-Share

What It Is

Think-pair-and-share is a prereading strategy that encourages group discussion and prediction about what students will read. Students work in pairs to discuss sentences selected from the text.

How to Introduce It

Break students into groups of two or three. Present three to six sentences from the selection. Ask group members to read the sentences and discuss what they mean and in what order they appear in the text.

Encourage groups to make predictions and generate questions about the reading.

Then read the selection.

Have groups discuss the selection and the accuracy of their think-pair-and-share sentences. How many were able to correctly predict the order in which they appeared? How many could predict what the selection was about?

Example

> **think-pair-and-share**
>
> **a.** "The fortunate ones milk and shut in the stock, but for most there is no stock to shut in, and their children do not know the milk from the family cow."
>
> **b.** "The rest of the evening is spent in silence."
>
> **c.** "Widowhood—a life of void and loneliness; a period of tension, unbalance and strenuous adjustment."
>
> **d.** "There will be bread, sugar, tea and a few extras for at least a few weeks. For others it is bad news."

Which sentence appears first in the story? Which one appears last?

What can you learn about the "widows" from these sentences?

How are the widows' lives like or unlike yours?

Why It Works

Think-pair-and-share can be a powerful tool for getting students motivated to read. Small-group work such as this gives students the chance to discover that they don't always have to come up with all the answers themselves; sometimes two or three heads *are* better than one. Working in groups also provides reluctant readers with the understanding that all readers bring different skills and schema to the reading task. The activity also begins the critical process of "constructing meaning" of the text.

Comments and Cautions

Enlist students in building the think-pair-and-share activity. Have each group member write one sentence from the text on a file card. Then ask groups to exchange file cards—one group pieces together the sentences of another group.

The active, social nature of this activity stimulates students, which can be highly motivational and beneficial if properly channeled into purposeful activity.

Word Web

What It Is

A word web is a prereading activity in which students brainstorm and make connections to a key concept from the reading material.

Example

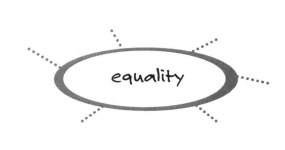

How to Introduce It

Word webs can be done independently or as a whole-group activity. You might want to do the initial word webs with the whole group and assign later word webs for independent learning.

Write a key concept in a circle. For example, in Lesson 23, "Harrison Bergeron," the concept is equality.

Have students brainstorm words related to the concept on spokes coming out of the circle.

Discuss with students how the key word is connected to the reading material.

Read the selection.

Return to the word web and add any new ideas brought about by reading the selection.

Why It Works

Word webs are excellent tools for developing students' conceptual knowledge. They tap into students' prior knowledge and help students make connections between what they know and what they will learn.

Comments and Cautions

Even though this is a brainstorming activity, do challenge incorrect assumptions about the concept, particularly when using the word web with a whole group. You want to be sure that students go into the reading assignment with an accurate impression of the concept.

If students get "stuck," encourage them to write down words, phrases, examples, or images they associate with the concept.

RESPONSE STRATEGIES

The response strategies are introduced at the beginning of each *Sourcebook* (pages 8–10). They are the heart of the interactive reading students are asked to do through the book. In Part II of each lesson, one or two response strategies are suggested to help teach students how to mark up a text and become active readers.

Struggling readers do not naturally know how to interact with a text, so these strategies are designed to help them get started. Examples are also provided in each lesson to model the strategy. The intent is to build the habit of reading with a pen in hand and marking up the text until it becomes a natural way to read.

Response Strategies

1. Mark or highlight

2. Question

3. Clarify

4. Visualize

5. Predict

6. React and Connect

Example

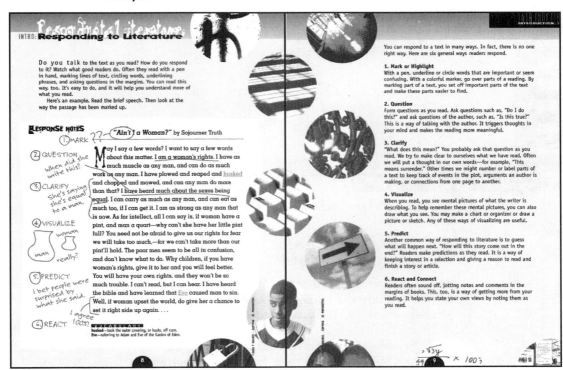

The purpose of these response strategies in each lesson is to

1. help students learn how to mark up a text

2. help students focus on specific aspects of a text and find the information they need

3. build lifelong habits for students by repeating good reading practices

COMPREHENSION STRATEGIES
Directed Reading

What It Is

Directed reading is a structured activity designed to guide students through a reading selection. Directed reading is composed of a series of steps, including readiness, directed silent reading, comprehension check and discuss, oral rereading, and follow-up activities. In the **Sourcebook**, students gain readiness in Part I, read silently in Part II, and then encounter questions that check their comprehension throughout the selection. Teachers are encouraged to have students go back through selections with this strategy and read the selection a second time. Repeated reading of a selection often increases reading fluency, which in itself often increases comprehension.

How To Introduce It

First, help students get ready to read by activating their prior knowledge, creating interest, and setting purposes. The prereading strategies described in Part I of the lesson offer suggestions for activities that promote reading readiness.

Next, have students read the selection silently. Guide them as they read by providing stopping points, such as the stop and think sections in the **Sourcebook**. Encourage them to focus on the purpose for reading that they established in Part I.

Example

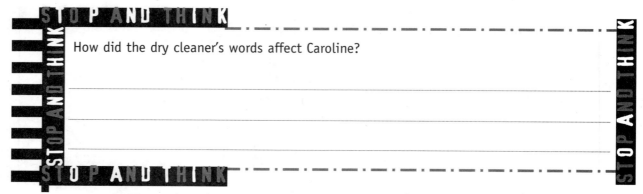

STOP AND THINK

How did the dry cleaner's words affect Caroline?

STOP AND THINK

After students have read the selection, take a moment to engage them in a discussion about what they read.

During or directly after the discussion, have students orally reread the selection to answer any remaining questions or clear up any confusion about the reading material.

During the discussion and oral rereading stages, you can get a sense of what kind of difficulties students are having with the material. Use follow-up activities to work on these areas of weakness and to extend students' understanding of the material, or use the additional comprehension activities included in each **Teacher's Guide** lesson. Follow-up activities range from direct skill instruction designed for individual or small-group work to response activities, such as those found in the **Sourcebook**.

Why It Works

Directed reading enhances students' ability to think critically and reflectively about the reading material. It helps them ask the questions good readers ask themselves as they read. The structured format ensures that students of all reading levels will be asking the right kinds of questions needed to comprehend the text.

Comments and Cautions

As with any comprehension strategy, directed reading needs to be modified to fit the needs of individual students.

Directed reading can be overly prescriptive, and overuse can contribute to passive reading, if it is relied on exclusively. Including activities that require student speculation and higher-level thinking will foster more active reading.

Prediction

What It Is

Prediction is both a comprehension strategy and a prereading strategy, but in the *Sourcebooks* it is formally used mostly as a comprehension strategy. Nearly all of the prereading strategies used in the *Sourcebooks* involve some level of prediction, but prediction is categorized as a comprehension strategy. When students predict during reading, they rely on information they have already read in the selection.

How to Introduce It

Break the selection into three or four parts.

Have students read to the first stopping point and then ask them to predict what they think will happen. Predictive questions include these:

- What will happen to the character?
- How do you think the problem will be resolved?
- How do you think the selection will end?

Example

What will happen when Polyphemus sees the men eating his goats?

As students read on, encourage them to reflect on their predictions and modify them as further information is provided.

After reading, discuss the accuracy of students' predictions, not to determine if the predictions were "correct," but to provide closure to the activity and validate students' responses. Reflecting back on the predictions will also help students see the information they might have used from the selection to predict but did not.

Why It Works

Because of the students' assertions about "what will happen," predicting gives students a stake in what they read. Their opinion is on the line, and this helps students set purposes for reading.

Comments and Cautions

Look for natural stopping points in texts; obvious spots to stop and predict what will happen next usually occur before episodes, or events, that occur in the story.

Prediction is best used with fiction, although it can also be applied to nonfiction with readers skilled at making predictions.

Graphic Organizers

What It Is

A graphic organizer is a visual representation of the key information for a reading selection. Graphic organizers can be as simple as a two-column chart or as complicated as a multi-dimensional diagram. They come in many sizes and shapes, such as plot charts, cause-effect charts, and character maps.

How to Introduce It

Begin by explaining the purpose of the graphic and the kind of information students should put into each of its parts.

Invite students to fill in the graphic organizer as they read, and then review it and make any modifications after completing the selection. For example, on page 147 in "A Sea of Dunes," students use the graphic organizer to keep track of the details about animal life in the Namib Desert. As they read, they write the name of an animal in each column and describe how it adapts to the desert.

Examples

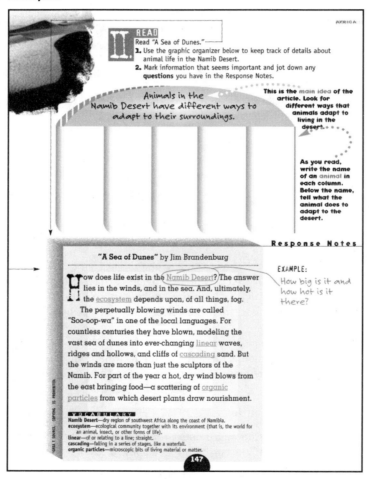

Examples

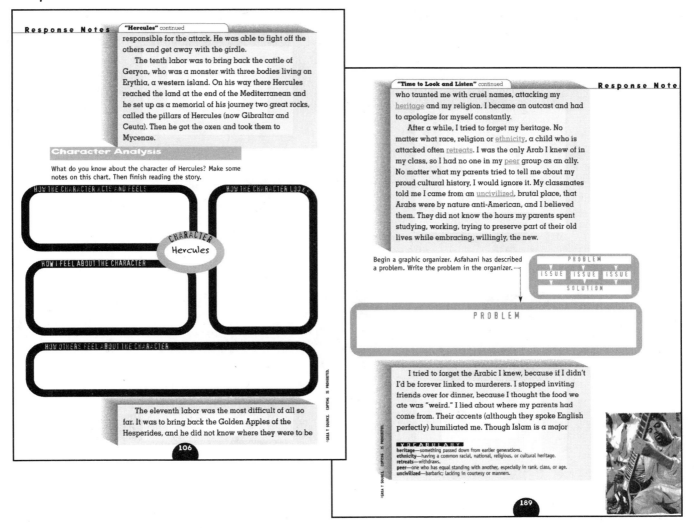

Why It Works

A graphic organizer is a useful tool for helping students to structure what they understand from their reading. It also helps students make connections between ideas, especially in flow charts or cause-effect charts.

Comments and Cautions

Some of the more common graphic organizers are these:

- Venn diagram for showing comparison and contrast
- Cause-and-effect chart for demonstrating causal relationships
- Sequence map for keeping track of a series of events
- Problem-solution map for identifying the problem and its solution(s)
- Word web for representing information about a particular concept

Graphic organizers are excellent tools for all students but are especially helpful for visual learners.

Reciprocal Reading

What It Is

Reciprocal reading is a small-group activity in which students take turns reading aloud to each other or with a tutor. It is such a powerful reading strategy that it has been modified for use in the ***Sourcebooks***. The power of the questions generated does not diminish when reciprocal reading is taken out of the group work or tutor/pupil setting and transferred to a pupil-and-text relationship. The strategy is characterized by asking students to ask questions, clarify, predict, and summarize.

How to Introduce It

Take a moment to introduce the strategy to the whole class. Explain that this strategy involves working with a partner or reading tutor and asking four kinds of questions: clarifying ones, predicting ones, exploratory ones, and summarizing ones.

Invite one student to read the title and opening paragraphs aloud. At the first question point, ask for a volunteer to answer the question. Work through the entire selection with students as a group. Then, ask students to reread the selection again in pairs, taking turns asking and then answering the questions.

Example

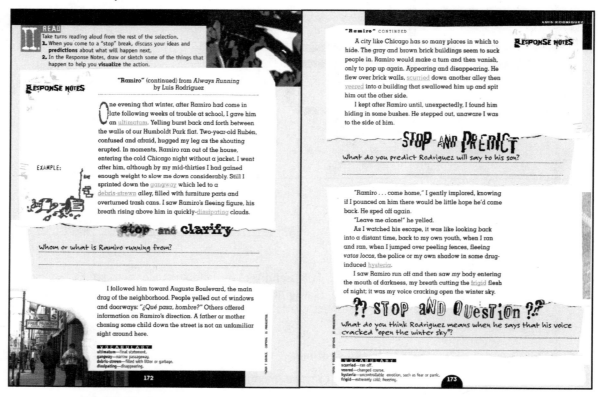

Why It Works

Reciprocal reading can be an excellent tool for both reinforcing listening skills (an often-overlooked skill) and improving reading fluency. It structures the work of students working with a reading partner and naturally helps them ask useful questions—the kinds good readers automatically ask—about a text.

Comments and Cautions

To ensure that the activity doesn't turn into a word-attack session, go over unfamiliar vocabulary before reading.

For reciprocal reading to be successful, it is important to introduce the idea to the whole class before turning students loose with a reading partner. Taking the time to walk through the process will prove beneficial later on when students are asked to work with their reading partners, because they will have a structured routine to fall back on.

Double-Entry Journal

What It Is

A double-entry journal is an adaptation of the more familiar response journal. Typically, the left column includes quotes or facts from a selection, while the right column offers students the opportunity to respond to the quotation or idea. It is a very good strategy to build students' ability to comprehend and interpret a text.

How to Introduce It

Begin by having students list quotations from the selection that interests them, or you can pull out some quotations yourself, as is done in the *Sourcebook*. The benefits of selecting the quotations for students are that the focus is then on interpreting passages of the text and that the task is simplified, making it easier for students to succeed.

Invite students to reflect on the meaning of each quotation and write their thoughts in the right column.

Example

Double-Entry Journal	
Quotation	My response (my thoughts and feelings)
"Here was the theory of racial equality about to be put into practice, and she only hoped she would be equal to being equal."	I think it is a funny comment and shows her intelligence.

Why It Works

Double-entry journals encourage students to become more engaged in what they are reading by focusing on just one part of the text at a time. With this kind of journal, students naturally make connections between the literature and their own lives. Double-entry journals expand on students' understanding of the material and build an initial interpretive response. By beginning the interpretation of literature, students will find writing about a text easier if they focus on the quotations they (or you) selected and their interpretations of them.

Comments and Cautions

Even if you structure the activity by selecting quotations, invite students to add those that have particular meaning to themselves as well.

Encourage students to use double-entry journals in other reading situations, including content-area reading.

Retelling

What It Is

Retelling is a comprehension strategy and assessment tool in which students retell a selection. It works best with chronological selections as a means of checking whether students followed the sequence of events.

How to Introduce It

Before reading the selection, let students know that they will be asked to retell or summarize their reading in their own words.

Either at the end of the selection or at certain stopping points within the selection (as done in the *Sourcebook*), have students retell what they have read as if they are telling it to a friend who has never heard it before.

Have students compare their retellings to examine each other's interpretations of the reading material.

Why It Works

Because retelling allows students to respond in their own words to what they've read, it increases both the quality and quantity of what is comprehended. Retelling also helps students make the text more personally meaningful and provides a deeper understanding of the reading material.

Comments and Cautions

You might have students tape-record the retellings and let students listen and assess their own work.

For fictional selections, try having students retell the story from another character's point of view to provide a different perspective to the tale.

A student's retelling offers a window into the student's thinking and is, therefore, a valuable assessment tool as well.

Story Frame

What It Is

A story frame is a visual representation of one or more of the key elements of a story: character, setting, plot, and theme. It helps students graphically construct the main elements of a story.

How to Introduce It

First, explain the idea of a story frame and its elements: plot, setting, characters, and themes. Be sure students understand that story frames can organize events, too. Just as there are many kinds of stories, students need to understand that there are many kinds of story frames.

Example

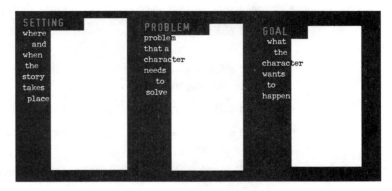

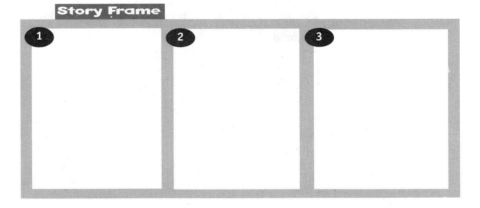

After completing the frame, have students use it as the basis for discussion about the selection or to help in their written responses.

Comments and Cautions

Story frames come in all shapes and sizes. Modify the frame to fit the needs of the students and the focus of the material. For instance, in "The Cyclops' Cave," the story frame focuses on the sequence of events; others focus on character development throughout a story. Other frames might focus on theme or other story elements.

For students who need more guidance filling in their frames, provide them with question prompts, such as "What happened first?" "What happened next? "Who did it happen to?" Let students know this is a strategy they are free to experiment with and use in whatever way they find is most helpful.

REFLECTIVE READING STRATEGIES

The reflective reading strategies occur in **Part V** of each lesson. They help students take away more from what they read. All too often students are asked, "Did you get it?" Reading seems like a code they have been asked to decipher but cannot. They feel stupid and think they have failed.

How can we turn around struggling readers if the only payoff for reading is "getting it"? Good readers read for a variety of reasons: to entertain themselves, to expand their understanding of a subject or develop their thinking in an area, or simply because they have to read. Yet good readers naturally take away more from what they read. For example:

- We read novels by Nobel Prize winners because of their writing **style**.

- We read sports pages because they are **enjoyable**.

- We read philosophy or religious meditations to add more **depth** to how we think about things.

- We read about such topics as Lamaze child-bearing techniques or natural foods because they are personally **meaningful** to us.

- We read cartoons and *People* magazine because they are **easy** to browse through.

- We read directions about setting up a computer because we **have to**; we need to have that particular understanding.

We read, in other words, for a variety of reasons. As teachers, we need to help struggling readers see that—and not just that they did not "get it" on the multiple-choice test. So, **Part V** of each lesson in the *Sourcebook* is a "reflective" assessment, a looking back, so students can see what they *gained* from the lesson, not what they failed to understand.

Example

V. **WRAP-UP**
What, if anything, did you like about Luis Rodriguez's style of writing?

READERS' CHECKLIST

STYLE
☐ Did you find the piece well written?
☐ Are the sentences well constructed and the words well chosen?
☐ Does the style show you how to be a better writer?

Doorway in Humboldt Park neighborhood

170

The purpose of the **Readers' Checklist** in each lesson is to:

1. model for students the questions good readers ask of themselves after reading.

2. expand the reasons for which students want to read.

3. build lifelong habits for students by repeating best reading practices.

Reflective Assessment

1. Understanding

Did you understand the reading?

Was the message or point clear?

Can you restate what the reading is about?

2. Ease

Was the passage easy to read?

Were you able to read it smoothly and without difficulty?

3. Meaning

Did you learn something from the reading?

Did it affect you or make an impression?

4. Style

Did you find the passage well written?

Are the sentences well constructed and the words well chosen?

Does the style show you how to be a better writer?

5. Depth

Did the reading make you think about things?

Did it set off thoughts beyond the surface topic?

6. Enjoyment

Did you like the reading?

Was the reading experience pleasurable?

Would you want to reread the piece or recommend it to someone?

Invite students regularly to provide examples and reasons for their answers to these questions.

Identity

Unit Background   **IDENTITY** (pages 11–32)

One's identity is shaped by many factors. Genetic heritage, name, birthplace, childhood, beliefs, and accomplishments all contribute to one's individuality. Some people live comfortably with their identity, accepting it unquestioningly. Others struggle to find their true selves, perhaps by trying on new names (and new clothes), accepting new beliefs and opinions, or rejecting a part of their heritage. In the two autobiographical selections in this first part, the writers recount their efforts to find an identity that seems both baffling and elusive.

Teaching the Introduction

The images on page 11 are designed to get students thinking about the many factors that influence identity.

1. Ask students whether they think one's identity is shaped by one's beliefs.

2. Ask: "In what ways do friends help to shape one's identity? What are the major ways friends can influence one?"

3. Ask students to discuss the influences of immediate and extended family on shaping who they are.

4. Ask: "How much does appearance play in establishing identity? Is appearance overemphasized in today's society?"

5. Finally, ask: "What are some other things on which your identity is based?" (*Students might mention where they live—country, city or town, and neighborhood—and language.*)

Opening Activity

Ask students to bring in a photo of themselves, or you can provide a disposable or Polaroid camera, and ask someone in the class to take an individual picture of each class member for posting on the bulletin board. Ask what students can conclude about the identity of the class as a whole. In addition, you might read Emily Dickinson's poem "I'm Nobody" and ask for comments.

The Good Daughter

Skills and Strategies Overview

THEME	Identity
READING LEVEL	average
VOCABULARY	✦queries ✦mirthless ✦flinched ✦flippant ✦abyss
PREREADING	quickwrite
RESPONSE	question
COMPREHENSION	directed reading
PREWRITING	narrowing a topic
WRITING	paragraph / capitalizing sentences and end punctuation
ASSESSMENT	understanding

BACKGROUND

"The Good Daughter" is a personal essay originally published in *Newsweek* as a "My Turn" (or guest) column. Caroline Hwang, who is an editor at *Mademoiselle,* is currently writing her first novel.

In "The Good Daughter," Hwang discusses the pull she feels from two different cultures. She was born and raised in the United States and knows that she is an American; yet she also has strong ties to her family's Korean ancestry. She feels robbed that she wasn't told much about her heritage as she was growing up, and she assumes that her parents didn't tell her more because they wanted her to be as "American as possible." As a result, Hwang feels as if she is "straddling" two cultures. More significantly, she admits that she has not been fully accepted by either culture. This has made it difficult for her to develop a sense of identity. In one of her most revealing sentences, Hwang explains that she and other children of immigrants are "living paradoxes. . . . We are in this country for its opportunities, yet filial duty binds us."

UNIT THEME Caroline Hwang questions her identity. Is she American, Korean, or Korean American? She maintains that she must learn who *she is* before she can decide who she wants to become.

GRAPHIC ORGANIZER A web like the one below might help students organize information about Caroline.

writing is her "passion"

feels "fully assimilated"

"straddles" two cultures

Caroline Hwang

is at a turning point

speaks Spanish, German, Latin

uncertain of her future

is looking for happiness

BEFORE YOU READ

Read through the introduction to the lesson with students. The purpose of the opening of the lesson is to motivate and focus students. Then introduce the prereading activity, a **one-minute quickwrite**. (Refer to the **Strategy Handbook** on page 40 for more help.)

Motivation Strategy

In "The Good Daughter," Caroline Hwang wonders who she is, and who she would like to become. Ask students to tell about a time they questioned who they were. Where did they go for answers? Involve students' egos by asking them to tell something about themselves.

ENGAGING STUDENTS Explain that "The Good Daughter" is a personal essay about a woman's search for identity. Ask students to complete this statement: "I think identity is _____." The question will help them begin thinking about the theme of the selection.

Vocabulary Building

Help students use **context clues** to figure out the meanings of difficult words as they read, especially the key vocabulary for this lesson: *queries, mirthless, flinched, flippant,* and *abyss*. Although footnotes define these words, model using context and then checking your ideas against the footnote: "I don't know the word *queries*. I see, though, that it follows two questions. Could *queries* mean 'questions'? I can check the footnote to see if my guess is correct." Be sure that students can pronounce the words. For additional practice with these words, see the **Vocabulary** blackline master on page 66.

STRATEGY LESSON: PREFIXES As students read, point out words with prefixes, such as *surname, unsatisfied, mispronounced, impossible,* and *disintegrating*. Model for students how to separate a prefix from the root word (un + fortunate). Remind the class that when a prefix is added to a word, the meaning of the word changes.

For additional practice on this strategy, see the **Vocabulary** blackline master on page 66.

Prereading Strategies

The purpose of a **quickwrite** is to get students writing almost before they know it. Always ask students to quickwrite with a particular topic in mind. In this case, they are asked to read the title and opening paragraph of "The Good Daughter" and write about a personal experience. Tell them it might be about a time they felt they didn't fit in, a time they thought about their name, and so on. Have them jot down whatever thoughts and memories come to mind.

PICTURE WALK As an alternate prereading strategy, ask students to do a picture walk. Have them tell you what the pictures remind them of. Based on what they've seen, what do they predict the selection will be about? When they've finished reading, they might return to the pictures and explain what connections they see between the art and the essay.

Spanish-Speaking Students

En "La hija buena" Caroline Hwang escribe del conflicto de encontrarse entre dos mundos diferentes. Ella nació en los Estados Unidos y sabe que es norteamericana. Pero como es la hija de padres koreanos, tiene lazos muy fuertes a su ascendencia extranjera. Como resultado de su dilema cultural, Hwang lo ha encontrado muy difícil desarrollar una identidad fija.

II. READ

As students begin to read, walk through the process of responding to literature. Introduce the strategy of questioning and point out the example given. Then begin reading. Start by reading the first selection aloud with the class. At the first **stop and think**, discuss an answer. Then ask students to write it in the book.

Response Strategy

QUESTION   Questions are bound to come up whenever students read. It's important that they make note of their questions right away, so that they don't lose track of what they want to ask. Tell them to write the questions they want to ask the author, another reader, and you in the **Response Notes**. When they've finished reading, have volunteers read their questions aloud. Work as a class to find answers.

Comprehension Strategies

Directed reading (stop and think) can help reluctant or low-level readers better comprehend what they are reading. In a directed reading, the teacher guides the reading by posing open-ended questions. You can set the stage for a directed reading by asking an open-ended question such as "How did the dry cleaner's words affect Caroline?"

GRAPHIC ORGANIZER   An alternate comprehension strategy is a problem/solution graphic organizer. As they read, students can make note of each problem Caroline Hwang presents. For example, she has problems talking with the dry-cleaning woman, she disagrees with her parents about what she should study in school, and so on. Next to each problem, students can write their advice to Hwang on how to solve the difficulty.

For more help, see the **Comprehension** blackline master on page 67.

Discussion Questions

COMPREHENSION   1. From which country did Caroline's parents immigrate? *(Korea)*

2. Why does the dry-cleaning woman laugh at Caroline? *(Caroline mispronounces her own last name.)*

3. Why does Caroline decide to drop out of graduate school? *(She has no passion for her studies.)*

CRITICAL THINKING   4. What do you think Caroline's parents want most for their daughter? *(They want her to follow traditional customs.)*

5. In what ways is Caroline Hwang "a good daughter"? *(Have students support their opinions. One idea is that Caroline seems to be trying to balance Korean and American ways.)*

Literary Skill

POINT OF VIEW   To introduce a literary skill with this lesson, explain to students that a personal essay is told from the first-person point of view. Caroline Hwang uses first-person point of view in her essay. In other words, she uses "I" to tell her story. Ask: In what ways would "The Good Daughter" be different had it been written by Caroline's mother or father? Help students see that if the vantage point changes, so does the essay.

III. GATHER YOUR THOUGHTS

The goal of these prewriting activities is first to help students collect what they have learned and then to build a topic to write about. Use the prewriting activities to show students how to take a large topic, such as "Finding an Identity," and break it into a more manageable size.

Prewriting Strategies

TOPIC SENTENCES After students limit their topics, you may also want to help them with topic sentences. Explain that a topic sentence must clearly state the subject of the paragraph. In addition, it should state a feeling or attitude about the subject. Have students use this simple formula when writing topic sentences:

Specific topic + attitude or feeling = a good topic sentence.

Have students use the **Prewriting** blackline master on page 68.

IV. WRITE

Set aside plenty of time for students to write. Many students will benefit from feeling relaxed about time. Ask students first to draft their **paragraph**. Remind students they need to include a topic sentence and three detail sentences. Then, after they have finished writing, ask them to revise using the **Writers' Checklist** in the student book.

WRITING RUBRIC Use the writing rubric below to help students focus on the assignment requirements and for help with a quick assessment of their writing.

Do students' paragraphs

- begin with a topic sentence?
- contain three or more details to support the topic sentence?
- stay focused on the topic "finding an identity"?

Grammar, Usage, and Mechanics

Draw students' attention to the **Writers' Checklist** as a way to introduce a mini-lesson. Remind students that every sentence must begin with a capital letter, end with a punctuation mark, and express a complete thought.

Incorrect: the author struggled

Correct: The author struggled to find an identity.

V. WRAP-UP

Take a moment at the end of the lesson for students to reflect on their **understanding** of the essay. Use the **Readers' Checklist** on page 20 to help students ask the questions good readers ask of themselves and to see that people read for a variety of purposes. This checklist asks students to reflect on their understanding of "The Good Daughter" and encourages them to think about how they might restate the main idea of the reading and what they might say the selection is about.

Assessment

To test students' comprehension, use the **Assessment** blackline master on page 69.

Name _____

VOCABULARY

Words from the Selection

DIRECTIONS Using context clues, fill in each blank with the most appropriate word from the list below.

> ◆queries   ◆mirthless   ◆flinched   ◆flippant   ◆abyss

1. Since we were lost in a strange city, we had to stop people with _____ about which bus to take.

2. Diego made a _____ remark to a man about how confusing the street signs were.

3. The man, a _____ type, was not amused.

4. He growled a remark at Diego, who _____ in surprise.

5. Diego's translation was that the man hoped we would fall into an/a _____.

Strategy Lesson: Prefixes

Prefixes are word parts that come before the root word (*pre-* = before). Some prefixes can change the meaning of a word from positive to negative. For example, when you add the prefix *mis-* to the word *understand,* you have a completely new word: *misunderstand.*

DIRECTIONS Write the prefix and root of each word. Then write what you think the word means.

> ◆impossible   ◆mispronounce   ◆unsatisfied   ◆disobey   ◆disintegrated

	prefix	+	root word	=	meaning
EXAMPLE: unable	un	+	able	= not able or can't	
6. impossible	_____	+	_____	=	_____
7. mispronounce	_____	+	_____	=	_____
8. unsatisfied	_____	+	_____	=	_____
9. disobey	_____	+	_____	=	_____
10. disintegrated	_____	+	_____	=	_____

Name _____

COMPREHENSION
Graphic Organizer

DIRECTIONS Use this Venn diagram to show how Caroline Hwang and her parents are similar and different. Feel free to look up details in your book if you need to.

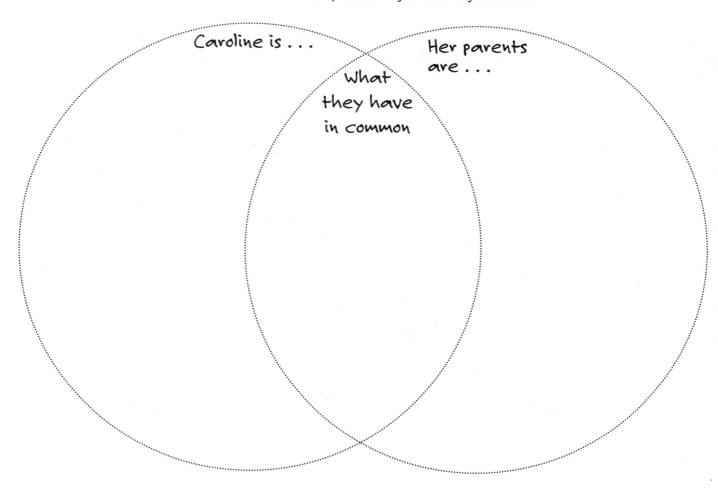

Name _____

PREWRITING

Writing a Topic Sentence and Details

DIRECTIONS Every paragraph you write must have a topic sentence. A topic sentence tells the subject of the paragraph and how you feel about the subject. You can use this formula to help you write a topic sentence.

A specific topic + a specific feeling or attitude = a good topic sentence.

Now follow these steps to write a topic sentence and supporting details.

1. Write a topic sentence for your narrowed topic about finding an identity.

Finding an identity is _____.

2. Now plan your paragraph.

Think of three details to support your topic sentence. Your details will be examples from your own life.

Then think of a concluding sentence that ties everything together.

Use the paragraph planner for your notes.

MY PARAGRAPH PLANNER

Topic sentence

Detail 1   Detail 2   Detail 3

Concluding sentence

Name _____

ASSESSMENT

Multiple-Choice Test

DIRECTIONS On the blanks provided, write the letter of the answer that best completes each statement or answers each question.

_____ 1. The woman at the dry-cleaning store asked Caroline if she was . . .
  A. Chinese.   C. Japanese.
  B. Korean.   D. Indonesian.

_____ 2. Why is the dry-cleaning woman confused about Caroline's heritage?
  A. She is distracted by other customers.   C. Caroline tries to mislead her.
  B. Caroline mispronounces her own name.   D. none of the above

_____ 3. When the dry-cleaner learns that Caroline can't pronounce her name, what does she do?
  A. apologizes   C. laughs
  B. cries   D. yells

_____ 4. What does Caroline's mother say when Caroline tells her about the dry-cleaning woman?
  A. "I'm sorry."   C. "Big deal."
  B. "How awful."   D. "Don't tell Dad."

_____ 5. Caroline can say "I am Korean" in . . .
  A. German.   C. English.
  B. Spanish.   D. all of the above

_____ 6. Caroline's parents wanted her to study. . .
  A. English.   C. law.
  B. nursing.   D. journalism.

_____ 7. Caroline wants to be a. . .
  A. doctor.   C. shopkeeper.
  B. writer.   D. veterinarian.

_____ 8. How does Caroline feel about her identity?
  A. confused   C. sad
  B. proud   D. surprised

_____ 9. How old is Caroline?
  A. 25   C. 18
  B. 32   D. 47

_____ 10. Why is Caroline worried about her love life?
  A. She and her boyfriend fight a lot.   C. She has trouble meeting nice men.
  B. She works too much to date.   D. Her parents expect her to marry a Korean man.

Short-Essay Test

What does Caroline mean when she says children of immigrants "are the first generation and the last"?

STUDENT PAGES 21–32

Skills and Strategies Overview

THEME Identity

READING LEVEL average

VOCABULARY
◇refrained ◇voraciously ◇angst ◇tenets ◇juvenile

PREREADING think-pair-and-share

RESPONSE highlight

COMPREHENSION directed reading

PREWRITING group discussion

WRITING personal experience paragraph / sentence fragments

ASSESSMENT meaning

BACKGROUND

As a child living in Harlem, the setting for many of his books, Walter Dean Myers had a chance to observe firsthand the poverty that many children today face. After dropping out of high school in 1954, Myers joined the army and then held positions with the New York Department of Labor, the post office, and a rehabilitation center. In 1969 his book *Where Does a Day Go?* won a contest sponsored by the Council on Interracial Books for Children. Since then, Myers has written full time.

"Bridges" is filled with the same emotions and conflicts that appear in Myers's stories. In this autobiographical piece, Myers focuses on his own uncertainties, describes his lifelong urge to read and write, and tells how it shaped the man he was to become. Myers is unflinching and honest when he talks about himself, readily admitting his weaknesses and revealing how he turned some into strengths.

UNIT THEME When confronted with the imminent death of his father, Walter Dean Myers here considers his own identity.

GRAPHIC ORGANIZER Students might try writing a bio-poem like the one below.

Bio-Poem:
Walter Dean Myers

Walter,
Writer.
Son, husband, thinker, worrier;
Lover of words, ideas, and dreams;
Who believes in fairness;
Who wants equality, justice, and peace;
Who keeps his words as protection, his memories as a shield,
    his father as his idol;
Who gives his words to children, his love to his family, and his
    ideas to those who will listen;
Who said, "I love you."
Role model.

BIBLIOGRAPHY Students might enjoy these other books by Walter Dean Myers: *Scorpions* (1988), *Fallen Angels* (1991), *Now Is Your Time!* (1992), *Somewhere in the Darkness* (1992), *Malcolm X* (1993), and *Slam!* (listed by the American Library Association as one of the best books for young adults, 1997).

BEFORE YOU READ

Explain that "Bridges" is Walter Dean Myers's emotional account of a journey he took to say good-bye to his dying father. Remind students to **highlight** passages that surprise or interest them. The sentences in the **think-pair-and-share** immediately immerse students in the drama of the text and launch discussion of what the reading will be about.

Motivation Strategy

ENGAGING STUDENTS Ask students to think about advice they would have for someone dealing with the death of a loved one. Or, have them consider a question that explores the grieving process (and relates to "Bridges") such as "Is it easier to accept a loved one's death if you've had the chance to say good-bye?"

Vocabulary Building

Draw attention to the key vocabulary words for this lesson: *refrained, voraciously, angst, tenets*, and *juvenile*. These words are emphasized in the "Words from the Selection" on the **Vocabulary** blackline master, page 74. The point is to help students add some new words to their vocabulary each time they read.

STRATEGY LESSON: CONTEXT CLUES Encourage students to figure out the meanings of difficult or unknown words, such as *unfamiliar*. Model the process by saying: "I don't know the meaning of the word *unfamiliar*. I see, however, that *unfamiliar* is used in a sentence describing something Myers doesn't know about (page 25), so I guess *unfamiliar* must mean something like 'don't know about.'"

For additional practice, see the **Vocabulary** blackline master on page 74.

Prereading Strategies

In the **think-pair-and-share,** students look at a series of quotations from the text and then decide a logical order for the sentences. What's most important here is that students start thinking about what they're about to read. Quotations for a think-pair-and-share have been chosen with the aim of giving students a brief introduction to the subject and—in many cases—the main idea of the piece. Students' judgments about the order of sentences will vary. The value of this activity comes when students talk about why they think the order is what they described and how well they use the clues, such as the word *dying*, in the sentences.

QUICKWRITE Another excellent prereading strategy is the quickwrite. Read aloud the first paragraph or two of Myers's memoir. Ask students to do a one-minute quickwrite about a topic from a list you write on the board. Items on your list might include: death, saying good-bye, parent-child relationships, my favorite childhood memory, and my worst childhood memory.

Spanish-Speaking Students

En la obra autobiográfica "Puentes," Walter Dean Myers describe su búsqueda de identidad y los intentos de entender a sí mismo. Frente a la muerte de su padre, quiere saber más sobre su propia vida y su papel en el mundo. Myers habla de su juventud con exactitud y honestidad, admitiendo a sus debilidades, fuerzas y pasiones.

II. READ

When students are ready to read, be sure they understand the response strategy of **highlighting.** If possible, ask students to use yellow markers. Ask a student to read the first paragraph while everyone follows along and marks the text. Have students share how they highlighted passages that surprised or interested them. Explain to students that responding to questions as in the **stop and think** spaces and sketching parts of the text are all ways to help them remember what they are reading.

Response Strategy

VISUALIZE An important reading strategy for reluctant readers is visualizing. As they read, students should try to form pictures in their minds of the people, places, and events the author describes. They can make quick sketches of what they've visualized as they read. These sketches will be a handy reference when it comes time to consider the meaning of the selection. Emphasize that artistic abilities are not necessary for sketching.

Comprehension Strategies

In **directed reading**, a reading coach helps struggling readers make sense of a passage. Here the **stop and think** questions coach readers through the selection. Whenever you think it's necessary, stop students and ask a comprehension question. Questions can be as simple as "What's Myers's mother like?" Help students get to the main idea of a selection. Ask such questions as, "What message does the author have for you?" and "Why might Myers have titled this piece 'Bridges'?"

GRAPHIC ORGANIZER Another comprehension strategy that works very well with nonfiction is the graphic organizer. Graphic organizers help students "see" a story unfold. For "Bridges," you might create and photocopy an organizer that uses time-sequence words such as *first, next, then, after that,* and *finally.* Students can make notes on the organizer as they read.

For more help, see the **Comprehension** blackline master on page 75.

Discussion Questions

COMPREHENSION 1. Who are the Deans? (*They are Walter Dean Myers's adoptive parents.*)

2. Why is Myers going to visit his father? (*His father is dying. Walter needs to say good-bye.*)

3. What does Walter later discover about his father? (*His father never learned to read.*)

CRITICAL THINKING 4. Why is Myers's trip to visit his father so painful? (*Besides his own grief, he is coming to grips with not knowing his father as well as he might have.*)

5. What do you think causes Myers the most sadness? (*Among the many possible answers is that his new appreciation for his father occurs right before his father's death.*)

Literary Skill

THEME One literary term to introduce in "Bridges" is theme, the main idea or underlying meaning of a work. Growing up, parent-child relationships, and identity all are possible themes of this selection. You might write a list of themes on the board and ask for volunteers to explain how they are developed in the selection. Ask students whether the title of this selection might provide a clue to them.

III. GATHER YOUR THOUGHTS

Students should stay in small groups to work through the **Discussion Guide**. By working cooperatively, students gain confidence in their own understandings about what they have read. Suggest that students use their answers to question 3 as possible topics for the personal experience paragraph they will write.

Prewriting Strategies

GROUP DISCUSSION A discussion can also show how rewarding it can be to build upon each other's ideas. Begin by answering the first question yourself and then asking volunteers to respond. Model the notes you would take on the board.

For more practice, see the **Prewriting and Writing** blackline master on page 76.

IV. WRITE

Set aside some time for students to write their **personal experience paragraph**. Explain that for the next fifteen minutes, students should write about the event they named in their title. Remind them to stay focused on this one event. Introduce a brief lesson on avoiding sentence fragments at the most opportune time.

WRITING RUBRIC Use the writing rubric to help students focus on the assignment and to help with a quick assessment of their writing.

Do students' paragraphs

- have the name of the event in the title?
- begin the same way that Myers begins?
- avoid sentence fragments?
- stay focused on just one event or thought?

Grammar, Usage, and Mechanics

Draw students' attention to the **Writers' Checklist** on sentence fragments. Remind them that they may need to add a subject or verb or combine a fragment with another sentence to fix a sentence that is not complete.

Fragment: Because the bus broke down.

Sentence: The bus broke down.

Sentence: Because the bus broke down, I was late for school.

Some students confuse short sentences with fragments. Help students realize that fragments can be long and complicated, such as, "The boy in the dog costume with the funny ears who came to your party."

V. WRAP-UP

At the end of the lesson, allow time for students to reflect on what they have learned and accomplished.

Assessment

As students answer the questions about the **meaning** of "Bridges," encourage them to make connections between their lives and families and Myers and his parents.

For a comprehension check, use the **Assessment** blackline master on page 77.

Name _____

VOCABULARY

Words from the Selection

DIRECTIONS Select the word from the list below that best describes each situation, and write the word on the blank.

> ✦refrained ✦voraciously ✦angst ✦tenets ✦juvenile

1. Raul lives his life according to two sayings: "Make hay while the sun shines" and "Do unto others as you would have them do unto you." These are his _____.

2. On weekends, he eats two eggs, hash browns, toast, and a glass of milk for breakfast. He eats _____.

3. We didn't say what we were thinking, but we wanted to. Instead, we
_____.

4. Raul is not worried about the math test tomorrow. He shows no signs of
_____.

5. He just laughed when someone spoke to him the way a five-year-old would. The remark was really _____.

Strategy Lesson: Context Clues

When you come to a word you don't understand, try using context to define the word. This means you look for clues about the unfamiliar word in the surrounding sentences.

EXAMPLE: Walter seemed <u>unfamiliar</u> with his old neighborhood, which was strange.
Clue: The strangeness happens in the neighborhood, which he should know. Maybe he doesn't recognize anything?

DIRECTIONS Read these sentences. Use context clues to help you figure out the meaning of the underlined words. Write the meaning of the word on the blank.

> ✦coaxed ✦irascible ✦significant ✦wages ✦decision

6. He <u>coaxed</u> the scared kitten down from the tree. _____

7. Since he was so easy to anger, the teacher called him <u>irascible</u>. _____

8. The scientist won a prize for his <u>significant</u> findings. _____

9. Thanks to the <u>wages</u> I earn at my job, I can afford a new bike. _____

10. It was my <u>decision</u> to say "yes" to public school and "no" to private. _____

Name _____

COMPREHENSION
Directed Reading
....

DIRECTIONS With a partner, decide on the answers to these questions, and write the answers on the blanks.

1. What three words would you use to describe Mr. Dean?

_____

_____

2. What words would you use to describe Mrs. Dean?

_____

_____

3. What secret does Mr. Dean keep from Walter?

_____

_____

4. How does Walter feel when he learns his father's secret?

_____

_____

_____

5. What is Myers's biggest regret about his father?

_____

_____

_____

6. How does Myers feel when his son says, "You're sounding a lot like Grandpa"?

_____

_____

_____

Name _____

PREWRITING AND WRITING

Writing a Personal Experience Paragraph

DIRECTIONS A personal experience paragraph tells a story. It should have a beginning, a middle, and an end. Follow these steps to write a paragraph about a personal experience.

STEP 1. WRITE A TOPIC SENTENCE. Complete this sentence in several different ways. Then choose one of your topic sentences.

I was _____ years old when _____

I was _____ years old when _____

I was _____ years old when _____

STEP 2. TELL WHAT HAPPENS. Next write three details or parts for your experience. Think of details that will help readers see and hear what you are describing.

#1 _____

_____

#2 _____

_____

#3 _____

_____

STEP 3. SHOW WHAT HAPPENS IN ORDER. Use this storyboard. Draw sketches, and then write about the sketches.

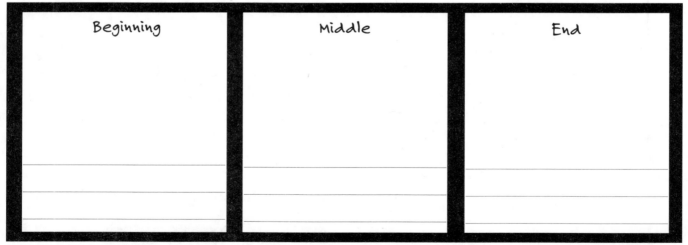

| Beginning | Middle | End |

STEP 4. WRITE A CONCLUSION. Write a concluding sentence that restates the topic sentence and tells what you learned from your experience.

My concluding sentence _____

_____

_____

Name _____

ASSESSMENT

Multiple-Choice Test

DIRECTIONS On the blanks provided, write the letter of the answer that best completes each statement or answers each question.

_____ 1. The Deans adopted Walter because . . .
    A. his mother had died.   C. he was neglected.
    B. he ran away.   D. none of the above

_____ 2. How does Myers feel about his journey to see his father?
    A. excited   C. unsure
    B. guilty   D. annoyed

_____ 3. When he was growing up, Walter was a . . .
    A. problem child.   C. criminal.
    B. gifted student.   D. none of the above

_____ 4. As a child, Walter loved to . . .
    A. read.   C. talk about ideas.
    B. write.   D. all of the above

_____ 5. Walter was not able to . . .
    A. find a job.   C. go to college.
    B. join the army.   D. learn to drive.

_____ 6. What does Walter want from his father?
    A. jokes   C. approval
    B. compassion   D. knowledge

_____ 7. What was Herbert Dean's secret?
    A. He drank too much.   C. He made bets.
    B. He couldn't read.   D. none of the above

_____ 8. Who tells the story?
    A. Walter Dean Myers   C. Herbert Dean
    B. Florence Dean   D. an outsider

_____ 9. After Herbert Dean dies, Walter feels . . .
    A. full of regret.   C. silly.
    B. full of relief.   D. embarrassed.

_____ 10. What emotions does Walter Dean Myers feel after the death of his father?
    A. compassion   C. gratitude
    B. love   D. all of the above

Short-Essay Test

What do you think Walter Dean Myers is trying to suggest with his title "Bridges"?

World War I

Unit Background   WORLD WAR I (pages 33–48)

World War I, the first war to involve countries from all over the world, literally reshaped the world. As a result of this war, boundaries shifted, alliances changed, and even the most peaceful nations began to rethink their military technology.

During the war, the Allies fought the Central Powers. The Allied Powers included Belgium, Great Britain, France, Italy (after late 1914), Japan, most of North Africa, Portugal, Romania, Russia, and the United States, which entered the war in 1917. The Central Powers included Germany, Austria-Hungary, Bulgaria, and the Ottoman Empire (Turkey). In all, more than ten million people were killed in the war.

One noteworthy aspect of World War I was the emergence of new technologies. The airplane, hand grenades, tanks, and machine guns were some of the new weapons that made a substantial impact during the war. One of the selections concentrates on a single aspect of the new technology: submarines. First used to cut off supplies, German submarines attacked supply ships bringing food and fuel to Great Britain and France. In fact, it was as a result of these attacks that the United States eventually entered the war. Its ships were being sunk and Americans were dying in these attacks.

Teaching the Introduction

The photographs and brief time line on page 33 are intended to help establish the general time of World War I and one of the most memorable results of the war, the new weapons of destruction that were first used, notably the airplane and submarine.

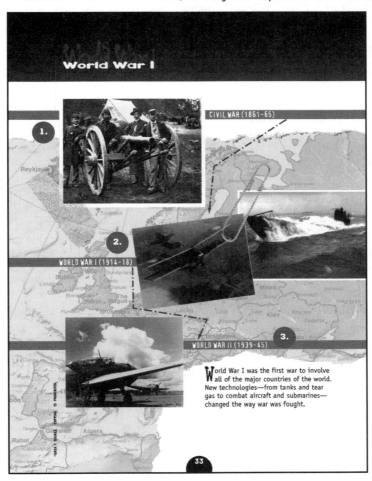

1. Ask students what they know about the Civil War. What were the two sides? What sort of weapons did they use? Try to establish major figures (Abraham Lincoln, Jefferson Davis, Ulysses Grant, and so on) and weapons (muskets and cannons).

2. Ask: "What do you know about World War I? Who fought in it? What sort of weapons were used? What differences can you see among the photographs?"

3. Ask students what they know about World War II. What is different about the kind of planes shown for this war?

Opening Activity

Bring copies of pictures from magazines and books of various people and weapons from the Civil War, World War I, and World War II. Ask a group of students to post pictures from World War I.

Pilots' Reflections

STUDENT PAGES 35–41

Skills and Strategies Overview

THEME	World War I
READING LEVEL	average
VOCABULARY	◆ fragile ◆ triumph ◆ perplexing ◆ idle ◆ vicinity
PREREADING	skimming
RESPONSE	question
COMPREHENSION	retelling
PREWRITING	main idea and details
WRITING	letter / greetings and closings of letters
ASSESSMENT	ease

BACKGROUND

Although most World War I planes were biplanes, there were also monoplanes and triplanes. The first planes were used for reconnaissance over enemy lines, but planes were soon armed. The English Sopwith Camel, for example, carried two machine guns, as did the French Spad XIII, a one-seater biplane.

Manfred von Richthofen, the famous German ace, became known as the Red Baron because he flew a red Fokker triplane.

UNIT THEME Two World War I pilots explain what it was like to be a pilot during the war. Their recollections will show students how terrifying war can be.

GRAPHIC ORGANIZER A time line like this one can help students see the major events of World War I.

Major Events: World War I

1914	1915	1916	1917	1918
Germany declares war on Russia, France, and Belgium. Britain declares war on Germany.	German submarine sinks *Lusitania*.	Battle of Verdun and Battle of the Somme; both are German defeats.	Germany sinks five U.S. ships. United States declares war on Germany.	President Woodrow Wilson proposes a fourteen-point peace plan. Germany signs a peace treaty.

BEFORE YOU READ

In "Pilots' Reflections," two men explain what it was like to fly solo missions during World War I. Explain to students that they'll be reading firsthand accounts of the war. Before they read, they'll **skim** the selection. This will help familiarize them with the topic and pique their interest about the two pilots.

Motivation Strategy

ENGAGING STUDENTS Tell students that a great way to learn history is to read a firsthand account. "Pilots' Reflections" gives them the chance to experience World War I through the eyes of soldiers who actually fought in the war.

Vocabulary Building

Read aloud to students the key vocabulary words for this lesson: *fragile, triumph, perplexing, idle,* and *vicinity*. These words are featured on the **Vocabulary** blackline master on page 84. Encourage students to familiarize themselves with the definition of each word. Later, they can practice using these words in sentences.

STRATEGY LESSON: PREFIXES For additional vocabulary work, teach a short lesson on prefixes. Remind the class that prefixes can change the meaning of a root word. Some common prefixes are *bi-* (two, having two, once every two) and *tri-* (three, having three, once every three). Show students these prefixes and have them try to build lists of words that contain the prefixes.

For additional vocabulary work, see the **Vocabulary** blackline master on page 84.

Prereading Strategies

During a **skim**, students glance through the selection quickly, looking for words and phrases that can reveal information about the topic. Skimming gives readers an idea of what they can expect during their close reads and can alert them to words or ideas that might cause them difficulty. If you like, work through the skimming questions on page 34 as a group. This can help students see that everyone skims differently. Not everyone will catch every detail.

PREVIEW As an alternate prereading strategy, ask students to preview the selection. This also will help familiarize them with the subject and writing style. Have them look at art, headlines, vocabulary words, and interrupter questions. Then ask: "What is the topic of this selection? Who are the narrators of the two pieces? What do you think the most difficult part(s) will be?"

Spanish-Speaking Students

"Las reflexiones de unos pilotos" expresa la realidad de la Primera Guerra Mundial por las experiencias diferentes de dos pilotos, un inglés y un alemán. El inglés explica cómo evadió una confrontación con el enemigo debido a un código de simpatía entre pilotos. El alemán, por otro lado, describe su determinación de entrapar y matar a un piloto enemigo. Los dos cuentos, sin embargo, muestran la complejidad de batalla y la incertidumbre de la vida diaria durante la guerra.

II. READ

As they read, students should **mark** the text by underlining, circling, highlighting, and writing notes in the margins. Read aloud the first paragraph while students follow along in their books. Then ask for volunteers to tell what they marked or highlighted in the paragraph and why. Explain to students that marking a text while they read is one way to keep themselves actively involved. Also point out that their notations will come in handy later, when they need to think critically about the selection.

Response Strategy

QUESTION In addition to having them mark and highlight the text, you also might want to ask students to write questions about what they're reading. This response strategy gives students a chance to note their immediate reactions to the pilots' reminiscences. Sometimes a reader's first thoughts about a piece end up being the most insightful of all.

Comprehension Strategies

RETELLING As students read, be sure they understand that they are to stop occasionally in order to retell the events described. Retelling a story or article can help readers make connections that they might not have noticed the first time around. When they retell, students should be brief but thorough. In a retelling, students should focus only on the major events and should ignore minor details.

For more help, see the **Comprehension** blackline master on page 85.

Discussion Questions

COMPREHENSION 1. What war are these men fighting, and when did it take place? *(They are fighting during World War I—1914–1918.)*

2. Who was Manfred von Richthofen? *(He was a German pilot who gained fame during World War I.)*

3. What was the "bond of sympathy" between pilots? *(Enemy pilots viewed each other as co-workers, rather than adversaries.)*

CRITICAL THINKING 4. What do you think were some of the difficulties of being a pilot during this war? *(Poorly built planes, no navigational equipment, no oxygen equipment, etc.)*

5. Judging from what you've read, would you say these pilots were brave or foolish? Explain. *(Answers will vary. Have students support their responses with evidence from the selection.)*

Literary Skill

TONE Take this opportunity to introduce tone, the author's attitude toward a subject or audience. Ask students which of the following words they would use to describe von Richthofen's tone or attitude toward his subject: matter-of-fact, humorous, mocking, angry, sympathetic, weary, serious, nasty, boastful.

III. GATHER YOUR THOUGHTS

After they finish reading, students will create a web that explores the **main idea** and supporting **details** of either Douglas's or von Richthofen's writing. If students are struggling to find the main idea, consider dividing the class into two groups. The first group can search for the main idea in Douglas's piece. The other group can look at von Richthofen's writing. Ask each group a series of questions that can lead them toward important ideas in the writing. For example, "What is Douglas's or von Richthofen's attitude toward war?" "How do they feel about their jobs as fighter pilots?" "How are the two men similar? How are they different?"

Prewriting Strategies

GROUP DISCUSSION As an alternate prewriting strategy, hold a group discussion. A discussion will be particularly helpful to students who are struggling with the selection. It can also show students how to build upon each other's ideas. During the discussion, ask factual and inferential questions that can help students see the main idea.

For more practice, have students use the **Prewriting and Writing** blackline master on page 86.

IV. WRITE

Remind students that their assignment is to write a **letter** to a friend in which they summarize the events either Douglas or von Richthofen describe. They should work directly from the main idea/details web they completed on page 39. Use the questions in the writing rubric to help them revise. During the revision session, you can introduce a brief lesson on proper letter form.

WRITING RUBRIC Do students' letters

- begin with a topic sentence that explains the event they "witnessed"?
- contain three or more details that help bring the event to life?
- use commas correctly?

Grammar, Usage, and Mechanics

Remind students to read through the **Writers' Checklist** on page 40 before they begin revising their letters. They should pay particular attention to the form of their greetings and closings. Also remind them to date their letters in the top right-hand corner.

V. WRAP-UP

At the end of the lesson, allow time for students to consider whether "Pilots' Reflections" was **easy** or difficult to read. Explain that it's not enough to say a piece is too hard. Readers need to think about the things that made the piece so hard. Was the language too challenging? Was the writing style too complex? Was the topic too abstract? If students have an idea of what is causing them problems, they'll have an easier time asking for help.

Assessment

For a comprehension check, ask students to complete the **Assessment** on page 87.

Name _____

VOCABULARY

Words from the Selection

DIRECTIONS Use the listed words in sentences that show you understand the meaning of each word.

✧fragile   ✧triumph   ✧perplexing   ✧idle   ✧vicinity

1. _____

_____

2. _____

_____

3. _____

_____

4. _____

_____

5. _____

_____

Strategy Lesson: Prefixes

Prefixes are word parts that come before a root word (*pre-* = before). Some prefixes can change the meaning of a word.

When you add the prefix *bi-* to the word *cycle*, you have a completely new word: *bicycle*.

When you add the prefix *mis-* to the word *understand,* you end up with a completely new word: *misunderstand*.

DIRECTIONS Write the prefix and root of each word. Then write what you think the word means.

✧tricycle   ✧triplane   ✧trilingual   ✧biplane   ✧bilingual

	prefix	+	root	=	meaning
EXAMPLE	bi	+	cycle	=	a two-wheeled vehicle
6. tricycle	_____	+	_____	=	_____
7. biplane	_____	+	_____	=	_____
8. triplane	_____	+	_____	=	_____
9. trilingual	_____	+	_____	=	_____
10. bilingual	_____	+	_____	=	_____

Name _____

COMPREHENSION
Storyboard
....

DIRECTIONS Use this storyboard to retell W. S. Douglas's adventure. Put one event in each box. Then draw a quick sketch of the event.

1.   *[sketch here]*

What happened:
_____

2.   *[sketch here]*

What happened:
_____

3.   *[sketch here]*

What happened:
_____

4.   *[sketch here]*

What happened:
_____

DIRECTIONS Use this storyboard to retell Manfred von Richthofen's adventure. Put one event in each box. Then draw a quick sketch of the event.

1.   *[sketch here]*

What happened:
_____

2.   *[sketch here]*

What happened:
_____

3.   *[sketch here]*

What happened:
_____

4.   *[sketch here]*

What happened:
_____

Name _____

PREWRITING AND WRITING
Writing Sensory Details

DIRECTIONS When you write, try to make your details as vivid and interesting as possible. If your details are boring, your writing will be boring. **Sensory details** can make your writing interesting. Sensory details are details that come to you through the senses *(smell, touch, taste, hearing, and sight)*. These kinds of details give the reader a "you are there" feeling.

EXAMPLE: I could feel the warmth of the fire and smell its smoke from a hundred yards away.

Imagine you are W. S. Douglas. What do you smell, see, taste, touch, and hear during your flight?

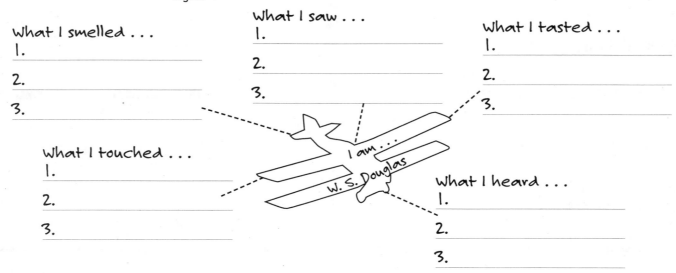

What I smelled . . .
1. _____
2. _____
3. _____

What I touched . . .
1. _____
2. _____
3. _____

What I saw . . .
1. _____
2. _____
3. _____

What I tasted . . .
1. _____
2. _____
3. _____

What I heard . . .
1. _____
2. _____
3. _____

I am . . . W. S. Douglas

Imagine you are Manfred von Richthofen. What do you smell, see, taste, touch, and hear during your flight? Write two or more details for each sense.

What I smelled . . .
1. _____
2. _____
3. _____

What I touched . . .
1. _____
2. _____
3. _____

What I saw . . .
1. _____
2. _____
3. _____

What I tasted . . .
1. _____
2. _____
3. _____

What I heard . . .
1. _____
2. _____
3. _____

I am . . . Manfred von Richthofen

Name

_____

ASSESSMENT

Multiple-Choice Test

DIRECTIONS On the blanks provided, write the letter of the answer that best completes each statement or answers each question.

_____ 1. At the beginning of the war, planes were mostly used for . . .
- A. exploring and bombing.
- B. attacking other planes.
- C. sightseeing tours.
- D. transportation.

_____ 2. WWI planes were made of . . .
- A. wood and canvas.
- B. steel and fiberglass.
- C. wood and steel.
- D. none of the above

_____ 3. Why does W. S. Douglas, author of the first pilot reflection, fly without a gun?
- A. He forgot it.
- B. It dropped when his plane turned.
- C. It would have made the plane too heavy to fly.
- D. It was stolen.

_____ 4. What is the purpose of Douglas's mission?
- A. He is looking for enemy troops.
- B. He is taking photos of enemy territory.
- C. He is on a mission to attack enemy planes.
- D. all of the above

_____ 5. What does Douglas do when he first spots the enemy?
- A. He takes out his gun.
- B. He radios for help.
- C. He curses.
- D. He waves.

_____ 6. Manfred von Richthofen is . . .
- A. English.
- B. German.
- C. American.
- D. none of the above

_____ 7. Manfred von Richthofen doesn't shoot down the other pilot because . . .
- A. it is too foggy to see him.
- B. he runs out of gas.
- C. he runs out of ammunition.
- D. he faints due to a lack of oxygen.

_____ 8. How does von Richthofen imagine the English would have felt to have fought and escaped "the red machine"?
- A. angry
- B. triumphant
- C. indifferent
- D. beaten

_____ 9. Whom does Manfred von Richthofen call "my Englishman"?
- A. his co-pilot
- B. the navigator
- C. the officer in charge
- D. the enemy

_____ 10. According to von Richthofen, what does a pilot do if he lands near the enemy?
- A. He sets his own plane on fire.
- B. He covers it with leaves.
- C. He pushes it to an area with trees.
- D. none of the above

Short-Essay Test

What do W. S. Douglas and Manfred von Richthofen have in common?

Adventures of the U-202

Skills and Strategies Overview

THEME	World War I
READING LEVEL	average
VOCABULARY	✦starboard ✦hare ✦nephew ✦rudder ✦insane
PREREADING	K-W-L
RESPONSE	question / clarify
COMPREHENSION	predict
PREWRITING	topic sentence and details
WRITING	summary / capitalizing names
ASSESSMENT	enjoyment

BACKGROUND

World War I was the first war in which submarines were used to any great extent. Prior to 1900, submarines had battery-powered engines and were limited by the constant need to surface and recharge. By 1911, however, several countries of the world—including Germany and the United States—were building diesel-powered submarines that could travel long distances without having to surface.

By the time the war started, Germany had the largest and most sophisticated fleet of submarines in the world. Germany's attack vessels, called *Unterseebooten,* or *U-boats,* had powerful engines that allowed U-boat navigators to "stalk" other ships in the sea. In retaliation, the Allies used "killer submarines" to track and fire on U-boats. Although the killer submarines were smaller than the U-boats, they were faster and could stay submerged longer.

UNIT THEME An excellent way to learn history is to "listen" to those who were there to see the events unfold. Eyewitness accounts give readers a chance to hear one person's version of what actually happened.

GRAPHIC ORGANIZER Some students may benefit by making a chart like the one below.

Sequence of Events: "Adventures of the U-202"

1. The U-202 slips closer to the British steamer.

2. The periscope operator determines the angle needed to fire the torpedo.

3. The periscope operator sees the captain and crew on deck of the steamer.

4. Although he experiences a twinge of conscience, Spiegel continues to prepare for the strike.

5. The periscope operator calls down to the command room, "Torpedo ready!"

6. The U-202 fires.

7. The British ship is hit and begins to sink.

BEFORE YOU READ

Look over the selection with students, and listen as a volunteer reads the title and first paragraph aloud. Discuss what students have heard about the war from friends or relatives. Then ask students to complete the **K** and **W** columns on page 42.

Motivation Strategy

ENGAGING STUDENTS Tell students that reading "Adventures of the U-202" will be something like watching a war movie on TV. There is plenty of intrigue, excitement, and danger, with the added advantage that this is fact, not fiction.

Vocabulary Building

Discuss with students the key vocabulary words for this selection: *starboard, hare, nephew, rudder,* and *insane.* Have them make a note when they come across these words in the reading, and then encourage them to define the words in context before checking the footnote definition. Students will benefit from the additional work with using context clues.

STRATEGY LESSON: SUFFIXES If you feel students need some additional vocabulary work, you might teach a short lesson on suffixes. Write this sentence on the board: *The U-202 slipped noiselessly closer.* Point out that *noiselessly* has two suffixes: *-less* (meaning "without") and *-ly* (meaning "in a certain manner or way"). Thus, the submarine slipped closer in a way that made no noise. Help students separate the suffixes from the root words *amazement* and *joyous.*

For additional vocabulary practice, see the **Vocabulary** blackline master on page 92.

Prereading Strategies

A **K-W-L** can be helpful to those students who have trouble settling down to read and write. In addition to assisting with organization, the K-W-L gives students the chance to activate prior knowledge about a subject. After recording what they already know, they can think carefully about gaps in their knowledge. This way, *they* (as opposed to *you*) decide what they need to learn.

QUICKWRITE As an alternate prereading strategy, ask students to do a quickwrite about World War I. Rather than writing everything they know, they should focus their quickwrites on the sensory images of the war. Later, they may want to use some of these images in their summaries.

Spanish-Speaking Students

Unas de las batallas mas ferozas de la Primera Guerra Mundial fueron luchadas en el mar. En "Las aventuras del U-202" un marinero alemán que se llama Baron Spiegel describe los momentos inmediatamente antes y después de la destrucción de una nave enemigo. Explica que un ataque siempre requiere mucho pensamiento, precisión, y concentración. Pero como el Baron también hace claro, no hay lugar para emociones durante una guerra así.

READ

Read aloud the directions on page 43. Make sure students understand that they should make a note of **questions** that occur to them as they are reading. Their questions can help them think critically about the selection and can be used to initiate interesting after-reading discussions.

Response Strategy

CLARIFY You might also explain how important it can be to visualize and then sketch the action as they read. Some of the maneuvers Spiegel describes are complicated. Students' sketches can help them clarify what he is describing.

Comprehension Strategies

Predicting can help students become involved in the text. It can also help them stay with a text that they might otherwise have put down. When a reader makes a prediction about a story's outcome, he or she has a stake in what happens. Many times, readers will keep reading to see if their prediction is correct.

GRAPHIC ORGANIZER As an alternate comprehension strategy, have students complete an organizer similar to the one on page 93. A sequence organizer can help students keep track of the events of a story. You can also use a sequence organizer to check a student's ability to retell events in chronological order.

For more work with comprehension, see the **Comprehension** blackline master on page 93.

Discussion Questions

COMPREHENSION 1. Which country owned the U-202? *(Germany)*

2. What bothers Spiegel about firing the torpedo? *(He sees horses on deck.)*

3. Why is the British steamer such an easy target for the torpedo? *(The crew doesn't know they are being tracked.)*

CRITICAL THINKING 4. Is Baron Spiegel a likable person? Explain. *(Answers will vary. Ask students to support their opinions with evidence from the selection.)*

5. Does Spiegel feel guilty after the ship begins to sink? Explain your opinion. *(Answers will vary, although students should note his reluctance to talk about the event, which might be a sign of guilty feelings.)*

Literary Skill

STYLE Style is the way in which the writer uses words and sentences to suit his or her ideas. Some writers have very distinctive styles (Ernest Hemingway, for example, with his short, terse sentences). Help students think about Spiegel's writing style. Ask: "What is the tone and mood of his writing? What imagery (sensory language) can you find?" Have them pay particular attention to his exclamations. How do these interruptions affect the style?

III. GATHER YOUR THOUGHTS

As a prewriting exercise, students will find the **topic** of the selection and then list four or five **details** about the topic that can be included in a summary of the selection. Remind the class to list only the most important details, such as information about people, places, and events. The easiest way to gather details for a summary is to return to the text and mark phrases and sentences that relate to the topic sentence. Have students write a number next to each detail they find. They can use the strongest three details in their summaries.

Prewriting Strategies

STORYBOARD As an alternate prewriting strategy, have students make a storyboard of the selection, listing the three most important events in chronological order and then drawing quick sketches of the events they describe. Storyboards are helpful because they are half drawing and half writing—a boon for students who have trouble putting words to their ideas. Have students use the **Prewriting and Writing** blackline master on page 94.

IV. WRITE

Students are asked to write a **summary** of the selection. As they are writing, review with them the tips for writing a summary listed on page 47. Remind them to stay focused on what actually happened in the article and avoid making statements about what should have or could have happened. Use the questions in the writing rubric to help them revise, and introduce a brief lesson on capitalization at an opportune time.

WRITING RUBRIC Do students' summaries

- begin with a clear topic sentence?
- include ideas in an order that makes sense?
- use words such as *first, next,* and *finally?*

Grammar, Usage, and Mechanics

Review with students the rules for capitalizing ship names, formal titles, names of places, the days of the week, months of the year, and events in history. If you like, put some practice sentences on the board. Have students edit each for capitalization errors.

EXAMPLE:

baron spiegel wrote the fascinating "adventures of the u-202."

V. WRAP-UP

At the end of the lesson, ask students what they **enjoyed** and did not enjoy about the article. Take note of what students thought was interesting or dull. You can use their comments to help you plan strategies for future lessons.

Assessment

For a comprehension check, ask students to complete the **Assessment** blackline master on page 95.

Name _____

VOCABULARY

Words from the Selection

DIRECTIONS Using context clues, fill in each blank with the most appropriate word from the list.

> ✧ starboard   ✧ hare   ✧ nephew   ✧ rudder   ✧ insane

1. I went sailing with my sister's son; that is, my _____.

2. A storm came up, and I was sitting on the _____ side to help balance the boat.

3. He suddenly grabbed the _____ and told me to duck.

4. I reacted like a frightened _____.

5. Sailing in that storm was an/a _____ experience.

Strategy Lesson: Suffixes

Suffixes come at the end of a word. A suffix can give you clues about the meaning of the word and how it should be used in a sentence. For example, if you add the suffix *-ous* to *nerve*, you get *nervous*, which means "full of nerves" or anxious.

DIRECTIONS Write the root word and then the suffix of each word. Then write what you think the whole word means.

> ✧ *-less* = without   ✧ *-ous* = full of *or* having to do with   ✧ *-er* = thing that does something

	root	+	suffix	=	meaning
EXAMPLE:	nerve	+	ous	=	full of nerves
6. steamer	_____	+	_____	=	_____
7. murderous	_____	+	_____	=	_____
8. desirous	_____	+	_____	=	_____
9. pointless	_____	+	_____	=	_____
10. fryer	_____	+	_____	=	_____

Name _____

COMPREHENSION
Graphic Organizer

DIRECTIONS Use this storyboard to show four memorable scenes from "Adventures of the U-202" in the order in which they occurred. Draw sketches of the scenes and then write brief descriptions.

Storyboard: "Adventures of the U-202"

1.

2.

3.

4.

Name _____

PREWRITING AND WRITING

Writing a Summary

DIRECTIONS To write a good summary, select the most important ideas and combine them into clear, easy-to-understand sentences. Follow these steps to write a summary for "Adventures of the U-202."

STEP 1. READ. Carefully read the selection. Highlight key words and phrases.

STEP 2. LIST. Make a list of the most important ideas and opinions in the selection.

Spiegel's important ideas:

• _____

• _____

• _____

• _____

STEP 3. CHOOSE. Select the most important idea or opinion from your list and make this the main idea of your summary. Write a topic sentence that states the main idea.

Spiegel's main idea in the article is: _____

_____

STEP 4. FIND DETAILS. Gather important details from the article. Names, dates, times, and places are examples of important details.

Spiegel's important details:

1. _____   6. _____

2. _____   7. _____

3. _____   8. _____

4. _____   9. _____

5. _____   10. _____

STEP 5. WRITE. Now write your summary. Begin with the topic sentence. Then summarize Spiegel's most important details. End with a concluding sentence that ties things together.

Name _____

ASSESSMENT

Multiple-Choice Test

DIRECTIONS On the blanks provided, write the letter of the best answer for each question.

_____ 1. What is a U-202?
A. a steamship
B. an aircraft carrier
C. an airplane
D. a submarine

_____ 2. What was Baron Spiegel's job on the U-202?
A. to steer
B. to fire the torpedo
C. to calculate the speed of the steamer
D. none of the above

_____ 3. Why is the crew of the U-202 "stalking" the steamship?
A. They are on a spy mission.
B. They want to destroy it.
C. They want to capture it.
D. all of the above

_____ 4. What does Spiegel see on the steamship that surprises him?
A. horses
B. the captain
C. a rowdy crew
D. none of the above

_____ 5. What is a periscope used for?
A. It steers the submarine.
B. It gives information about ocean depth.
C. It shows objects on the surface.
D. It helps the crew watch for sharks.

_____ 6. How does Spiegel feel after the torpedo hits the ship?
A. a little surprised
B. a little tired
C. a little guilty
D. a little bored

_____ 7. What alerts the British crew that a torpedo is on its way?
A. They see the torpedo hovering over the water.
B. They see it on their radar.
C. They see its path in the water.
D. They receive a warning over the radio.

_____ 8. Who narrates "Adventures of the U-202"?
A. a sailor on the submarine
B. a journalist in a chase boat
C. a sailor on the British ship
D. none of the above

_____ 9. What word best describes Baron Spiegel?
A. shy
B. serious
C. worried
D. funny

_____ 10. Who owns the U-202?
A. Germany
B. the United States
C. Great Britain
D. Russia

Short-Essay Test

What does Spiegel mean when he says, "War is war"?

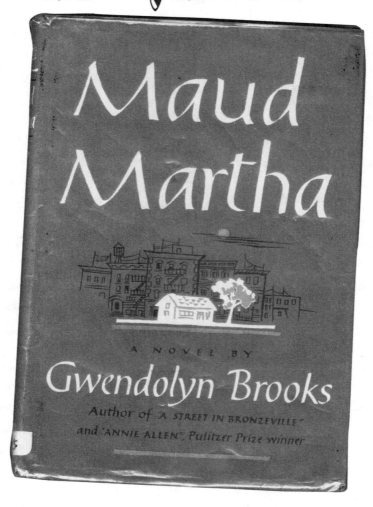

Unit Background   GWENDOLYN BROOKS (pages 49–64)

Gwendolyn Brooks has had a long and illustrious career. Born in Topeka, Kansas, she has spent nearly all of her life in Chicago. She began writing poetry at an early age, and when she was sixteen, she regularly contributed poetry to and was published in the *Chicago Defender*.

After graduation from Wilson (now Kennedy-King) Junior College, she worked as a maid and a secretary, took a writing course, and had a poem accepted by *Poetry* magazine. She was married in 1939 to Henry Lowington Blakely II, and she and her husband had two children.

Her first volume of poems, *A Street in Bronzeville* (1945), resulted in an award from the American Academy of Arts and Letters. Her second book, *Annie Allen*, won the Pulitzer Prize for poetry in 1950.

Brooks subsequently won two Guggenheim Fellowships, was elected to the National Institute of Arts and Letters, and was made Consultant in Poetry at the Library of Congress in 1985–1986. She published *Maud Martha* in 1953 and *In the Mecca* in 1968, the same year she was made poet laureate of Illinois.

She has traveled widely and given many workshops and continues to make racial identity a strong theme in her works.

Other works by Brooks include *The Bean Eaters* (1960), *Selected Poems* (1963), *Primer for Blacks* (1980), *The Near-Johannesburg Boy and Other Poems* (1986), and *Selected Poems* (1999).

Teaching the Introduction

Point out that the center photograph is of a young Gwendolyn Brooks holding a copy of her book, *A Street in Bronzeville*, and that the upper-right photo is of a rather typical urban greystone dwelling. The bottom-right photo is of an urban area with an elevated commuter train in the distance.

Gwendolyn Brooks

Gwendolyn Brooks

Maud Martha

Gwendolyn Brooks

Gwendolyn Brooks (1917–), an American writer and poet, grew up in Chicago. In 1950, she became the first African American to win a Pulitzer Prize. Her 1953 novel, *Maud Martha*, traces the growth of an African-American girl from the age of seven through adulthood.

Gwendolyn Brooks

1.

2.

49

1. Tell students that many awards and fellowships have been established to honor or aid writers and scholars. One such award, which Brooks received twice, is the Guggenheim Fellowship. A fellowship is a sum of money. Ask students why they think someone would want to grant a fellowship to a writer.

2. Brooks has given much time to encouraging young writers. Ask students whether they think people have an obligation to give back in some way what they have received in life or whether this idea is only relevant for wealthy people.

Opening Activity

Ask students how they think being an African American influenced Gwendolyn Brooks's writing.

STUDENT PAGES 50–56

Skills and Strategies Overview

THEME	Gwendolyn Brooks
READING LEVEL	easy
VOCABULARY	✧dignity ✧shuddered ✧maneuvered ✧taut ✧impulse
PREREADING	walk-through
RESPONSE	question
COMPREHENSION	double-entry journal
PREWRITING	character cluster
WRITING	descriptive paragraph / run-on sentences
ASSESSMENT	depth

BACKGROUND

Gwendolyn Brooks has had an unparalleled career in American literature. A poet, novelist, and essayist, Brooks is the first African American to win the Pulitzer Prize for poetry. Brooks, whose personal philosophy is "[t]o be clean of heart, clear of mind, and claiming of what is right and just," is currently the poet laureate of Illinois.

UNIT THEME This selection is an excerpt from Brooks's only novel, *Maud Martha*. It chronicles the life of Maud Martha Brown from the age of seven until the birth of her own daughter. Because she is African American, Maud Martha is subjected to racial prejudice both inside and outside of her community. Her day-to-day life offers little excitement and few rewards. In this selection, an impending visit from Charles, a white classmate, makes Maud Martha feel that her life is very commonplace.

GRAPHIC ORGANIZER For extra work on sequence and plot, you might have students record the events of this excerpt on a plot line.

I. BEFORE YOU READ

Read the unit opener on page 49 with students. Next ask a volunteer to read aloud the introduction on page 50. Use the motivation strategies below to help students consider what they already know about the topic of the story. Then have students complete the **walk-through** of the story on page 51.

Motivation Strategy

Tell students that this selection is about a girl waiting for a date. Ask students to offer suggestions about how the girl might feel as she is waiting.

ENGAGING STUDENTS You might further set up the story by telling students it is about interracial dating. Ask students how they feel about that subject.

Vocabulary Building

Help students use context as they read to figure out the meanings of difficult or unknown words. Ask them to pay particular attention to the key vocabulary words for this lesson: *dignity, shuddered, maneuvered, taut,* and *impulse.* Although the footnotes define these words for students, you'll want to model using context clues and then checking your ideas against the footnote: "I'm not sure of the meaning of the word *dignity*. I notice in the sentence that the chairs are disgusted with the family but that they used to have dignity. Dignity must mean the opposite of disgusted. I can look at the footnote to see if my idea is correct." For additional practice, see the **Vocabulary** blackline master on page 102.

STRATEGY LESSON: NEGATIVE PREFIXES As students read, point out words with negative prefixes such as *unspeakably, nonsense,* and *unafraid.* Write the words on the board, separating the prefixes from the root words. Remind students that when the negative prefix *non-* or *un-* is added to a word, the meaning of the word changes.

For additional practice with this strategy, see the **Vocabulary** blackline master on page 102.

Prereading Strategies

The **walk-through** of the selection encourages students to become actively engaged in the text. Students will make personal connections when they consider what they already know about the author, the subject, and situations depicted in the art. Ask a volunteer to read aloud the title and author's name as students copy the information onto their diagrams on page 51. Thumb through the selection with them to help them get an idea of the story's length. Ask leading questions that can assist students in describing the art. Also have students tell you words or phrases they noticed as they were thumbing through the selection. Students can note these on the diagram as well.

QUICKWRITE As an additional prereading strategy, have students do a quickwrite about the selection. Tell students that the story is about a girl named Maud Martha who is waiting for someone. Ask students to write for whom and what she is waiting. Remind students that quickwriting is not "right or wrong." Instead, they should jot down whatever thoughts first come to mind.

Spanish-Speaking Students

En "estás siendo tan bueno, tan simpático" autor, Gwendolyn Brooks examina como la raza afecta las relaciones entre los seres humanos. Maud Martha es una adolescente negra y una mimebra de la clase media. Está esperando una visita de Charles, un compañero blanco, cuyo mera raza le hace a Maud Martha sentirse muy insegura. Ella se siente avergonzada de la condición de su casa y se preocupa mucho por cómo Charles le va a percibir. Es como si Charles le estuviera haciendo un favor por visitarla. Maud Martha se da cuenta luego, sin embargo, lo absurdo de tal pensamiento.

II. READ

Ask a student to read the directions on page 52. To introduce the response strategy, point out the example question in the **Response Notes**. To make sure that students understand the comprehension strategy of **double-entry journals**, go through the first one on the bottom of the page as a class.

Response Strategy

Encourage students to list **questions** under the **Response Notes** columns as they read. Model this for students, suggesting questions such as, "Why make the chairs seem human? Why is Maud Martha so sad? Is it hard to write descriptions like this? What makes it difficult?" Use students' questions as the basis for a whole-class discussion after the reading.

VISUALIZE As an alternative strategy, ask students to visualize the scene by drawing in the margin what they see in their mind as they read. Allow time after reading for students to share their drawing and discuss what they think Brooks's answers might be.

Comprehension Strategies

Using a **double-entry journal** encourages active response to text. Students find statements, quotes, ideas, or events in the selection, record them, and then write their thoughts and reactions. Rather than paraphrase, they raise questions about what they're reading and note their reactions. (Remind them to go beyond "I like/don't like this sentence.") Work through the first entry with the entire class, discussing their reactions to and ideas about the quotation from the story. Once students understand the quotation and discuss their ideas, encourage them to note their ideas in their journals.

RECIPROCAL READING Another comprehension strategy that will work well with this selection is to have students do a reciprocal reading with a partner. They should take turns reading aloud, switching readers after every page. As students read, they 1. clarify the problem, characters, and setting of the story; 2. predict what will happen; 3. summarize the events; and 4. raise questions about the literature. Encourage students to stop during reading to discuss any questions their partners have and to figure out meanings of new or difficult vocabulary.

For additional practice, see the **Comprehension** blackline master on page 103.

Discussion Questions

COMPREHENSION 1. Where is Maud Martha at the beginning of the story? *(at home)*

2. Why is Maud Martha so uneasy about having this boy come over? *(She is ashamed of her house and perhaps unsure of herself.)*

CRITICAL THINKING 3. What do you think Gwendolyn Brooks means by the title "you're being so good, so kind"? *(Answers will vary. Accept reasonable responses.)*

4. How would you have reacted if you were in Maud Martha's shoes? *(Ask students to connect the selection to their own ideas and experiences.)*

Literary Skill

THEME The novel excerpt "you're being so good, so kind" suggests a variety of themes: self-concept, issues of interracial dating, doubts and fears, and much else. You might ask students what they think is the author's theme or the point she makes.

III. GATHER YOUR THOUGHTS

Completing **character clusters** helps students solidify their ideas about Maud Martha's characteristics. If students have trouble getting started, read them sentences or passages from the story that highlight particular characteristics. After each, ask: "What does this tell you about Maud Martha?" Encourage them to find "proof" for their descriptions in the text.

Prewriting Strategies

TOPIC SENTENCES For more prewriting, students can work on formulating topic sentences about Maud Martha. Show students how to take a larger topic and narrow it into a topic sentence. Students can then list details to support their topic sentences. When they write their descriptions, remind them to start with their topic sentences and explain each of the details.

For more practice, see the **Prewriting and Writing** blackline master on page 104.

IV. WRITE

Set aside some time for students to write their **descriptive paragraphs** about Maud Martha. Explain that for the next fifteen minutes, they should write what comes into their head about the topic. Encourage students to write and not procrastinate, explaining that writing is a practice one needs to get in the habit of doing.

WRITING RUBRIC Use this writing rubric to keep students focused on the assignment and to help with a quick assessment of their writing.

Do students' paragraphs

- begin with a topic sentence?

- contain three or more facts to support the topic sentence?

- stay focused on the topic of Maud Martha?

Grammar, Usage, and Mechanics

When students have finished writing, have them revise using the **Writers' Checklist** as a guide. At this point you might want to teach a brief mini-lesson on run-on sentences. Remind students to avoid run-on sentences and to use compound sentences instead. Point out that a compound sentence joins two separate ideas with a comma and a conjunction such as *and*, *or*, or *but*. When complete thoughts are not joined by a conjunction and a comma, they are run-ons.

Incorrect: Maud Martha liked the boy she was waiting for him at her house they are going on a date.

Corrected: Maud Martha liked the boy. She was waiting for him at her house, and they are going on a date.

V. WRAP-UP

Take a moment for students to reflect. Ask them to look back at what they have read and written. The point of this informal assessment is to remind students of what they have accomplished and learned. Focus on the **depth** of their understanding. Help students see the benefits of a reading experience.

Assessment

For a comprehension check, ask students to complete the **Assessment** test on page 105.

Name _____

VOCABULARY

Words from the Selection

DIRECTIONS Using context clues, fill in each blank with the most appropriate word from the list.

> ✧dignity   ✧shuddered   ✧maneuvered   ✧taut   ✧impulse

1. Marisa _____ when she saw the alien monster in the horror movie.

2. She felt _____ with fear.

3. Courtney's _____ was destroyed when she stumbled on the way to her seat.

4. Tim _____ his way to a seat next to the wall.

5. Luis's first _____ was to buy a large box of popcorn, but he got candy instead.

Strategy Lesson: Negative Prefixes

The negative prefixes *un-* and *non-* change the meaning of a word.

EXAMPLE: un- + lucky = unlucky (not lucky)

non- + violent = nonviolent (not violent)

DIRECTIONS On the blanks provided, write the underlined word from each sentence. Then add the prefix *un-* or *non-* to the words. (HINT: Add the prefix *un-* to three of the words.)

6. During a test, students shouldn't make <u>needed</u> noise._____

7. The path of a tornado is <u>predictable</u>. _____

8. Dad prefers <u>dairy</u> products. _____

9. We were <u>aware</u> of storm warnings. _____

10. Don't worry about garter snakes. They are <u>poisonous</u>. _____

Name _____

COMPREHENSION
Reciprocal Reading

DIRECTIONS With a partner, work through the answers to these questions.

CLARIFY What parts of the story were not clear? List them. Then go back and reread the story with your partner, looking to clarify these parts.

_____

_____

_____

_____

PREDICT What will happen when Charles comes to Maud Martha's house? Write your predictions below.

_____

_____

_____

_____

QUESTION What questions do you have about Maud Martha while she waits for Charles? Write your questions here.

_____

_____

_____

_____

SUMMARIZE Tell what happens in the selection. What does the narrator mean by the words, "It's so good of you. You're being so good"?

_____

_____

_____

_____

Name _____

PREWRITING AND WRITING

Writing a Topic Sentence and Details

DIRECTIONS The first sentence of a paragraph should set the stage for what you want to tell readers. The first sentence is your topic sentence. Follow these steps to write a topic sentence and list supporting details.

STEP 1. List details about Maud Martha. Don't worry about writing complete sentences. Just list words that you think describe her.

WORD BANK

nervous

STEP 2. Look at your word bank. Circle the words that you think best describe Maud Martha. Choose no more than three words. Imagine that someone has never met or heard of Maud Martha. What would be the most important words in a description of her?

Use the words as you write a topic sentence. Fill in the blanks.

My Topic Sentence: The character Maud Martha is

_____

_____ , and _____ .

STEP 3. Now plan the rest of your paragraph. Use the list of descriptive words in Step 1 above. For each detail, give specific "proof" from the story that supports each detail.

Detail #1: _____

proof: _____

Detail #2: _____

proof _____

Detail #3: _____

proof _____

Use your "proof" as you write your paragraph. Each sentence after the topic sentence should include one proof.

Name _____

ASSESSMENT

Multiple-Choice Test

··

DIRECTIONS On the blanks provided, write the letter of the item that best answers each question.

_____ 1. In the beginning of the story, where does Maud Martha wait for Charles?
- A. in the kitchen
- B. in the living room
- C. on her front porch
- D. none of the above

_____ 2. Which answer best tells how Maud Martha feels about her home?
- A. sparkling
- B. impressive
- C. dull
- D. dirty

_____ 3. How does Maud Martha feel about Charles's visit?
- A. worried
- B. excited
- C. bored
- D. content

_____ 4. What does Maud Martha do to prepare for Charles's visit?
- A. She moves the sofa.
- B. She bakes cookies.
- C. She opens the window.
- D. both A. and C.

_____ 5. Why doesn't Maud Martha want to see Charles at her home?
- A. She really doesn't like Charles.
- B. It is too hard for Charles to travel to her home.
- C. She is embarrassed by her home.
- D. She has other friends who are coming over to visit.

_____ 6. How does Maud Martha's father walk to the door when Charles rings?
- A. quickly and angrily
- B. slowly and patiently
- C. fearfully and noisily
- D. none of the above

_____ 7. When Charles rings the bell, how does Maud Martha think that he feels?
- A. regretful
- B. eager
- C. angry
- D. bored

_____ 8. Who tells the story?
- A. Maud Martha's father
- B. Maud Martha
- C. an outside narrator
- D. Charles

_____ 9. What words best describe Maud Martha?
- A. nervous and upbeat
- B. proud and terrified
- C. worried and uncertain
- D. confident and lucky

_____ 10. Why does Maud Martha feel gratitude toward Charles?
- A. She thinks that his coming to her house is a gift.
- B. Charles brings Maud Martha a gift.
- C. Charles is going to help her with her homework.
- D. Maud Martha is going to give Charles a gift.

Short-Essay Test

··

Why do you think Maud Martha is sickened at the idea of feeling gratitude toward Charles?

Maud Martha and New York

Skills and Strategies Overview

THEME	Gwendolyn Brooks
READING LEVEL	average
VOCABULARY	✦ plush ✦ antique ✦ figurines ✦ pore ✦ caviar
PREREADING	read-aloud
RESPONSE	react / visualize
COMPREHENSION	directed reading
PREWRITING	draw a place
WRITING	descriptive paragraph / comma splices
ASSESSMENT	style

BACKGROUND

In much of her writing, Gwendolyn Brooks focuses on the conflict between individual African Americans and various social pressures on the African-American community. In *Maud Martha,* as in many of her other works, she also explores the theme of race relations between blacks and whites.

"Maud Martha and New York" differs from "you're being so good, so kind" in that the tone of the writing is more exuberant—although careful readers will notice the same undercurrent of sadness in this piece. An older, though still naive Maud Martha dreams about leaving her hometown behind in order to become a part of "glittering" New York City life. Maud Martha's yearnings will seem familiar to any child or adult who has said even once: "Watch out world, here I come."

UNIT THEME In this second excerpt from *Maud Martha,* Brooks uses sensory details to depict Maud Martha's dreams of New York.

GRAPHIC ORGANIZER Students might make a circular story map like the one below to help them follow the sequence of events.

Circular Story Map: "Maud Martha and New York"

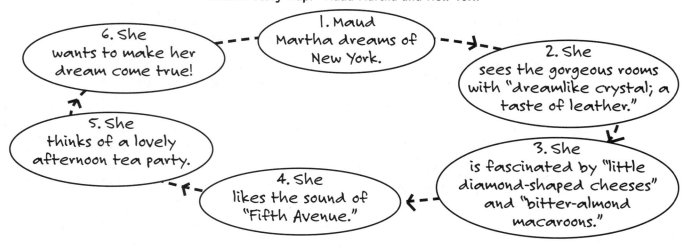

6. She wants to make her dream come true!

1. Maud Martha dreams of New York.

2. She sees the gorgeous rooms with "dreamlike crystal; a taste of leather."

5. She thinks of a lovely afternoon tea party.

4. She likes the sound of "Fifth Avenue."

3. She is fascinated by "little diamond-shaped cheeses" and "bitter-almond macaroons."

BIBLIOGRAPHY In addition to the Gwendolyn Brooks works listed on page 96, students might enjoy: *Annie Allen* (awarded the Pulitzer Prize in 1950), *Family Pictures* (1970), *To Disembark* (1981), *Report from Part One* (1972; part one of her autobiography) and *Report from Part Two* (1995; part two of her autobiography).

I. BEFORE YOU READ

Explain that "Maud Martha and New York" is the story of one girl's dream to live a whole new life. The Maud Martha of this story is the same girl as the one who waits for her visitor in "you're being so good, so kind," although in this selection, she is several years older. Have a student read the title and opening paragraphs, and then ask students to complete the **listener's guide.**

Motivation Strategy

ENGAGING STUDENTS Introduce the story by telling students it's all about New York City. Ask students to share what they know about "the city that never sleeps."

Vocabulary Building

Draw attention to key vocabulary words for this selection: *plush, antique, figurines, pore,* and *caviar*. Some of these will be familiar to students, although they may be a little uncertain about definitions and pronunciations. Help students learn the new words and reinforce their understanding of the words they already know. For practice work, turn to the **Vocabulary** blackline master on page 110.

STRATEGY LESSON: CONTEXT CLUES Have students pay particular attention to unfamiliar words as they read. Before they check the footnote definitions, however, students should try to define the words in context. They can search surrounding words and sentences for clues about meaning. Tell students: "I see the word *grating*, which is an unfamiliar word. Instead of going right to the footnote, I look for clues in surrounding sentences. I see that the word appears in a sentence describing the sound a train makes. This must mean that it is a harsh sound like the sound of metal on metal."

For additional help, see the **Vocabulary** blackline master on page 110.

Prereading Strategies

Although it might at first seem "babyish" to listen as a story is **read aloud**, students will soon see that listening can make a story easier to understand. Encourage students to follow along in the book as they listen. This way, they can mark passages that they think are important or confusing.

PICTURE WALK As an alternate prereading strategy, have students do a picture walk. This strategy will be particularly helpful for students who have never visited New York City—although even those who have been there have certainly not seen the city exactly as Maud Martha sees it. After they've finished their picture walks, ask students: "Is this how you envision New York City? Why or why not?"

Spanish-Speaking Students

Como "estás siendo tan bueno, tan simpático," "Maud Martha y Nueva York" es un cuento conmovedor a lo cual muchos lectores se pueden relacionar. En esta selección Maud Martha es mayor, pero no menos ingenua. Ella sueña con trasladarse de su pueblo natal, donde todo le aburre, para vivir en la Ciudad de Nueva York, donde hay diversión y aventura. A lo largo del cuento tiene que considerar la persona que es, y las persona que quiere ser.

II. READ

When students are ready to read, be sure they understand the response strategy of **visualizing** the people, places, and events of the story. Visualizing can make a story come alive for readers and can even serve to deepen the bond between character and reader. Students' sketches will help them feel involved in the story—as if they too are a part of Maud Martha's dream. As an added benefit, their during-reading sketches will help them when it comes time to complete the assignments in **Part III. Gather Your Thoughts**.

Response Strategy

HIGHLIGHT Encourage students to highlight the text as they read, noting anything that particularly interests them.

Comprehension Strategies

Directed reading can help reluctant or low-level readers better understand what they are reading. Since students are reading "Maud Martha and New York" aloud to one another, try having students pose the **stop and think** questions aloud to the rest of the reading group. If they get stuck, jump in and redirect the discussion. Otherwise, let students work through the comprehension and critical thinking questions on their own.

DOUBLE-ENTRY JOURNAL For an alternate comprehension strategy, consider asking students to complete a double-entry journal that explores their reactions to the story. Have the class pull a few interesting quotations from the story. Next to each quotation, they should write how the sentence makes them feel. To get them started, suggest that they react to the quotation: "It was not for her. Yet."

For additional work on comprehension skills, see the **Comprehension** blackline master on page 111.

Discussion Questions

COMPREHENSION 1. What does Maud Martha love about New York City? *(She loves the glamour, the wealth, and the possibilities for freedom.)*

2. Is there anything she doesn't like about it? *(Answers will vary. Encourage students to support their ideas with evidence from the text.)*

3. What clues tell you this story is really a dream? *(Help students spot clues in the story. Have them pay particular attention to the penultimate paragraph on page 61.)*

CRITICAL THINKING 4. Would you say Maud Martha has a realistic view of New York City? *(Students should note that her view of New York and what it's like to be a "grown-up" is pretty idealized—no place or person in the world is this glamorous and trouble-free.)*

5. What three adjectives would you use to describe Maud Martha? Explain. *(Ask students to discuss their choices along with others' ideas.)*

Literary Skills

IMAGERY Ask students to notice how important imagery is in this story. Gwendolyn Brooks shows a poet's love for language when she describes "gemlike surfaces" and steps that never "grated." Reading this selection is like taking a five-senses tour through New York City. For fun, have students count how many images they can find that appeal to sight, hearing, taste, smell, and touch.

STYLE Gwendolyn Brooks uses a dreamlike, stream-of-consciousness style to tell this story. Some of her sentences are short or choppy or even incomplete. Others are long and meandering— they flow together in the same way that our dreams flow together during deep sleep.

GATHER YOUR THOUGHTS

Before they write, students are asked to **draw** a picture of the New York that Maud Martha envisions. Explain to students that drawing can help get the creative juices flowing. Their sketches will come in handy when it comes time to build word pictures.

Prewriting Strategies

WEB As an additional prewriting strategy, have students create a five-senses web that shows their own important place. They can incorporate these sensory details into the descriptive paragraph they write.

For more practice, see the **Prewriting** blackline master on page 112.

IV. WRITE

Allow plenty of time for students to complete their **descriptive paragraphs**. Explain that their assignment is to write a paragraph about a place that is important to them. Remind the class that the language they use should help readers see, hear, smell, taste, and touch the places they describe. If needed, present a brief lesson on comma splices before they begin the revision process. Then use the questions in the writing rubric to assess students' writing.

WRITING RUBRIC Do students' paragraphs

- begin with a topic sentence?
- offer enough details so that readers can visualize the place described?
- avoid comma splices?

Grammar, Usage, and Mechanics

Review the definition of a comma splice and explain why it should be avoided. Point out that comma splices are more than just irritating; they can affect meaning. Remind students that a comma alone is not strong enough to hold up the two parts of a compound sentence.

V. WRAP-UP

Show students how to evaluate various aspects of the writing **style** so that they can think about what they did and did not like about the piece as a whole. Ask them what they think of Brooks's word choices, sentence construction, and so on. For example, point out the final sentence on page 59 and the first sentence on page 60, and ask students to talk about the connotations of some of the words.

Assessment

For a comprehension check, ask students to complete the **Assessment** blackline master on page 113.

Name _____

VOCABULARY

Words from the Selection

DIRECTIONS Write the words from the list below that best fit each of the following descriptions.

> ✧plush   ✧antique   ✧figurines   ✧pore   ✧caviar

1. An old and priceless table stood in one corner of the room. _____

2. Miniature china animals were scattered about the tabletop. _____

3. Leslie sank onto the sofa cushions, which were deep and soft. _____

4. A bowl of something that looked like tiny dark pearls rested on the coffee table.

   _____

5. She found a diary nearby and began to look through it carefully. _____

Strategy Lesson: Context Clues

When you come to a difficult word, be sure to look at surrounding words and phrases. You might be able to pick up hints or clues about the word's meaning. This is called using context clues.

EXAMPLE: Louisa is tired of <u>trite</u>, worn-out expressions such as "A rolling stone gathers no moss." *Clue: Trite* must have something to do with being "worn out" or overused.

DIRECTIONS Read these sentences. Use context clues to help you figure out the meaning of the underlined words. Write the meaning of the word on the line.

> ✧grating   ✧shimmering   ✧ferns   ✧nebulous   ✧remote

6. The <u>grating</u> sound was so harsh it made my ears feel raw.

_____

7. The lantern gave a steady light, but we preferred the <u>shimmering</u> candles.

_____

8. It was my job to water the <u>ferns</u> that grew in huge pots and decorated the lobby.

_____

9. Because of the rain and mist, the school building looked <u>nebulous</u> in the distance.

_____

10. Although our relatives once lived nearby, they are now <u>remote.</u>

_____

Name _____

COMPREHENSION
Directed Reading

DIRECTIONS With a partner, decide on the answers to these questions, and write the answers on the blanks.

1. Who is Maud Martha?

_____

_____

_____

_____

2. Why does she love New York so much?

_____

_____

_____

_____

3. How many times has she visited the city? Explain how you know.

_____

_____

_____

_____

4. What is "Maud Martha and New York" about? Summarize it here.

_____

_____

_____

_____

_____

Name _____

PREWRITING
Sketch a Place

Drawing and writing go hand in hand. When you draw, you add details so that your reader can see the object. In writing, your details can help your readers "see" what you are describing.

DIRECTIONS Draw a sketch of a place that is important to you. Add plenty of details.

Write Details

Now write the details that you just drew. Write the name of your important place in the middle of the web. Then describe how the place looks, sounds, smells, feels, and even tastes. List as many words as you can.

What I hear . . .   What I see . . .

Name of Place

What I taste . . .   What I smell . . .   What I touch . . .

Name _____

ASSESSMENT

Multiple-Choice Test

DIRECTIONS On the blanks provided, write the letter of the answer that best completes each statement or answers each question.

_____ 1. What is Maud Martha's dream?
- A. to ride in a taxi
- B. to eat fine food
- C. to wear expensive clothes
- D. all of the above

_____ 2. More than anything else, Maud Martha is . . .
- A. a thinker.
- B. a talker.
- C. a dreamer.
- D. a doer.

_____ 3. What does Maud Martha like so much about New York?
- A. the luxury
- B. the good schools
- C. the job opportunities
- D. its parks

_____ 4. How often do you think Maud Martha has visited New York?
- A. once
- B. twice
- C. many times
- D. never

_____ 5. What is Maud Martha's main source of information about New York?
- A. magazines and newspapers
- B. movies
- C. television
- D. books

_____ 6. What does Maud Martha's mother think of New York food?
- A. It is delicious.
- B. It is boring.
- C. It is foolish.
- D. It doesn't taste good.

_____ 7. Maud Martha thinks life should be . . .
- A. fancy.
- B. perfect.
- C. glittering.
- D. all of the above

_____ 8. Judging from what you've read, would Maud Martha most like to be . . .
- A. a movie star?
- B. a scientist?
- C. a stay-at-home mom?
- D. a librarian?

_____ 9. Maud Martha will count on _____ to make her dream come true.
- A. her parents
- B. herself
- C. her teachers
- D. her friends

_____ 10. How sure is Maud Martha that her New York dream will come true?
- A. not sure at all
- B. pretty sure
- C. completely sure
- D. She has given up on her dream completely.

Short-Essay Test

Describe Maud Martha to a person who has never read about her. Explain what she likes and dislikes. Also explain her hopes for the future.

New Lands

Percentage of U.S. Population That Is Foreign Born

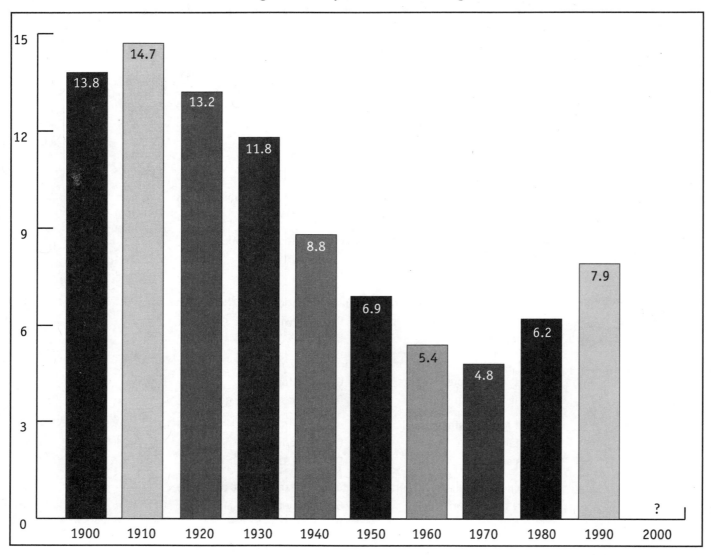

Unit Background **NEW LANDS** (pages 65-84)

Show students the above graph. Now, as always, the United States is a nation of immigrants, and all have brought their own ideas and customs to enrich the nation as a whole. But being an immigrant is not always easy, as the two writers in this section attest to.

Teaching the Introduction

The photographs on this page show a variety of types of people in the United States, some wearing distinctive dress and hairdos.

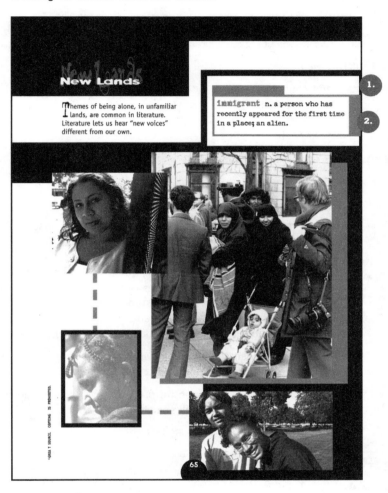

1. Ask whether anyone in the class has immigrated to the United States or has visited a foreign country. If so, ask what the most unusual aspect of that experience was.

   What do or did they miss most about their home country?

2. Tell students that one way the United States has become enriched is through the traditional foods favored by immigrants. Ask students to tell or make some guesses about where the following foods or dishes originated: tacos, sauerbraten, borscht, pumpernickel, kimchee, piroshki, ravioli, wonton, couscous, quiche, crepes, chicken curry, eggroll, and blintzes. If they can name other foods they think were imported along with various immigrants, urge them to do so.

Opening Activity

Ask students to assume they are to prepare a booklet welcoming new citizens to the community. What kinds of things would they want to tell them? What kinds of things would be essential for these new citizens to know, and what can they expect?

Legal Alien and Immigrants

Skills and Strategies Overview

THEME New Lands

READING LEVEL easy

VOCABULARY

◇ paneled   ◇ exotic   ◇ fringes   ◇ discomfort   ◇ bi-laterally

PREREADING picture walk

RESPONSE react and connect

COMPREHENSION double-entry journal

PREWRITING brainstorm/web

WRITING poem / capitalizing proper nouns

ASSESSMENT meaning

BACKGROUND

Multiculturalism continues to be an important topic in today's schools. Every day, students wrestle with questions such as: "How do I fit in?" and "What is my place in the world?" Pat Mora, who was born in 1942 in El Paso, Texas, explores these questions in her poems "Legal Alien" and "Immigrants." Of course, every child, no matter what his or her race or nationality, feels "bicultural" at times. Family values can conflict with peer values, which can conflict with school values. These poems show students that all people struggle with these conflicts. Mora reminds us that we are all immigrants of a sort, and as such, we are all asked at times to mask "the discomfort/of being pre-judged/Bi-laterally."

UNIT THEME New Lands helps students think about what it's like to be a stranger in a new place. What can we do to make ourselves and others feel "at home"?

GRAPHIC ORGANIZER Students might create a word web for *bi-lateral,* which is at the thematic heart of both poems. Students' webs might look something like this:

Word Web: Bi-lateral

Use words together to describe: Having or involving 2 sides. This means two different opinions—two sides to a coin. Not disagreeing, but working in harmony.

What is it like?
having two faces
seeing two sides to an issue
discussion

Bi-lateral

What it does:
promotes unity
causes conflict
helps me reassess who I am

Example:
My school
my city
my state
my country

BEFORE YOU READ

Before they read Mora's two poems, students should walk through the pictures on pages 66–72 and then say how the pictures make them feel. A **picture walk** can offer clues about the topic of the reading and at the same time motivate students to read. A simple strategy like this one will be particularly useful to students who are intimidated by poetry.

Motivation Strategy

ENGAGING STUDENTS Explain that Mora's poems are about moving to a new land. Ask students to imagine themselves in this situation. What would they do first? Would they look for friends, learn the language, learn the customs, or what?

Vocabulary Building

Point out the key vocabulary words for this lesson: *paneled, exotic, fringes, discomfort, bilaterally*. These words appear in an exercise on the **Vocabulary** blackline master on page 120. Encourage students to learn the definitions for these words so that they can begin incorporating the words into their own vocabularies.

STRATEGY LESSON: CONTEXT CLUES Help students use context clues to figure out the meanings of difficult words. Model using context and then show how to check provisional definitions against the footnotes. Say to the class, "I don't know the word *exotic*. I see, though, that it appears in a sentence with the word *different*. Could *exotic* mean 'strange'? I can check the footnote to see if my guess is correct."

For additional practice, see the **Vocabulary** blackline master on page 120.

Prereading Strategies

During their **picture walks**, students should look carefully at each drawing and photograph in the selection. Then they will write their reactions to the images that interest them most. The art for this section was chosen with the aim of giving students a glimpse of Mora's main idea—that all people are in some ways "bi-lateral" and "bicultural." The art introduces an idea that Mora explores in some detail in her writing.

QUICKWRITE Another excellent prereading·strategy is the quickwrite. Read aloud the first few lines of "Legal Alien." Then ask students to do a one-minute quickwrite about a topic that you suggest. You might ask them to write about the topic of "family relationships," "moving to a new land," "learning a new language," or "learning new customs."

Spanish-Speaking Students

"Extranjero legal" e "Inmigrantes" dan un retrato de la vida multicultural en los Estados Unidos. "Extranjero legal" muestra las ventajas y desventajas de ser parte de dos culturas, y señala las dificultades de definir a una persona de una manera concreta. "Inmigrantes" también examina el dilema de adoptar o adaptar a una cultura para ser aceptado en la sociedad total. En este poema, son obvios los deseos y miedos de mezclar con la masa.

II. READ

As they read, students should **react and connect** to the author's topic and words by writing in the **double-entry journal**. Ask them to make notes about how individual lines make them feel. Do they agree or disagree with the speakers? Do they have an experience from their own lives that they'd like to share out loud or in writing? They can use their responses later, when they write their own poems.

Response Strategy

HIGHLIGHT In addition to the strategy of **react and connect**, suggest that students **mark** or **highlight** words or phrases that stand out for them. Ask students to write in the **Response Notes** their interpretation of what these words or phrases mean.

Comprehension Strategies

In a **double-entry journal**, students note their individual responses to the specific phrases, sentences, or lines from the selection. Have students comment on lines from the poems that they find interesting, confusing, or relevant. A double-entry journal serves two purposes: 1. It gives readers the chance to do a line-by-line analysis of the text; 2. It helps students see that their responses to the text can help them uncover the author's meaning.

GRAPHIC ORGANIZER As an alternate strategy, have students work on a graphic organizer that can help them think about the meaning of the two poems. Your advanced readers can make a stylistic comparison of the two poems, focusing on language, rhythm, tone, and form. Other readers can compare and contrast Mora's messages. Are they exactly the same in both poems? If not, what's different?

For additional work, see the **Comprehension** blackline master on page 121.

Discussion Questions

COMPREHENSION 1. According to both poems, what do legal aliens and immigrants do to feel more American? *(They speak English, they eat American food, they give their children American names, and so on.)*

2. In "Legal Alien," how do Americans treat immigrants? *(as exotic, inferior, different)*

3. In the same poem, how do Mexicans view immigrants? *(They are wary of those who have become too "assimilated" into the American culture.)*

4. According to the speaker in "Immigrants," what fear do immigrant parents have? *(that their children won't be accepted)*

CRITICAL THINKING 5. What does it mean to be a "hyphenated" American? *(Not only are you bilingual and bi-cultural, you may be known as Mexican-American, Polish-American, Japanese-American, and so on.)*

6. Do you think the feeling of being a "hyphenated" American ever goes away? If so, when? *(Accept any reasonable answers.)*

Literary Skill

FREE VERSE Take this opportunity to introduce free verse to students. Free verse is a type of poetry that is written with rhythm and other poetic devices but without a fixed pattern of meter and rhyme. In free verse, sound is important, as is the way individual lines flow together. When they read free verse, students should look at the poem as a whole, rather than try and understand any one line by itself. To make this easier, rewrite one of the poems as a paragraph on the board. Then ask: "What is the main idea of this paragraph?" Once they understand the message, students can begin to think about Mora's poetic patterns.

III. GATHER YOUR THOUGHTS

Students can work alone or with a partner to create a web that explores how the speaker of one of the two poems feels about living in a new land. **Brainstorming** ideas and then creating a **web** can help students see connections in a work that they didn't notice on a first reading. Then have students complete a web about a time when they were in a new place as preparation for writing their own poems.

Prewriting Strategies

BRAINSTORM As an alternate prewriting strategy, have students brainstorm types of "new" places while you or a student write them on the board. For example, a new home, a new family, a new route to a new school, or a new classroom. Students might also suggest places where new experiences happen, such as a gym, a summer camp, a swimming pool, or a stage.

For more practice, see the **Prewriting and Writing** blackline master on page 122.

IV. WRITE

On page 72, students are asked to write a **poem** about being somewhere new. Students who feel intimidated at the thought of writing a poem might work together in small groups. Each group can produce one poem. (Later, after students see that the process is not so difficult, they can try writing their own verse.) Before they revise, teach a brief lesson on capitalization. Then use the writing rubric to assess the poems.

WRITING RUBRIC Do students' poems

- explore a new experience?
- have details that help the experience come alive for readers?
- follow the model of Mora's "Immigrants"?

Grammar, Usage, and Mechanics

Explain that there are no set capitalization rules in poetry. Still, students might benefit from some additional help with capital letters. Remind them that in most writing, proper nouns and titles such as Mr. and Dr. are capitalized.

V. WRAP-UP

Take a moment at the end of the lesson for students to talk about what the two poems **meant** to them. If appropriate, have them explain why they found themselves unable to connect to Mora's writing. Which reading strategies could they have used to forge a stronger connection?

Assessment

For a comprehension check, ask students to complete the **Assessment** blackline master on page 123.

Name _____

VOCABULARY

Words from the Selection

DIRECTIONS To help you learn new words from "Legal Alien," try answering these five questions. Then write the meaning of the underlined words on the lines.

1. What might a <u>paneled</u> office have on its walls?

_____

2. Can a cat be <u>exotic</u>?

_____

3. If I'm planning a fence for the <u>fringes</u> of my property, where am I going to build it?

_____

4. If I feel <u>discomfort</u>, am I happy?

_____

5. Is a coin <u>bi-lateral</u>?

_____

Strategy Lesson: Context Clues

When you come to a word you don't understand, try defining the word in context. This means you look for clues about the unfamiliar words in surrounding phrases or sentences.

EXAMPLE: I felt <u>uncertain</u> of myself. I was not sure I'd be able to do the job.
Clue: In the sentence following the one with *uncertain*, I see that the speaker feels "not sure" about doing a job. This tells me that *uncertain* must have something to do with being unsure.

DIRECTIONS Read these lines from Mora's poems. Use context clues to help you figure out what the underlined words mean.

. . . <u>drafting</u> memos in smooth English,

able to order in <u>fluent</u> Spanish

at a Mexican restaurant,

American but <u>hyphenated</u> . . .

6. drafting means: _____

7. fluent means: _____

8. hyphenated means: _____

Name _____

COMPREHENSION

Directed Reading

DIRECTIONS Answer these questions about Mora's poems. They can help you think about her main ideas.

1. What does it mean to be "bilingual"?

_____

_____

2. According to the first poem, how do Anglos feel about a "legal alien"? How do some Mexicans feel about a "legal alien"?

_____

_____

3. In "Immigrants," what do the immigrant parents say to their children?

_____

_____

4. Why do they say these things?

_____

_____

5. Why do the parents "wrap their babies in the American flag,/feed them mashed hot dogs and apple pie . . ."?

_____

_____

Name _____

PREWRITING AND WRITING

Writing a Free-Verse Poem

DIRECTIONS Follow these steps to help you write a free-verse poem. Remember that free-verse poetry does not follow a specific form, and it does not have to rhyme.

STEP 1. READ THE ASSIGNMENT. Your book asks you to write about a new experience.

My subject: _____

STEP 2. COLLECT YOUR THOUGHTS. Write freely for a few minutes about your subject. Don't worry about spelling and punctuation. Just get your ideas down.

My free-write: _____

_____

_____

_____

_____

_____

STEP 3. WRITE A FIRST DRAFT. Now take your free-write and insert some line breaks. Try to put breaks where you hear natural pauses in the sentences.

My free-write with line breaks: _____

_____

_____

_____

_____

_____

_____

STEP 4. IMPROVE YOUR WRITING. Move words or phrases around to make the poem sound better. Replace words as necessary. Remember to use words that carry some emotional weight. For example, *sad* doesn't say nearly as much as *wept* or *cried*.

STEP 5. REVISE YOUR WRITING. Read the poem aloud to yourself. If a line sounds odd, rewrite it. If a word doesn't seem to work, replace it. Then write your finished poem here.

_____

_____

_____

_____

_____

_____

Name _____

ASSESSMENT

Multiple-Choice Test

DIRECTIONS On the blanks provided, write the letter of the answer that best completes each statement or answers each question.

_____ 1. The speaker in "Legal Alien" can read and speak . . .

A. Spanish only.

B. two languages.

C. English only.

D. three languages.

_____ 2. In "Legal Alien," the speaker feels . . .

A. uncomfortable.

B. pre-judged.

C. part of two cultures.

D. all of the above

_____ 3. What do the parents in "Immigrants" want most for their children?

A. They want them to fit into American society.

B. They want them to eat properly.

C. They want them to learn to play football.

D. They want them to learn to read well.

_____ 4. How do the parents in "Immigrants" help their children?

A. by giving them American food

B. by giving them American names

C. by speaking English to them

D. all of the above

_____ 5. How do you think the parents in "Immigrants" feel about their children?

A. proud

B. worried

C. hopeful

D. all of the above

_____ 6. What example of American food does Pat Mora give in "Immigrants"?

A. pumpkin pie

B. apple pie

C. blueberry pie

D. cherry pie

_____ 7. Which names in "Immigrants" are an example of American names?

A. Bob and Mary

B. Jeff and Betty

C. Bill and Daisy

D. John and Jane

_____ 8. How old are the children in "Immigrants"?

A. babies

B. elementary-school age

C. high-school age

D. college age

_____ 9. What fear do the parents in "Immigrants" have?

A. that they will have to leave the U.S.

B. that they'll lose their jobs

C. that their children won't be liked

D. that they'll never make enough money

_____ 10. When do the parents in "Immigrants" speak in their native languages?

A. on holidays

B. when the children are asleep

C. when relatives are visiting

D. on Sundays

Short-Essay Test

Are the speakers of the two poems happy, sad, or angry? Explain how you know.

A Simple Proposition

Skills and Strategies Overview

THEME	New Lands
READING LEVEL	average
VOCABULARY	✦cackle ✦permanent ✦reproof ✦arrogant ✦proposition
PREREADING	anticipation guide
RESPONSE	clarify
COMPREHENSION	plot chart
PREWRITING	group discussion
WRITING	review / capitalizing place names
ASSESSMENT	understanding

BACKGROUND

Lensey Namioka was born in China but has lived most of her life in the United States. Much of her writing reflects her strong cultural ties to her Chinese heritage and to her husband's Japanese ancestry. Namioka is most known for her works *Ties That Bind, Ties That Break: A Novel* (1999), *Yang the Youngest and His Terrible Ear* (1998), and *April and the Dragon Lady* (1994).

UNIT THEME In "A Simple Proposition," Lensey Namioka poses the thematic question: "Is fitting in worth sacrificing your own self-esteem?" Namioka's protagonist learns the answer to this question the hard way.

GRAPHIC ORGANIZER A story pyramid like the one below can help students focus on the main elements of the story.

Story Pyramid: "A Simple Proposition"

1. Emma Hu
Name of main character

2. smart nice
Two words describing main character

3. Boston today high school
Three words describing setting

4. kids resent Emma's genius
Four words stating problem

5. Emma Arthur win math prize
Five words describing one event

6. Arthur asks Emma: competition or prom?
Six words describing second event

7. Emma is shocked. She refuses the proposition.
Seven words describing third event

8. Emma says competition and self-esteem are most important.
Eight words describing solution

I. BEFORE YOU READ

Read through the introduction to the lesson with students. The purpose of the opening of the lesson is to motivate and focus students. Then have students complete the **anticipation guide**. (Refer to the **Strategy Handbook** on pages 40–59 for more help.)

Motivation Strategy

ENGAGING STUDENTS Explain that in "A Simple Proposition," a girl is ridiculed and alienated because she is a math whiz. What advice do students have for her? Discuss the problem as a class.

Vocabulary Building

Draw attention to the key vocabulary words for this lesson: *cackle, permanent, reproof, arrogant*, and *proposition*. Ask students to volunteer definitions for the words. Also have them use the words in sentences of their own. A series of quick vocabulary exercises can help students become more comfortable with any words that are new to them. For more practice work, have students complete the **Vocabulary** blackline master on page 128.

STRATEGY LESSON: PREFIXES If students would benefit from more vocabulary work, you might teach a brief lesson on prefixes. Hundreds of words contain the prefix *un-*. In this story the following words appear: *unfeminine, unnatural, uncomfortable,* and *unable*. Ask students to guess what the prefix means ("not" or "the opposite of"). Then ask them to think of five more words that contain this prefix.

For additional practice, see the **Vocabulary** blackline master, page 128.

Prereading Strategies

The **anticipation guide** on page 73 will get students thinking about the topic of Namioka's story. Tell students that you are interested in their responses to the statements. Since no adult will see their answers, they should be as honest as possible. After they've finished reading the story, have students return to the anticipation guide to see if their attitudes have changed. This is an excellent way of showing students that what they read really can change the way they view the world.

PICTURE WALK As an additional strategy, have students do a quick picture walk after they complete their anticipation guides. This strategy will serve as another introduction to the topic—and main idea—of the selection. From the art, students should be able to infer that "A Simple Proposition" has something to do with an Asian-American girl, math, and boy-girl relationships. Ask students to make a one-sentence prediction of the story: "'A Simple Proposition' is probably about a girl who . . ."

Spanish-Speaking Students

"Una proposición simple" retrata el gran deseo de una mujer de sentir parte de la multitud. Lensey Namioka cuenta su lucha en el colegio, donde se enfrentaba con el racismo y sexismo. Explica su anhelo de ser "normal" como sus compañeros de clase, y su determinación de mantener su orgullo personal e individualidad. Al final, tiene que escoger entre sus dos deseos.

READ

As they read, students should **underline** the main events. You might suggest that they number each new event so that they can keep an eye on story sequence. Later, if they are asked to summarize or retell the action of the story, they can return to the numbered items.

Response Strategy

CLARIFY As they read, students should watch for events and ideas that they will need to clarify. Have them note their questions in the **Response Notes**. These questions will help them when it comes time to write a review of the story.

Comprehension Strategies

A **plot chart** can help students keep track of the events of a plot. Plot charts work well with students who have trouble reading longer selections or remembering the sequence of events in a story. As they read "A Simple Proposition," students will make notes on three different charts plus a character development organizer. Encourage them to be brief in their responses so that they have time to finish the whole selection. Remind them that plot charts (and other graphic organizers) are for brief notes, not full paragraphs.

DIRECTED READING As an alternate comprehension strategy, you might do a directed reading of the story, stopping along the way to ask fact-based questions about character, setting, and plot. Questions as simple as "What is Emma's opinion here?" can lead students to a deeper understanding of the story.

For additional work, see the **Comprehension** blackline master, page 129.

Discussion Questions

COMPREHENSION 1. What does Emma Hu's father do for a living? *(He's a math professor at M.I.T.)*

2. Why do the kids and teachers poke fun at her? *(She is gifted in math, which is uncommon for a girl.)*

3. What is Emma's concern about the prom? *(She doesn't have a date.)*

CRITICAL THINKING 4. What "proposition" does Arthur make to Emma? *(He'll take her to the prom if she'll drop out of the math contest.)*

5. Why does she turn it down? *(She knows it's more important to feel good about yourself than to do what others expect of you.)*

Literary Skill

PLOT LINE For extra work on sequence and plot, have students record the events of "A Simple Proposition" on a plot line similar to the one below.

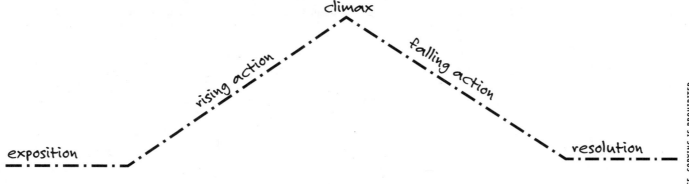

III. GATHER YOUR THOUGHTS

A **group discussion** can help students get more out of a story or article. When they share ideas, they see that not everyone will interpret an action or character in the same way. To keep their discussions centered and productive, students should talk mostly about the graphic organizer they completed after reading the story. Once they've finished with their organizer, they can begin a discussion of the problem and resolution Namioka sets up in her story. Be sure that students read the discussion tips on pupil's page 82.

Prewriting Strategies

TOPIC SENTENCES As an additional prewriting strategy, have students practice writing topic sentences that they can use for their reviews of the story. Begin by asking them to read the sample topic sentence on page 83. Ask them to use this sentence as a model for their own topic sentences. They key here is to give students the chance to experiment with topic sentences. They might be surprised to see that the best topic sentence is one that is clear and direct.

For more practice, see the **Prewriting and Writing** blackline master on page 130.

IV. WRITE

Remind students that their assignment is to write a **review** of "A Simple Proposition." They should work directly from the organizers they completed on page 82. When they've finished, they can use the questions in the writing rubric to help them revise. During the revision session, you might introduce a brief lesson on capitalization of place names.

WRITING RUBRIC Do students' reviews

- start with a topic sentence that states an opinion of the story?
- contain ideas that support the opinion?
- capitalize place names?

Grammar, Usage, and Mechanics

Remind students to capitalize the names of proper nouns, including the names of cities and states. Also remind them that if they name a particular place *(Afton High School)*, they use capital letters. If they simply name the type of place it is *(school)*, no capital letters are needed.

V. WRAP-UP

Help students see that one of the reasons they dislike a story or think it's boring is because they don't really **understand** it. Ask: "What about Namioka's story was difficult to understand? What are some strategies you could use to improve your comprehension?"

Assessment

For a comprehension check, ask students to complete the **Assessment** blackline master on page 131.

Name _____

VOCABULARY

Words from the Selection

DIRECTIONS Use the vocabulary words from the list below in sentences that show you understand the meaning of each word.

✧ cackle   ✧ permanent   ✧ reproof   ✧ arrogant   ✧ proposition

1. _____

_____

2. _____

_____

3. _____

_____

4. _____

_____

5. _____

Understanding Prefixes

A prefix is a word part added to the beginning of a word that changes the word's meaning. For example, when the prefix *pre-* (which means "before") is added to the word *war,* you have a new word: *prewar*—or "before the war."

DIRECTIONS Write the prefix and root word of each word. Then write what you think the word means.

✧ immeasurable   ✧ semi-final   ✧ impersonal   ✧ discourage   ✧ unattractive

	Prefix	+	Root	=	Meaning
EXAMPLE:					
transatlantic	trans	+	Atlantic	=	across the ocean
6. immeasurable (*im-* = not)	_____	+	_____	=	_____
7. semi-final (*semi-* = partly)	_____	+	_____	=	_____
8. impersonal (*im-* = not)	_____	+	_____	=	_____
9. discourage (*dis-* = lack of)	_____	+	_____	=	_____
10. unattractive (*un-* = not)	_____	+	_____	=	_____

Name _____

COMPREHENSION
Graphic Organizer

DIRECTIONS Decide what you like and don't like about "A Simple Proposition." Use this chart to keep track of your ideas. Be sure to explain your reasons.

"A Simple Proposition"

What I liked about the story . . .	What I didn't like about the story . . .	My reasons:

If you had written the story, what would you have done differently?

_____

_____

_____

_____

_____

_____

Name _____

PREWRITING AND WRITING
Writing a Review

DIRECTIONS In a story review, you give your opinion, offer support for your viewpoint, and then say whether or not you would recommend the story. Follow these steps to write a review.

STEP 1. **WRITE A TOPIC SENTENCE.** In your topic sentence, say if you liked the story and whether or not you want to recommend it to a friend.

my topic sentence: _____

STEP 2. **WRITE PARAGRAPH 1.** Use the first few sentences of your review to tell a little about the story. Give the story's name, the author's name, and a brief plot summary.

story name: _____

author's name: _____

what the story's about: _____

_____

_____

_____

STEP 3. **WRITE PARAGRAPH 2.** Next you will need to support your opinion of the story. Your support should come directly from the story.

support #1: _____

support #2: _____

support #3: _____

STEP 4. **WRITE A CONCLUDING SENTENCE.** Say whether or not you want to recommend the story. Use this as your closing sentence.

my closing sentence: _____

_____

_____

Name _____

ASSESSMENT

Multiple-Choice Test

DIRECTIONS On the blanks provided, write the letter of the item that best completes each statement or answers each question.

_____ 1. Why does Emma Hu feel like a freak?

    A. because of her name   C. because her mother is a professor

    B. because she is a math whiz   D. because she doesn't have a prom date

_____ 2. Her teachers and classmates think it's strange that Emma is so good at math because . . .

    A. she is a girl.   C. she used to be a poor math student.

    B. she dislikes math.   D. she never studies.

_____ 3. How does Emma feel about math?

    A. excited   C. fearful

    B. bored   D. neutral

_____ 4. Why does Emma like her teacher, Mr. Antonelli?

    A. He is an easy grader.   C. He tells funny jokes.

    B. He is handsome.   D. He thinks it's OK that she's good at math.

_____ 5. What does Mr. Antonelli do that makes Emma feel comfortable in class?

    A. He keeps his manner impersonal.   C. He treats the kids as adults.

    B. He calls everyone by their last names.   D. all of the above

_____ 6. What does Arthur want Emma to do?

    A. drop out of the math contest   C. transfer to a new school

    B. look over his homework   D. study for the contest with him

_____ 7. What does Arthur offer in return?

    A. money   C. help getting into a good college

    B. a date for the prom   D. tickets to an upcoming concert

_____ 8. Why do you think Arthur makes his proposition?

    A. He likes Emma.   C. He is afraid Emma is better at math.

    B. He feels sorry for Emma.   D. none of the above

_____ 9. How does Emma feel about Arthur's offer?

    A. angry   C. shocked

    B. triumphant   D. all of the above

_____ 10. What answer does Emma give?

    A. She says she'll think about it.   C. She turns Arthur down.

    B. She says yes.   D. She asks her friend Katey for advice.

Short-Essay Test

Would you say Emma did the right thing when she turned down Arthur? Explain.

Myths and Monsters

TVT . JO.

Unit Background

MYTHS AND MONSTERS (pages 85–110)

Myths or stories have originated in many cultures throughout the world. Originally transmitted orally, their purpose was often to explain creation, phenomena in the heavens or on earth, or the mysteries of life and death, but sometimes they simply told a good story. They also tell the adventures of gods and heroes. Heroes in myth are always men of action, and Greek and Roman heroes are often depicted in art engaged in a struggle of some kind. Ulysses, the Roman name for the Greek hero Odysseus, is the main character of Homer's epic poem, the *Odyssey*. The *Odyssey* tells the tale of an adventurer who, after the Trojan War, tries to make his way home to Ithaca. One of his many escapades is his encounter with the Cyclops, a one-eyed giant who devours men, a story retold here.

Hercules, the Roman name for the Greek hero Heracles, was the son of the Greek god Zeus and Alcmene, who was married to Amphitryon. Hera, the wife of Zeus, hated Hercules. She drove him mad, and he murdered his wife Megara and all their children. When he recovered from his madness, he was overcome with grief and consulted the oracle at Delphi, who advised him to go to the king of Mycenae and vow to serve him for twelve years. The king devised twelve labors for the mighty Hercules to accomplish, promising him immortality if he succeeded. Although he eventually died, he is supposed to have gone to Olympus, the home of the gods.

Many writers have retold the Greek and Roman myths, and students intrigued by the story of Ulysses will enjoy reading of his other adventures as retold by Bernard Evslin.

Teaching the Introduction

Capturing Cerberus, the three-headed dog in Hades, was Hercules' last labor. Hercules took the dog back, however. Originally Hades, sometimes known as Pluto, a brother of Zeus and Poseidon, was ruler of the underworld, but later the gloomy place itself became known as Hades.

The illustration of the Cyclops shows Ulysses putting out his eye. The center drawing shows Hercules wrestling with the Nemean lion. At the bottom is Hercules temporarily taking over the duties of Atlas. The drawing at bottom right shows a classical warrior with helmet and shield.

1. Ask students whether they are familiar with myths from any culture and if so, to mention some of them.

2. Ask students to tell what characteristics or traits a hero has. What makes a hero a hero? (*bravery, strength, goodness*)

3. Have students describe what they think of as a monster. Is it big? Dangerous? Ugly?

Opening Activity

Ask students to tell about monsters they have read about or seen in films. Why do monsters in literature and on the screen seem to appeal to people?

The Cyclops' Cave

Skills and Strategies Overview

THEME Myths and Monsters

READING LEVEL challenging

VOCABULARY

◆savage ◆vigil ◆heed ◆aghast ◆niche

PREREADING preview

RESPONSE clarify

COMPREHENSION predict

PREWRITING storyboard

WRITING tale or story / using consistent verb tense

ASSESSMENT enjoyment

BACKGROUND

According to Bernard Evslin, a renowned storyteller of classical mythology, the Greek gods and monsters "had more powers than mortals could ever imagine. They could change day to night, turn people into animals, and punish men with eternal torture. Their whims and desires changed the course of human destiny. No legends are more fabulous than those of the Greek gods."

Evslin's retelling of "The Cyclops' Cave" follows closely the original story, which was first told by Homer toward the end of the eighth century B.C. This story, which is actually a small part of Homer's masterwork, the *Odyssey*, tells the story of the hero Ulysses (called Odysseus by the Greeks), who left his homeland of Ithaca in order to fight in the Trojan War. According to legend, Odysseus spent more than ten years battling the Trojans. When the war ended, the mighty warrior was eager to return home to his family. Unfortunately, his return trip would take him another ten years. On his voyage home, one of the first stops he made was to the island of the Cyclopes.

UNIT THEME Classical and world mythology is the foundation for most stories and legends told since the eighth century B.C. The selections in "Myths and Monsters" offer students an engaging, easy-to-understand introduction to classical Greek and Roman mythology.

GRAPHIC ORGANIZER Students might be helped by filling in a story frame like this one.

Story Frame: "The Cyclops' Cave"

1. THE STORY TAKES PLACE on the island of the Cyclopes.

2. Ulysses IS A CHARACTER IN THE STORY WHO lands on the island and is captured (along with his crew) by the terrible Cyclops.

3. Polyphemus IS ANOTHER CHARACTER IN THE STORY WHO is the fiercest and hungriest of all the Cyclopes.

4. A PROBLEM OCCURS WHEN Polyphemus decides to make a meal of Ulysses and his crew. He captures the men and imprisons them in his cave.

5. AFTER THAT, a desperate Ulysses gives wine to Polyphemus hoping to get him drunk.

6. AND when Polyphemus passes out, Ulysses thrusts a sword in Polyphemus's eye.

7. THE PROBLEM IS SOLVED WHEN Ulysses and his men hide under the bellies of Polyphemus's goats and escape from the cave. Polyphemus, now half-blind and crazy with pain, can't catch them.

8. THE STORY ENDS WITH Ulysses taunting Polyphemus from the boat. An angry Polyphemus asks the god Poseidon to condemn Ulysses to all kinds of agony as punishment for his pride.

BIBLIOGRAPHY You might assign extra reading in one of the following books: *One Hundred and One Read-Aloud Myths and Legends* (Joan C. Verniero, 1999—easy), *D'Aulaire's Book of Greek Myths* (Ingri and Edgar D'Aulaire, 1962—easy), *The Children's Homer* (Padraic Colum, 1918—average), or *Mythology* (Edith Hamilton, 1940—challenging).

BEFORE YOU READ

Explain that this is the story of a brave warrior who is imprisoned in a cave by a one-eyed monster. On their **previews**, students should watch for information about the warrior and the monster. This will help them begin exploring Evslin's thematic question of whether the monster is truly worse than the man.

Motivation Strategy

ENGAGING STUDENTS Tell students that not all of them will take the side of man over monster in this story. Can they imagine a situation in which they *wouldn't* root for the good guys?

Vocabulary Strategy

As students read, point out key vocabulary words such as *savage, vigil, heed, aghast,* and *niche.* Ask for volunteers to pronounce and offer definitions of these words. Then ask for sample sentences that use the words. Help students become accustomed to hearing the words in many different contexts.

STRATEGY LESSON: PREFIXES Knowing the prefix of a word can help students figure out the meaning of the word. Show this list of words from the selection: *disembark, undiluted,* and *unslung.* Tell the students what the prefixes mean, and have them help you separate the prefixes from the root words.

For additional practice, see the **Vocabulary** blackline master on page 138.

Prereading Strategies

Before they read, students will do a **preview** of the myth. A preview is a helpful prereading strategy because it gives readers a glimpse of what's to come. Thumbing through the pages they are about to read can help students learn about the subject and anticipate any comprehension problems they might have. A preview is also a good way to ease reluctant readers into a long or complicated text.

PICTURE WALK As an alternate strategy, ask students to do a picture walk of the selection. A picture walk is similar to a preview in that it asks students to thumb through the selection they're about to read. A picture walk can also reveal valuable clues about the subject of the story and, in some cases, the author's main idea. These clues can help readers when it's time to talk about the plot, characters, and setting of the selection.

Spanish-Speaking Students

"La Cueva del Cíclope" relata parte de la obra maestra de Homer, *La odisea.* El gran heroe, Odysseus, ha luchado en la Guerra de los Trojans durante diez años, y quiere volver a su familia en Ítaca. Su decisión de desembarcar en la tierra de los Cíclopes, sin embargo, es un error que le costará los próximos diez años intentando remediar.

As they read, students should watch for events and ideas that they will need to **clarify**. Students should ask themselves, "What does this mean?" or "What's happening here?" and then make notes in the **Response Notes**. These kinds of clarification questions can help them make sense of the action, keep track of the author's main idea, and make connections from one page to another.

Response Strategy

REACT AND CONNECT As an alternate prereading strategy, have students react and connect to the topic and message of the myth. Ask them to make comments in the **Response Notes** about how the writing makes them feel, and how the characters' actions, thoughts, and feelings might apply to themselves. These comments can help them feel more involved in the reading.

Comprehension Strategies

Making **predictions** is an excellent strategy for low-level or reluctant readers because it helps them become engaged in what they're reading. Prediction questions ask students to consider outcomes and encourage them to ponder issues such as character motivation. As they read, students should pay particular attention to the **stop and predict** questions about Ulysses. Their predictions about what he might do will help them understand both his triumphs and his defeats.

STORY FRAME As an alternate comprehension strategy, ask students to complete a story frame as they read. A story frame can help students keep track of important events in the plot. This strategy is a particularly good one to use with long, more complicated selections. (See page 134 in this guide.)

For additional practice, see the **Comprehension** blackline master on page 139.

Discussion Questions

COMPREHENSION 1. Why does Polyphemus capture Ulysses and his men? *(He wants to eat them.)*

2. Why does Ulysses give him wine to drink? Why does Polyphemus accept it? *(Ulysses wants to get him drunk, which might allow the men to escape. Polyphemus drinks the wine because he is curious.)*

3. How does the crew manage to escape from the cave? *(They hide under the rams' bellies after blinding Polyphemus.)*

CRITICAL THINKING 4. What is Ulysses' tragic mistake at the end of the story? *(He boasts about his deeds and is punished for his pride.)*

5. Is Ulysses a likable person? Explain why or why not. *(Answers will vary. Ask students to explain their opinions.)*

Literary Skill

PLOT Plot is the action or sequence of events in a story. A plot can be diagrammed on a plot line. A plot line for "The Cyclops' Cave" might look something like this:

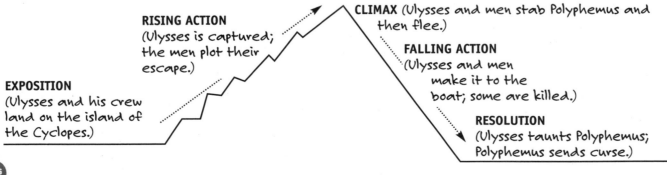

RISING ACTION (Ulysses is captured; the men plot their escape.)

CLIMAX (Ulysses and men stab Polyphemus and then flee.)

FALLING ACTION (Ulysses and men make it to the boat; some are killed.)

EXPOSITION (Ulysses and his crew land on the island of the Cyclopes.)

RESOLUTION (Ulysses taunts Polyphemus; Polyphemus sends curse.)

III. GATHER YOUR THOUGHTS

Students should work alone or in pairs to complete the **storyboard** on page 96 that shows the sequence of events in the selection. A storyboard can help students keep track of the most important events in a plot. Since it combines both writing and drawing, it is particularly useful for students who have trouble getting started on a writing project. Before they begin the storyboard on page 96, you might have students list the six most important events from the plot. Have them compare what they wrote with a partner and then make revisions as needed.

Prewriting Strategies

GRAPHIC ORGANIZER As an additional prewriting strategy, ask students to create a Venn diagram in which they compare Ulysses to Polyphemus. Traits the two characters have in common should go in the center of the diagram. This exercise helps students see that "good" and "evil" characters are never as cut-and-dried as they first appear.

For additional help, see the **Prewriting** blackline master on page 140.

IV. WRITE

Explain to students that they'll be writing a **continuation** of Evslin's **story**. It's important that they reread the last few paragraphs of "The Cyclops' Cave" so that they know how to set up their continuations. Students who have trouble getting started might want to talk over their ideas in a small group or with a writing partner. Use the rubric to assess students' writing. Also teach a brief lesson on verb tense.

WRITING RUBRIC Do students' continuations

* focus on the storm, shipwreck, or sorcery mentioned in Evslin's story?

* tell a series of events in a clear, straightforward manner?

* use past tense verbs?

Grammar, Usage, and Mechanics

Many students have trouble maintaining one verb tense throughout an entire piece of writing. Explain how important it is to choose one tense and stay with it throughout. In their continuations, they should write in the past tense *(sailed, screamed, ran,)* just as Evslin does in his story.

V. WRAP-UP

Take a moment at the end of the lesson for students to talk about what they did and did not like about this myth. Ask students: What would have made the story more **enjoyable** for you? What changes would you make to the story if you could?

Assessment

Ask students to complete the **Assessment** blackline master on page 141.

Name _____

VOCABULARY

Words from the Selection

DIRECTIONS Some words look almost the same as other words. There are two possible choices in each sentence below. Pick the word that correctly fits in the sentence and write it on the blank.

1. The giant was a/an (savage–average) monster who ate men. _____

2. It was a good idea to appoint someone to keep a constant (visible–vigil) on the giant.
   _____

3. Ulysses tried to keep his men from running toward the giant, but they paid no (heed–head).
   _____

4. The giant picked up men and stuck them in a (nick–niche) in the wall.
   _____

5. Ulysses was (aghast–a guest) at the size of the giant. _____

Vocabulary Strategy: Prefixes

Prefixes are word parts that come before a root word (*un-* = not). Understanding the meaning of some prefixes can help you figure out the meaning of a word.

DIRECTIONS Circle the prefix of each italicized word. Underline the root word. Then write what the word means.

EXAMPLE:

(un)able   can't _____

6. *disembark* from a ship _____

7. *unwatered* wine _____

8. *unslung* a flask _____

9. *unconscious* man _____

10. *unwanted* stranger _____

Name _____

COMPREHENSION
Predict

DIRECTIONS Fill in this prediction chart. In the second column, write what you predicted. In the third column, write what really happened. Then answer three questions about the story.

My Predictions: "The Cyclops' Cave"

page number	I predicted . . .	What really happened . . .
88		
89		
92		

Questions

1. What three words would you use to describe Ulysses?

_____

_____

2. Do you feel sorry for Polyphemus at the end? Why or why not?

_____

_____

3. Why does Polyphemus beg Poseidon to punish Ulysses?

_____

_____

Name _____

PREWRITING
Storyboard

DIRECTIONS Use this storyboard to plan what will happen in your continuation. Make a sketch in each box. Write one sentence underneath each sketch to explain what happens.

Storyboard: What Happens Next

1.	2.

3.	4.

Name _____

ASSESSMENT

Multiple-Choice Test

DIRECTIONS On the blanks provided, write the letter of the item that best completes each statement or answers each question.

_____ 1. What is the most noticeable thing about the Cyclops?
A. He has three hands.　　　　　　C. He has four ears.
B. He has two mouths.　　　　　　D. He has one eye.

_____ 2. What is the Cyclops' favorite food?
A. wild goat　　　　　　　　　　C. human flesh
B. tree tops　　　　　　　　　　D. wild pig

_____ 3. Why do Ulysses and his men get off their boat?
A. to hunt for food　　　　　　　C. to make repairs
B. to take a rest　　　　　　　　D. to search for fresh water

_____ 4. How does Ulysses feel as he and his men explore the island?
A. relaxed　　　　　　　　　　　C. nervous
B. tired　　　　　　　　　　　　D. happy

_____ 5. What does Ulysses do to save his men from Polyphemus?
A. He tells Polyphemus that men are poison.　C. He makes Polyphemus drunk.
B. He makes friends with Polyphemus.　　　D. none of the above

_____ 6. After Polyphemus crashes to the cave floor, Ulysses . . .
A. stabs him in the back.　　　　　C. ties him up.
B. puts out his eye.　　　　　　　D. cuts off his ears.

_____ 7. How do the men get out of Polyphemus's cave?
A. They wait until he leaves.　　　　C. They run when he moves the stone.
B. They find a second exit.　　　　　D. They hide under the rams' bellies.

_____ 8. Why does Polyphemus tell the other Cyclopes that Nobody put out his eye?
A. He thinks that is Ulysses's name.　　C. He is embarrassed.
B. He wants to catch Ulysses himself.　　D. He thinks he injured himself.

_____ 9. Nine crew members make it to the boat. How many survive Polyphemus's final attack?
A. two　　　　　　　　　　　　C. five
B. three　　　　　　　　　　　　D. seven

_____ 10. Polyphemus asks _____ to punish Ulysses.
A. the other Cyclopes　　　　　　C. the chief judge of the Cyclopes
B. the god Poseidon　　　　　　　D. Zeus

Short-Essay Test

The myth says that "the gods honor courage but punish pride." What does this mean?

STUDENT PAGES 99–110

Skills and Strategies Overview

THEME Myths and Monsters

READING LEVEL challenging

VOCABULARY ✧impulse ✧bewilderment ✧defiled ✧loathing ✧immortal

PREREADING think-pair-and-share

RESPONSE highlight

COMPREHENSION graphic organizer

PREWRITING clustering

WRITING descriptive paragraph / subject-verb agreement

ASSESSMENT ease

BACKGROUND

Thanks to Walt Disney and other filmmakers, just about everyone knows Hercules. But not nearly as many people know the real story of Hercules and his twelve tasks. Hercules is the Roman name for the Greek mythological hero Heracles, who was famous for his courage and strength. Many plays and operas have been written about Hercules over the centuries. Some of the first were Euripides' *Heracles,* Sophocles' *The Women of Trachis,* and Seneca's *Hercules Furens*.

Many scholars call Hercules literature's first great tragic character. Despised by Hera, Zeus's wife, because of Zeus's affair with Hercules' mortal mother, Alcmene, Hercules spent his entire mortal life trying to escape the goddess's evil eye. As a result of Hera's scheming, Hercules kills his own family. Hoping to atone for the murders, Hercules performs the twelve tasks that made him legendary.

UNIT THEME In "Myths and Monsters," students can explore the theme of good and evil.

GRAPHIC ORGANIZER The student clusters on page 108 might look something like this.

Character Analysis: Hercules

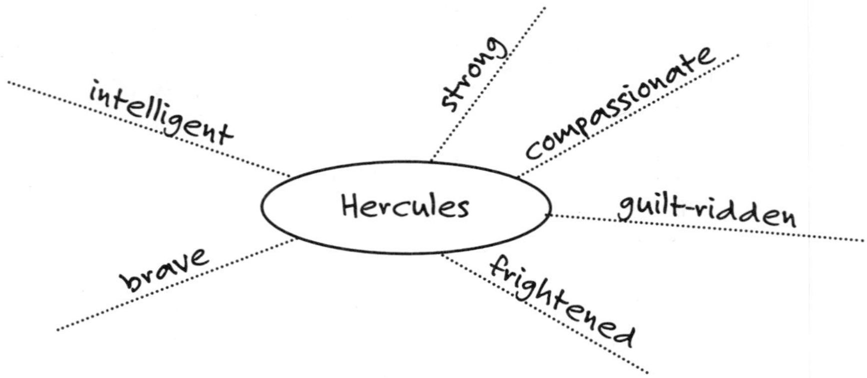

BIBLIOGRAPHY Encourage students to read other tales in Edith Hamilton's *Mythology,* which is one of the best-selling books of all time. In her book, Hamilton offers stories of the twelve gods and goddesses of Mount Olympus, as well as other Greek and Roman myths.

BEFORE YOU READ

Introduce the story by explaining that Hercules was a mighty and strong man in mythology. As they read, students should watch carefully for clues about his character. The sentences in the **think-pair-and-share** should immediately immerse students in the story and provide their first clues about Hercules.

Motivation Strategy

ENGAGING STUDENTS Set up the story by saying that the central character commits a murder as a young man. Ask students to think about what leads people to commit terrible crimes. How are they punished? Do they ever try to punish themselves?

Vocabulary Building

Draw attention to the key vocabulary words for this lesson: *impulse, bewilderment, defiled, loathing,* and *immortal*. Students should add some new words to their vocabulary each time they read. For additional practice, see the **Vocabulary** blackline master on page 146.

STRATEGY LESSON: GREEK AND LATIN ROOTS Long or complex words sometimes can be broken down into smaller units that can give clues about their meaning. Since more than half the words in English come from Greek or Latin sources, it's important for students to know a little about Greek and Latin word families—for example, *graph* (writing), *pathos* (suffering, feeling, disease), and *chronos* (time).

For additional practice, see the **Vocabulary** blackline master on page 146.

Prereading Strategies

The **think-pair-and-share** strategy is based on the notion that two minds are better than one. Your students will benefit from group discussions before, during, and after reading. In a think-pair-and-share, students consider a series of quotations from a selection and then make guesses about the proper ordering. Their work will familiarize them with the topic of the selection, and help them feel involved with the reading from the very start. Help them see that the fourth sentence probably comes first.

K-W-L As an alternate or additional prereading strategy, have students create a K-W-L organizer. K-W-L organizers help students activate prior knowledge about a topic. They can also help students see where the gaps in their knowledge base fall. If you like, set up a K-W-L on the board, and then have students make some "what they know" notes in their books. When they've finished the story, ask them to return to the L column and say what they've learned. They might be surprised to see that their L columns turn out to be longer than their K columns.

Spanish-Speaking Students

En la mitología griega Hercules es el hijo de Zeus, el reino de todos los dioses y seres humanos, y de Alcmena, una mujer mortal. Hera, la esposa de Zeus, se pone celosa de la aventura y decide a castigar a Hercules. Usando sus poderes mágicos, le causa a Hercules a matar a su propia familia. Para expiar su gran pecado él hace doce labores, pero ni arrepiento ni trabajo puede liberarse de su culpabilidad.

II. READ

As they read, students should **highlight** words, sentences, and ideas that they think are interesting, important, confusing, or puzzling. Have them underline words and phrases and write notes in the **Response Notes**. Their notations will help them when it comes time to think about what the selection really means.

Response Strategy

QUESTION As an alternative response strategy, ask students to keep a running list of questions they'd like to ask the author, another reader, or you. Have them jot these questions in the **Response Notes**. When they've finished reading, they can discuss their questions in small groups. They might find that many of their author and teacher questions can be answered by their peers.

Comprehension Strategies

On page 106, students are asked to complete a character analysis designed to help them think about the many facets of Hercules' personality. A **graphic organizer** like this one can help students explore a character in some detail. The organizer is set up in such a way that students will need to return to the text to look for specific information. Students' during-reading notes can help them with this task.

RECIPROCAL READING As an alternate comprehension strategy, you might do a reciprocal reading of the selection. This strategy is a particularly good one to use when the selection is long or the vocabulary is challenging. During a reciprocal reading, you ask a series of questions that allow you to diagnose and then address problems with comprehension and inferencing. During your reciprocal reading of this selection, you might stop every other page or so and ask questions that encourage students to 1. clarify the problem, characters, or setting; 2. predict what will happen next; 3. summarize the events; and 4. raise questions about the literature.

For additional comprehension practice, see the **Comprehension** blackline master on page 147.

Discussion Questions

COMPREHENSION 1. Why does Hercules kill his music tutor? *(He does it by accident because he doesn't know his own strength.)*

2. How does he feel after he murders his family? *(guilty; grief-stricken)*

3. Who sent the madness on Hercules? *(Hera)*

CRITICAL THINKING 4. Which of Hercules' tasks prove to be most difficult? *(Answers will vary. Have students support their ideas with evidence from the selection.)*

5. Does Hercules feel better about himself after he completes the twelve tasks? *(Not really. He is still unhappy and continues to feel crippling guilt about his family.)*

Literary Skill

CHARACTERIZATION You might use "Hercules" as the basis for a brief lesson on characterization. Characterization is the method by which an author describes a character in a written work. A writer can describe a character's physical appearance, personality, behavior, thoughts, feelings, and speech. Sophisticated readers know that clues about character can be found in all parts of a story. Help students see that Hercules' actions, speech, and interactions with other characters reveal information about his personality.

III. GATHER YOUR THOUGHTS

Clustering is a useful prewriting strategy because it can help students see links between different elements of a text. You can have students do a plot cluster, character cluster, or even a setting cluster for "Hercules."

Prewriting Strategies

GROUP DISCUSSION As an alternate prewriting strategy, you might hold a group discussion about Hercules—who he is, what he's like, and why he does the things he does. During the discussion, model for students how to support their inferences about the character. Say: "I think that Hercules is a kind and loving man. To support the idea that Hercules is compassionate, I return to the selection and find places where he shows a kindness to another character. I see, for example, that Hercules says after killing his family: 'And I myself am the murderer of my dearest. . . . Shall I spare my own life then? . . . I will avenge upon myself these deaths.' This quote shows the depth of Hercules' feelings for his family."

For more practice, see the **Prewriting and Writing** blackline master on page 148.

IV. WRITE

On page 109, students will write a brief **character description** of Hercules. In a character description, the writer makes inferences about a character and then supports those inferences with information from the selection. Use the questions from the writing rubric to help them revise, and introduce a short lesson on subject-verb agreement at an opportune time.

WRITING RUBRIC Do students' paragraphs

- begin with a topic sentence?
- contain thoughtful inferences about the character?
- have subjects and verbs that agree?

Grammar, Usage, and Mechanics

The subject and verb of a sentence must always agree. Write the following sentences on the board. Then ask someone to suggest a sentence with a plural subject and a plural noun.

Incorrect: Hercules <u>perform</u> many tasks.

Correct: Hercules <u>performs</u> many tasks.

V. WRAP-UP

After they've finished the writing assignments, ask students to reflect on the story. Ask them to tell you what they found **easy** or difficult about the story. Were the names hard? Were the sentences too long? Their comments will help you choose appropriate strategies for the next lesson.

Assessment

For a comprehension check, ask students to complete the **Assessment** blackline master on page 149.

Name _____

VOCABULARY

Words from the Selection

DIRECTIONS To help you learn new words from the selection, answer these five questions. Then write the meaning of each underlined word on the line.

1. If I have an <u>impulse</u>, does it come on all of a sudden or build gradually?

_____

_____

2. When I'm in a state of <u>bewilderment</u>, am I confused or level-headed?

_____

_____

3. Has a wall been <u>defiled</u> if it is covered with graffiti?

_____

_____

4. If I look at you with <u>loathing</u>, do I like you or hate you?

_____

_____

5. Will someone who is <u>immortal</u> live forever?

_____

_____

Strategy Lesson: Greek and Latin Roots

DIRECTIONS The words in the word box are made up of Greek and Latin roots. Write the word from the word box that best completes each sentence.

> **capture/captive** [from Latin *capere, captum*: to take]
> **sympathy** [from Greek *pathos*: suffering, feeling]
> **predict** [from Latin *dicere, dictatum*: to say]
> **chronology** [from Greek *chronos*: time]

6. Often, readers can _____ what will happen in a story.

7. What is the _____ of events in Hercules?

8. Hercules had to _____ a great boar.

9. Theseus expressed his _____ for Hercules.

10. A stag with golden horns was made a _____ by Hercules.

Name _____

COMPREHENSION
Graphic Organizer

DIRECTIONS Use this graphic organizer to show what happens to Hercules in the story. Add boxes if you need to.

Story String: "Hercules"

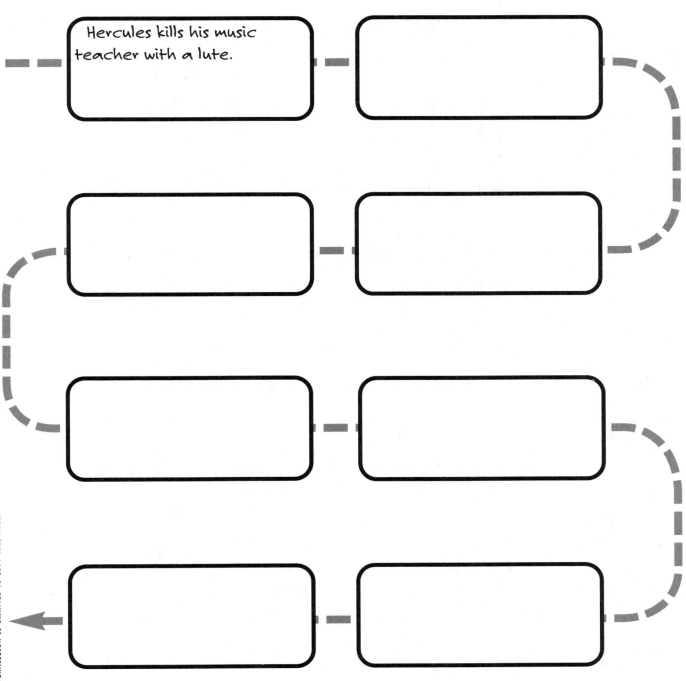

Hercules kills his music teacher with a lute.

Name _____

PREWRITING AND WRITING
Character Organizer

DIRECTIONS **A.** Use this graphic organizer to show how Hercules changes over the course of the story. Write three words that describe Hercules at each stage of his life.

Character Development: Hercules

As a young boy, Hercules is	During his tasks, Hercules is	After he finishes his tasks, Hercules is

B. Now write a topic sentence that tells how Hercules changes from the beginning of the story to the end.

In the story, Hercules changes from a _____ to a _____ .

C. List three fact or events from the story that support your topic sentence.

support #1 _____

support #2 _____

support #3 _____

D. Now write a paragraph about Hercules. Tell how he changes over the course of the story. Remember to support what you say.

_____

_____

_____

_____

_____

_____

_____

Name _____

ASSESSMENT

Multiple-Choice Test

DIRECTIONS On the blanks provided, write the best answer for each question.

_____ 1. What is Hercules' most memorable quality?
   A. his love of animals   C. his skill as a parent
   B. his strength   D. his skill as a musician

_____ 2. Who is Hercules' chief enemy among the gods and goddesses?
   A. Zeus   C. Poseidon
   B. Atlas   D. Hera

_____ 3. Why does Hercules kill his wife, Megara, and his three sons?
   A. They made fun of his powers.   C. He is temporarily insane.
   B. He thinks they want to kill him. D. He is very angry.

_____ 4. How does Hercules feel after he kills his family?
   A. guilty   C. neutral
   B. excited   D. peaceful

_____ 5. Why does Theseus try to help Hercules?
   A. because they are friends   C. because the gods have ordered him to help
   B. because he doesn't like Megara   D. because they are family

_____ 6. Why does Hercules go to visit Eurystheus?
   A. to grieve   C. to meet a new wife
   B. to pay a penalty for the killings D. to rest

_____ 7. What does Eurystheus tell Hercules to do?
   A. complete twelve difficult tasks   C. pray to Zeus for forgiveness
   B. apologize to Megara's family   D. forgive himself

_____ 8. Why does Hera dislike Hercules?
   A. because he is strong   C. because he is Zeus's son
   B. because he wears a lion skin as a cloak   D. because he is handsome

_____ 9. What job does Atlas have?
   A. He is master of the sea.   C. He supports the sky on his shoulders.
   B. He helps humans fall in love.   D. He protects the earth's animals.

_____ 10. How does Hercules feel after he completes his tasks?
   A. happy and at ease   C. tired and relieved
   B. forgiven and peaceful   D. guilty and sad

Short-Essay Test

According to the myth, Hercules was "never tranquil and at ease." Why do you think he wasn't?

Dorothy West

Unit Background   DOROTHY WEST (pages 111–124)

Dorothy West was born in Boston and studied journalism and philosophy at Columbia University. Her first published short story appeared in the *Boston Post*. She and Zora Neale Hurston (see page 224) both submitted stories for a competition given by *Opportunity* magazine and split the second-place award. West's story, "The Typewriter," was later included in *The Best Short Stories of 1926*.

West went to live in Harlem, where she founded and edited the magazine *Challenge* in 1937. The magazine suffered from financial problems, however, and West complained about the poor quality of writing she received from young writers. The successor to *Challenge* was *New Challenge*, but that magazine also failed for lack of funds.

For more than a year West worked as a welfare investigator and then joined the WPA Federal Writers' Project. From 1940 to 1960, she published more than twenty-six stories, perhaps the most famous one being "Jack in the Pot." She went to live on Martha's Vineyard in the 1940s and published her only novel, *The Living Is Easy*, in 1948.

Teaching the Introduction

The photographs at the top and bottom of page 111 depict people at leisure. The center photograph, taken in an earlier period, could represent the two women in the story.

Dorothy West (1910–1998) has written fiction, newspaper columns, essays, and articles for literary magazines. *The Richer, the Poorer* (1995) is a collection of stories, sketches, and memoirs about African-American middle-class life.

111

1. Tell students that during the Depression, the Federal Writers' Project was established in 1935 by the Works Projects Administration (originally the Works Progress Administration), which was known as the WPA. The Federal Writers' Project was funded by the government and continued until 1939. Its purpose was to help writers who were out of work. Dorothy West was a member of the Writers' Project, as were thousands of others. Ask students to speculate about why writers were in particular need of help during the Depression.

2. As is true of many writers, much of West's work was based on her own life. Ask students to discuss why people write autobiographies, memoirs, or reminiscences.

Opening Activity

Ask students to write in their journal about the earliest thing they can remember as a child and about how old they were at the time.

The Richer, the Poorer

STUDENT PAGES 112–118

Skills and Strategies Overview

THEME Dorothy West

READING LEVEL easy

VOCABULARY
◇ possessions ◇ skimping ◇ clerking ◇ wardrobe ◇ ambition

PREREADING compare/contrast chart

RESPONSE predict

COMPREHENSION directed reading

PREWRITING organize details

WRITING compare and contrast paragraph / using commas in compound sentences and in a series

ASSESSMENT style

BACKGROUND

Dorothy West was a novelist, short-story writer, editor, and journalist who had a profound impact on the direction and form of African-American literature. When she was in her twenties, West contributed articles to many of the journals of the Harlem Renaissance. Later, she was influential in the naturalistic realism of the 1930s and 1940s. Her book, *The Richer, the Poorer,* which is a collection of stories and reminiscences, was published in 1995.

UNIT THEME In "The Richer, the Poorer," Dorothy West explores the choices people make in life and presents this question: "Which is preferable, to think about today's happiness or save for future happiness?"

GRAPHIC ORGANIZER You might share this "Lottie" character attribute map with students.

Character Attribute Map: Lottie

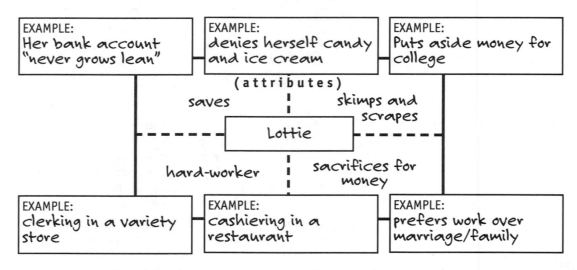

EXAMPLE:
Her bank account "never grows lean"

EXAMPLE:
denies herself candy and ice cream

EXAMPLE:
Puts aside money for college

(attributes)

saves

skimps and scrapes

Lottie

hard-worker

sacrifices for money

EXAMPLE:
clerking in a variety store

EXAMPLE:
cashiering in a restaurant

EXAMPLE:
prefers work over marriage/family

BIBLIOGRAPHY You might choose excerpts from the following West works for students to read: *The Living Is Easy* (1948), *The Richer, the Poorer* (1995), *The Wedding* (1995).

BEFORE YOU READ

> Read through the introduction to the lesson and then explain that "The Richer, the Poorer" is the story of two sisters, one of whom is "rich" and the other "poor." They can keep this topic in mind as they work on their **compare and contrast** charts.

Motivation Strategy

ENGAGING STUDENTS Tell students that the story shows two different viewpoints about money. Is it best to spend what you have and enjoy yourself now, or save for some future enjoyment? Students can think about and then respond to this question.

Vocabulary Building

Introduce the lesson's key vocabulary words to students: *possessions, skimping, clerking, wardrobe,* and *ambition.* After you discuss definitions, ask students to use words in sentences of their own. The more they use the words, the easier it will be for students to make them a part of their vocabularies.

VOCABULARY STRATEGY: SYNONYMS As an alternate vocabulary strategy, teach a short lesson on synonyms. Explain to students that sometimes it's easier to memorize the synonym for a word rather than its full dictionary definition. Show students a list of words from the selection. What synonyms can they come up with off the top of their heads? If one or more words cause problems, have students consult a dictionary or a thesaurus. You might include these words from the selection on your list: *miserly, beau,* and *sentimental.*

For additional practice, see the **Vocabulary** blackline master on page 156.

Prereading Strategies

Compare and contrast charts are important exercises for students because they help to improve students' vocabularies, which in turn can improve their understanding of a text. Focusing on a particular word such as *rich* or *poor* allows students to explore both the connotations and the denotations of the word. Ask students to relate these two words to their own lives. What are "rich" people like? What are "poor" people like? Is it a good idea to generalize?

READ-ALOUD As an alternate prereading strategy, ask students to do a read-aloud of the first several paragraphs of the story. A read-aloud can ease reluctant readers into a story and arouse enough curiosity that they'll want to continue reading on their own. For your read-aloud, choose a reader who will read with expression. Ask students to follow along in their books, making notes in the **Response Notes** about words or sentences that interest or puzzle them.

Spanish-Speaking Students

Lo más rico, lo más pobre es una colección de cuentos escritos por Dorothy West. Las siguientes selecciones introducen la gran pregunta: Prefieres pensar en la alegría de hoy, o en ahorrar para la alegría en el futuro? Lottie y Bess son hermanas muy distintas. Lottie cree que es necesario ahorrar y preparar para lo inesperado. Bess vive de una manera completamente diferente, creyendo en la importancia de aprovechar de cada día como si fuera el último. Cuando su marido se muere, Bess tiene que depender de, y vivir con Lottie.

II. READ

As they read, students will make **predictions** about characters and events. Their predictions will help them become more involved in the story. In addition, their predictions will allow them to begin exploring the differences between the two main characters. Questions such as "What do you think will happen to Lottie?" and "What do you think will happen to Bess?" will encourage them to begin the process of comparing and contrasting the two characters.

Response Strategy

REACT AND CONNECT For an alternate strategy, have students react and connect to the story as they read. Ask students to jot their opinions about the characters and plot in the **Response Notes**. Encourage them to describe people in their own lives who seem similar to Lottie and Bess. Do they see a little of themselves in one of these characters?

Comprehension Strategies

Directed reading can help reluctant or low-level readers better comprehend what they are reading. During directed reading of "The Richer, the Poorer," stop every other page or so and ask a question that can help clarify the action or main idea. These questions will allow you to keep track of problems and cope with reading difficulties as they come up. If you like, begin your directed reading by asking a question that calls for prediction. For example: Why might being past age 60 be a time for 'summing up'?

DOUBLE-ENTRY JOURNAL As an additional comprehension strategy, you might have students work on a couple of double-entry journals that explore quotations from the story that seem interesting or meaningful. This strategy will help them become more personally involved in the story. Encourage students to use their entries to say what they would have done had they been in the character's shoes or why they agree or disagree with what a character says or does.

For additional practice, see the **Comprehension** blackline master on page 157.

Discussion Questions

COMPREHENSION 1. Why does Lottie save her money? *(for her retirement)*

2. What does Bess do with her money? *(She uses it to buy things that make her happy, such as clothes, travel, and so on.)*

CRITICAL THINKING 3. In what ways is Bess rich? In what ways is Lottie poor? *(Encourage students to explore West's definition of rich and poor.)*

4. Are either of the sisters happy at the end of the story? Why or why not? *(Answers will vary. Have students support what they say with evidence from the selection.)*

5. Which sister reminds you most of yourself? Explain. *(Have students fully explain the comparison they make between themselves and the character.)*

Literary Skill

IRONY "The Richer, the Poorer" presents a perfect opportunity to introduce irony to students. Irony is a contrast between what appears to be and what really is. In verbal irony, the writer says one thing but means another. We are told that Lottie is rich and Bess is poor, but are they? Help students see the irony of West's title, "The Richer, the Poorer." Questions such as "Which character is rich at the end of the story? Which character is poor?" and "Judging from what you've read, does Dorothy West equate money with happiness?" will help students move beyond the literal meanings of the words *rich* and *poor*.

III. GATHER YOUR THOUGHTS

On page 116, students are asked to **organize details** about Bess and Lottie. Their goal will be to gather several details that they can use to write a compare and contrast paragraph about the two sisters. When they compare and contrast, students use higher-level thinking skills. Instead of merely stating facts, they will put the facts into two separate categories: similarities and differences. As such, this strategy can help students move beyond literal response and into the realm of inferential response.

Prewriting Strategies

GRAPHIC ORGANIZER As an alternate prewriting strategy, have students complete a Venn diagram that explores similarities and differences between the two sisters. A Venn diagram can also help students think more critically about the text. Encourage them to begin with the "Lottie" circle first, and then move on to the "Bess" circle. Any similarities between the two belong in the middle section, where the two circles intersect.

For additional help, see the **Prewriting** blackline master on page 158.

IV. WRITE

Allow plenty of time for writing the **compare and contrast paragraph**. When students have finished their rough drafts, ask them to exchange papers with a partner. Their partner can read the paragraph for problems with content, style, and mechanics. Later, you might want to review some rules for comma usage.

WRITING RUBRIC Do students' paragraphs

- begin with a topic sentence that states the purpose of the comparison?

- contain details that support the topic sentence?

- use commas correctly?

Grammar, Usage, and Mechanics

Writers are often confused about where and when to use commas. Remind the class that commas are used before a conjunction in a compound sentence and between items in a series of three or more. For example:

I feel sorry for Lottie, but I admire Bess. Bess is fun, fancy, and full of life.

V. WRAP-UP

Before they leave this first excerpt from "The Richer, the Poorer," have students discuss West's writing **style**. Students might enjoy the chance to comment on a published writer's word choices, grammatical structures, and so on.

Assessment

For a comprehension check, ask students to complete the **Assessment** blackline master on page 159.

Name _____

VOCABULARY

Words from the Selection

DIRECTIONS Use the words from the list to write a paragraph about Lottie and Bess.

◆possessions ◆skimping ◆clerking ◆wardrobe ◆ambition

_____

_____

_____

_____

_____

_____

_____

_____

_____

_____

Strategy Lesson: Synonyms

A synonym is a word that has the same or almost the same meaning as another word. For example, *scared* is a synonym for *afraid*. Knowing the synonym for a word is like knowing a shortcut for the word's definition.

DIRECTIONS Find the word in column B that most closely matches the meaning of the word in column A. Then draw a line between the matching words. If there's a word you don't know, skip it and come back to it when you've finished the whole column.

Column A	Column B
6. sentimental	boyfriend
7. expanding	tender
8. miserly	growing
9. beau	meagerly
10. halfway	partly
11. encounter	delicious
12. mouth-watering	meet

Name _____

COMPREHENSION
Venn Diagram

DIRECTIONS Use this Venn diagram to show how Bess and Lottie are similar and different. Remember to compare

- how they act
- how they talk
- how they feel about themselves
- how they feel about others

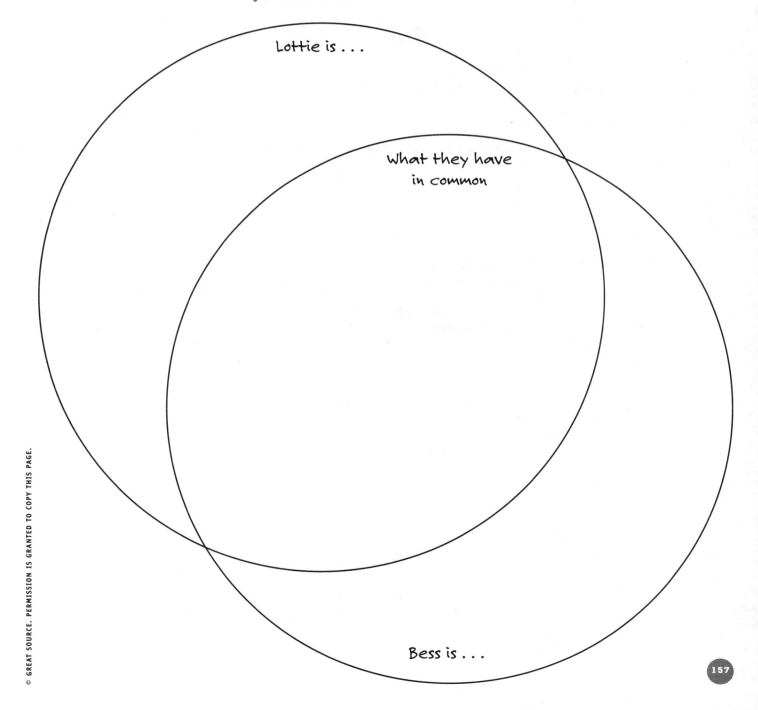

Name _____

PREWRITING

Comparing and Contrasting

DIRECTIONS Use your Venn diagram to help you write a compare and contrast paragraph about Lottie and Bess. Follow these steps:

STEP 1. WRITE A TOPIC SENTENCE. Write a topic sentence that prepares the reader for the comparison. Start your sentence like this:

Although they are sisters, Bess and Lottie are _____

_____

STEP 2. LIST DETAILS. Write your details from the "Lottie" circle here:

detail #1 Lottie is _____

detail #2 Lottie is _____

detail #3 Lottie is _____

STEP 3. LIST DETAILS. Write your details from the "Bess" circle here:

detail #1 Bess is _____

detail #2 Bess is _____

detail #3 Bess is _____

STEP 4. WRITE A SUMMARY SENTENCE. Write one sentence that sums up their similarities. Use information from the center of the Venn diagram in this sentence. Start your sentence like this:

Of course, both Lottie and Bess are _____

_____

STEP 5. WRITE A CONCLUDING SENTENCE. Write a concluding sentence that will come right after the summary sentence. Your concluding sentence should be a restatement of your topic sentence.

Name _____

ASSESSMENT
Multiple-Choice Test

DIRECTIONS On the blanks provided, write the letter of the answer that best completes each statement or answers each question.

_____ 1. How are Lottie and Bess related?
A. They are sisters.   C. They are cousins.
B. They are mother and daughter.   D. They are just friends.

_____ 2. To Bess, money is for . . .
A. school.   C. enjoyment.
B. saving.   D. retirement.

_____ 3. To Lottie, money is for . . .
A. spending.   C. saving.
B. traveling.   D. enjoyment.

_____ 4. When she was a child, Lottie watched as her parents . . .
A. favored one child over another.   C. scrimped and saved.
B. spent money like crazy.   D. lost money in the lottery.

_____ 5. What job did Lottie have after school?
A. She worked at a McDonald's.   C. She shelved books in a library.
B. She was a mother's helper.   D. She was a clerk in a variety store.

_____ 6. What job did Bess have after school?
A. She never had a job.   C. She shelved books in a library.
B. She worked at all kinds of jobs.   D. She was a clerk in a variety store.

_____ 7. Why didn't Lottie marry?
A. She never found the right man.   C. She didn't trust men.
B. She didn't want to give up her job to be a homemaker.   D. She was dumped by her fiancé shortly before the wedding.

_____ 8. What is Lottie's most private and precious possession?
A. her bankbook   C. her birth certificate
B. her wardrobe   D. a photo of her parents

_____ 9. What is Bess's reaction when her husband Harry dies?
A. She is relieved.   C. She is confused.
B. She is very upset.   D. all of the above

_____ 10. Why does Lottie send for Bess after Harry dies?
A. She feels trapped by a blood tie.   C. She wants to ask Bess for money.
B. She adores her sister.   D. She wants to meet Bess's children.

Short-Essay Test

Which of these two women has had a better life: Lottie or Bess? Explain why.

The Richer, the Poorer (continued)

Skills and Strategies Overview

THEME Dorothy West

READING LEVEL easy

VOCABULARY

◆ parlor ◆ gleaming ◆ clarity ◆ basting ◆ finery

PREREADING anticipation guide

RESPONSE react and connect

COMPREHENSION double-entry journal

PREWRITING theme and details

WRITING expository paragraph / using commas with adverbs

ASSESSMENT depth

BACKGROUND

As you might expect, the second half of "The Richer, the Poorer" follows in the same vein as the first. West continues her story of two sisters and the choices they made over the course of their lives. As is typical of West's works, this part of "The Richer, the Poorer" has a lesson to teach, although the writing style is never didactic. Instead, West presents the facts and expects the reader to make his or her own judgments about the two sisters' behavior. Life is for living, West tells us. Those who squander opportunities will live to regret it.

UNIT THEME Dorothy West explores the universal themes of family, happiness, and the choices we make in life. Is it possible, she asks, to create your own happiness, no matter what your circumstances?

GRAPHIC ORGANIZER Students will benefit from working on a character attribute map for either character.

Character Attribute Map: Bess

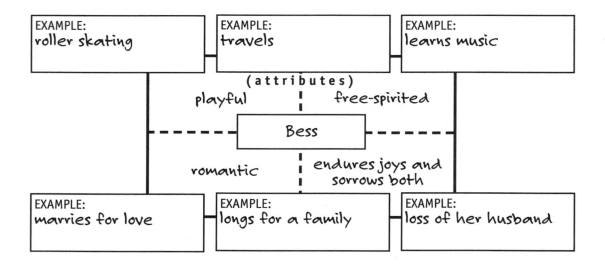

BEFORE YOU READ

Read through the introduction to the lesson with students. The purpose of the opening of the lesson is to motivate and focus students. Then ask students to begin work on the **anticipation guide.** For more information, refer to the **Strategy Handbook** on page 40.

Motivation Strategy

Tell students that this story is about a change of heart. Have them discuss a time they changed their minds about something important. What brought about the change? Did it end up being for the better? Why or why not?

ENGAGING STUDENTS Remind students of the title of the selection. Then have them give their own definitions for rich and poor.

Vocabulary Building

Draw students' attention to the lesson's key vocabulary words: *parlor, gleaming, clarity, basting,* and *finery.* The footnotes define these words for students, although you'll want to encourage them to define in context as often as they can. Help students build their vocabularies by modeling how to use these words in several different sentences. For additional practice with these words, see the **Vocabulary** blackline master on page 164.

STRATEGY LESSON: ANTONYMS As an alternate vocabulary strategy, teach a lesson on antonyms. Knowing an antonym for a word may serve to reinforce the definition for a given word. To make things interesting, have students race to see how many antonyms they can find for a set of words from the selection, such as *shabby, elderly, sorrow.*

For additional practice on this strategy, see the **Vocabulary** blackline master on page 164.

Prereading Strategies

Anticipation guides are easy to create and interesting for students to do. They work especially well for longer selections that you plan to use over several class periods. In an anticipation guide, students predict what they think will happen in the story. In most cases, they use their own ideas and experiences to help form their predictions. Almost without thinking about it, students will activate prior knowledge and make personal connections to themes, characters, and events.

K-W-L As an alternate prereading strategy, try using a K-W-L with students. A K-W-L will be particularly helpful since students are about to read a continuation of a story they started in a previous lesson. In the K column, students should write down everything they know so far about Lottie and Bess. Then have them think about the question, "What do you suppose will happen when Bess returns after the death of her husband? What will she say to Lottie? What will Lottie say to Bess?" Their answers to these questions belong in the W column.

Spanish-Speaking Students

Lottie no quiere mantener a su hermana porque se preocupa por el sumo de dinero que le va a costar. Pero en preparación para la llegada de Bess, Lottie empieza a cambiar de opinión. Después de una noche hablando y compartiendo historias de los años anteriores, Lottie se da cuenta que mientras estaba ahorrando dinero, estaba gastando su vida. Aunque Bess no tiene dinero, ha guiado una vida llena de diversión y placer. Inspirada de su hermana, Lottie decide que no es demasiada tarde para divertirse, y le pide a Bess que le muestre cómo vivir.

II. READ

Many of your students will want to **react** to Lottie's change of heart. Have them consider whether the change in her character is realistic or not. Could such a dramatic change happen in real life? Encourage students to **connect** what happens in the story to events or experiences from their own lives.

Response Strategy

VISUALIZE West uses quite a bit of detailed description in the second part of "The Richer, the Poorer." As an alternate response strategy, have students visualize the places and people she describes. If you like, have students draw "before" and "after" sketches to show Lottie's transformation. These sketches will help them when it comes time to write a paragraph about the story.

Comprehension Strategies

Double-entry journals send a message to students that says: "Your ideas can be as valuable as the author's ideas." As they are reading "The Richer, the Poorer," students will write their reactions to particular lines from the story. Help them see that the ideas and experiences that they bring to a text can strongly affect their interpretations. For some, a line such as "She was living each hour for itself" might mean very little. For others, especially those who have struggled or known difficulty in their lives, the line might mean a world of things.

For additional practice, see the **Comprehension** blackline master, page 165.

RETELLING As an alternate comprehension strategy, ask students to stop and retell parts of the "The Richer, the Poorer." Retelling can help students with their comprehension of the story. Once they've shown they understand the story, they can move to a more sophisticated analysis of the text and begin thinking about the style, main idea, and so on.

Discussion Questions

COMPREHENSION 1. How does Lottie change in the second part? *(She fixes up herself and her house and begins to take a renewed interest in life.)*

2. What brings about this change? *(Bess's expected arrival and then her encouragement. Lottie recognizes, however, that the desire to change must come from within.)*

CRITICAL THINKING 3. Why does Lottie say she's "had a life never lived"? *(She never enjoyed life. She feels she allowed it to pass her by.)*

4. How does Lottie feel about her sister? *(She admires her and is happy that her sister loves her.)*

5. Which character, Lottie or Bess, can you relate to most? *(Answers will vary. Remind students to fully explain their answers.)*

Literary Skill

CHARACTERS You might use "The Richer, the Poorer" as an opportunity for introducing dynamic vs. static characters. In literature, a dynamic character is one who undergoes a change over the course of the story. A static, or flat, character stays the same throughout the story. Usually, many forces bring about a change in character. Plot events or action can precipitate a change. Ideas or information from another character can also initiate change. Ask students which of the two characters is dynamic.

III. GATHER YOUR THOUGHTS

On page 123, students are asked to find the **theme** and supporting **details** of "The Richer, the Poorer." Explain that the main underlying meaning of a novel, short story, or poem is its theme. A theme may be directly stated; but it is usually implied. Most often students can find clues about theme
in the characters, action, images, or tone. Theme is different from the topic of a work in that the theme makes a statement or offers an opinion about the topic. Help students uncover the theme by asking: "What is the topic of the story?" (*Money or attitudes about riches*). Then, " What does the author have to say about the topic?"

Prewriting Strategies

SEQUENCING As an additional prewriting activity, you might have students create an organizer that shows the sequence of events in the story from start to finish. This activity will help students keep track of the events of the plot, which they'll need to know in order to write their paragraphs about theme.

For more practice, see the **Prewriting** blackline master on page 166.

IV. WRITE

For this writing assignment, students will identify West's theme and then explain how she supports it. Encourage students to refer to the book as necessary when they are writing their **expository paragraphs**. Afterward, have them read their writing for revision, keeping the questions on the writing rubric in mind. During the revision stage, you might also teach a short lesson on commas with adverbs and parenthetical expressions.

WRITING RUBRIC Do students' paragraphs

- clearly state West's theme in a topic sentence?

- offer three or four reasons in support of that theme?

- use commas correctly?

Grammar, Usage, and Mechanics

This mini-lesson is a follow-up to the lesson on commas on page 117. Remind the class that commas are used to set off parenthetical expressions and conjunctive adverbs such as *however, furthermore, and finally*. If you like, supplement the examples in the book with some of your own.

V. WRAP-UP

Students can use their reading as springboards for new thoughts and ideas. Have students say what the selection made them think about. Focus on the **depth** of their understanding. Did it change their ideas or attitudes in some way? If so, how?

Assessment

For a comprehension check, ask students to complete the **Assessment** blackline master on page 167.

Name _____

VOCABULARY

Words from the Selection

DIRECTIONS   Answer these questions that use words from the selection. Then write the meaning of the underlined words on the lines.

1. Is a <u>parlor</u> the same as a kitchen?

_____

2. If a light is <u>gleaming</u>, has it burned out?

_____

3. If I see something with <u>clarity</u>, am I having trouble focusing?

_____

4. Where would you be if you were <u>basting</u> a turkey?

_____

5. If I have a lot of <u>finery</u>, does it mean that I have a lot of ugly things?

_____

Strategy Lesson: Antonyms

An antonym is a word that means the opposite of another word. For example, *love* is an antonym for *hate*.

DIRECTIONS   Find the word in column B that means the opposite of the word in column A. Then draw a line between the two words. If there's a word you don't know, skip it and come back to it when you've finished the whole column.

Column A	Column B
6. dismal	unhappy
7. marveling	ignoring
8. sorrow	serious
9. lumpy	ugly
10. rigid	bearable
11. giddy	bright
12. intolerable	happiness
13. magnificent	flexible
14. satisfied	smooth

Name _____

COMPREHENSION
Thinking about Theme

DIRECTIONS Answer these questions. They will help you think about the theme of "The Richer, the Poorer."

1. In what ways is Bess "rich"?

_____

_____

_____

_____

2. In what ways is Lottie "poor"?

_____

_____

_____

_____

3. Which of the two characters do you think Dorothy West approves of most? What makes you think so?

West approves of _____ . I know this because _____ :

fact #1 _____

fact #2 _____

fact #3 _____

4. Does this story have a happy ending? Explain why or why not.

_____

_____

_____

Name _____

PREWRITING

Fact and Opinion

Sometimes it's hard to figure out what's a fact and what's an opinion. An **opinion** is a view or belief held by a person. A **fact** is a specific statement that can be checked or proven to be true. For example,

Fact: Lottie and Bess are sisters.

Opinion: Bess is more interesting than Lottie.

DIRECTIONS Look at these facts and opinions from the story. Write F next to the facts and O next to the opinions.

1. Lottie redoes the upstairs and downstairs of her house.

2. Lottie is a hard worker.

3. Bess is lazy.

4. Bess visits Lottie at her house.

5. Bess tells Lottie to live her life as if every minute counts.

Sorting Details

Read the theme statements in the box. Then read the five facts from the story. Decide which facts best support the theme. Write them in the organizer.

THEME STATEMENT: Money can't buy happiness. Happiness comes from within.

Fact: Lottie cleans her house while waiting for Bess.

Fact: Bess has no money, but she loves life.

Fact: Bess feels content with her life.

Fact: Lottie has allowed her house to go to ruin.

Fact: Lottie has a fat bank account but no friends.

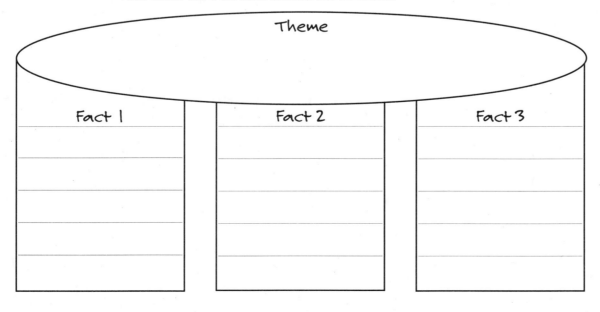

Theme

Fact 1   Fact 2   Fact 3

Name_____

ASSESSMENT

Multiple-Choice Test

DIRECTIONS On the blanks provided, write the letter of the best answer for each question.

_____ 1. Why does Lottie begin cleaning and redoing her house?
   A. She's tired of looking at it.   C. She wants to sell it.
   B. Bess is coming for a visit.   D. She's tired of saving her money.

_____ 2. How does Lottie feel once she has made over her whole house?
   A. ashamed of herself   C. worried about money
   B. tired but proud   D. anxious that Bess won't like it

_____ 3. Why does Lottie go to the specialty shops and beauty salon?
   A. It's her habit.   C. She sees herself in the mirror and hates
                                                what she sees.
   B. Her friend invites her for a treat. D. Bess insisted that she fix herself up.

_____ 4. How does Lottie feel as she waits for Bess's arrival?
   A. excited   C. bored
   B. angry   D. none of the above

_____ 5. What does Bess talk to Lottie about?
   A. her travels   C. her husband
   B. her friends   D. all of the above

_____ 6. Why doesn't Bess say anything about the finery and beauty of Lottie's house?
   A. She doesn't even see them.   C. She is used to beautiful things.
   B. She is jealous.   D. She's paying so much attention to Lottie.

_____ 7. What advice does Bess have for Lottie?
   A. Buy a new house.   C. Have a child.
   B. Quit spending.   D. Learn to live.

_____ 8. What is Lottie's reaction to Bess's advice?
   A. She's thrilled.   C. She's confused.
   B. She's bored.   D. She's angry.

_____ 9. Why does Lottie feel giddy at the end of the story?
   A. She's happy about herself.   C. She's too old for a party.
   B. She's had too much wine.   D. none of the above

_____ 10. What does Lottie mean when she says that she "didn't use them" [the years]?
   A. She wishes she had bought a bigger house. C. She feels she hasn't made enough money.
   B. She wishes she had worked at better jobs. D. She feels she's wasted her life.

Short-Essay Test

Does "The Richer, the Poorer" have a happy ending? Support your response.

Protest and Revolt

Unit Background **PROTEST AND REVOLT** (pages 125–144)

"I hold it, that a little rebellion, now and then, is a good thing, and as necessary in the political world as storms in the physical."
    Thomas Jefferson, 1787

People all over the world for centuries have protested or revolted against injustices—curtailment of liberty, taxes, and conscription, to give just a few causes. The two selections in this cluster are about two different types of rebellion. In the excerpt from George Orwell's *Animal Farm*, a satire on Stalinist Russia, Major, a pig, proposes a revolt against Man, who has subjected the farm animals to endless labor and repression. As readers of the entire novel know, however, the result of the animal revolt is a government as repressive and tyrannical as the one they had hoped to escape.

The excerpt from Mohandas K. Gandhi's autobiography is a description of a protest that prompted his fast, a passive resistance technique he often used. Gandhi was the driving force for Indian independence from British rule and was imprisoned several times for civil disobedience. A Hindu ascetic, he was assassinated in 1948 by a Hindu nationalist protesting Gandhi's support of Pakistan as a separate Muslim state.

Teaching the Introduction

The photographs on page 125 set the tone for this cluster.

1. Read aloud the Jefferson quotation on the facing page, or write it on the board, and ask students whether they agree with his statement.

2. Ask students whether they have previously read stories in which animals talk and act like humans. Tell them that the characters in the first selection, a novel excerpt, are animals who talk and that the author's purpose was satirical; that is, his purpose was to expose human misdeeds and vices.

3. Students may know that Martin Luther King, Jr. (pictured on page 125), was an admirer of Indian leader Mohandas K. Gandhi and his nonviolent methods of protest. Ask whether King's nonviolent methods were successful in his quest for equal rights for African Americans.

4. Ask which method to correct social ills takes more courage—armed revolt or passive resistance. Why?

Opening Activity

Bring to class or ask students to bring to class newspaper pictures of people protesting, and discuss reasons for these particular protests. Do students think the protests will be effective?

STUDENT PAGES 126–135

Skills and Strategies Overview

THEME Protest and Revolt

READING LEVEL challenging

VOCABULARY ✧ensconced ✧foal ✧plaited ✧slaughtered ✧abolished

PREREADING prediction

RESPONSE clarify and question

COMPREHENSION directed reading

PREWRITING graphic organizer

WRITING descriptive paragraph / comparative adjectives

ASSESSMENT understanding

BACKGROUND

George Orwell (1903–1950), the pen name for Arthur Eric Blair, was born in Bengal, India, and was taken to live in England when he was a young boy. Orwell's two best-known books, *Animal Farm* (1945) and *Nineteen Eighty-Four* (1949), reflect his lifelong distrust of government, be it of the left or the right.

"Animals Unite!" is an excerpt from the opening chapters of Orwell's *Animal Farm*. This protest novel, written in the form of a fable, is the story of a group of domestic animals who rebel against their human oppressors. At first, the intention of the animals is good—they seek to improve their lives and choose revolution as the most effective means of bringing about change. Later, however, the animals in power create a society that is even more tyrannical than the one that preceded it. From just this short excerpt, it is clear that Orwell's *Animal Farm* was meant to be a satire on postrevolutionary Russia. In the full novel, Orwell shares his belief that the dictatorship established after the revolution was more oppressive than the government that came before.

UNIT THEME This unit offers a brief introduction to the theme of social protest. In "Animals Unite!" a group of animals—who are very much like humans—protest their treatment at the hands of a tyrant: man.

GRAPHIC ORGANIZER To help students focus on the main idea, have them create an organizer like this one.

Main Idea and Supporting Details: "Animals Unite!"

Main Idea			
Man is the enemy.			
Detail #1 He feeds the animals just enough to keep them alive.	Detail #2 He separates mother from young.	Detail #3 He forces animals to labor for no reward.	Detail #4 He puts to death animals who can no longer work.
Topic: Man vs. animals			

Bibliography Other books by Orwell include *Down and Out in Paris and London* (1933) and *Keep the Aspidistra Flying* (1936).

BEFORE YOU READ

Read through the introduction to the lesson with students. If you like, ask students to say what they know about Orwell's *Animal Farm*. It's possible that many have seen a film adaptation of the novel. Ask students to keep their prior knowledge in mind as they read this excerpt. Then have them begin work on the **prediction guide** on page 127.

Motivation Strategy

Explain that "Animals Unite!" is about a group of animals who are angry at the way humans treat them. Ask students to imagine a group of barnyard animals staging a protest. What grievances would the cow have? What would the pig, horses, and ducks be angry about?

ENGAGING STUDENTS As an additional motivation strategy, explain that this story has to do with the rights of animals. What do students think about this topic?

Vocabulary Building

Help students use **context clues** as they read to figure out the meanings of unfamiliar words. Remind them that using context clues can make their job as reader easier and more enjoyable. Ask students to use context clues to figure out the meaning of these words from the story: *ensconced, foal, plaited, slaughtered,* and *abolished.* For more practice with these words, see the **Vocabulary** blackline master, page 174.

STRATEGY LESSON: HOMOGRAPHS A homograph is a word having the same pronunciation and often the same spelling as another word but a different meaning. Help students see that context can tell them which meaning of a word is appropriate. Put the following sentence on the board:

Man is the root cause of hunger and overwork.

Ask: Does *root* mean "part of a plant that grows downward" or "essential part"?

For additional practice with this strategy, see the **Vocabulary** blackline master, page 174.

Prereading Strategies

Students' before-reading predictions will motivate them to read more of Orwell's story. Before they begin writing in the **prediction guide** on page 127, direct them to make thoughtful guesses about the story using what they know from the first paragraph. As they read the rest of the story, they can note their additional predictions in the **Response Notes**.

READ-ALOUD As an alternate prereading strategy, have students do a read-aloud of the first part of the story. Students might find "Animals Unite!" easier to understand if they sit back and listen to it read aloud. Then they can do a second reading by themselves, marking the text as needed with their comments and questions.

Spanish-Speaking Students

"¡Los animales se unen!" es una parte de los primeros capítulos de la novela *Animal Farm,* escrito por George Orwell. Esta obra famosa se trata de un grupo de animales domésticos que se rebela contra sus opresores humanos. Al principio los animales tienen buenas intenciones, esperando que la revolución mejore sus vidas. Pero cuando los animales ganan poder, crean una sociedad incluso más opresiva que antes.

It's important that students keep clear in their minds the many problems Major lists as support for his opinion that it's time for a rebellion. Each time Major explains a new problem, students should **clarify** the point he is making by writing a comment in the **Response Notes**. Later, when students need to think critically about Major's argument and his qualities as a leader, they'll be able to return to their notes.

Response Strategy

QUESTION As an additional response strategy, you might want to have students keep track of questions that occur to them as they are reading. Because the sentence structure and vocabulary of "Animals Unite!" can be challenging, students should be extra vigilant in marking parts of the text that they don't understand and need to ask questions about. When they've finished reading, students can return to their notes to see if they can answer their own questions. Have them save questions they can't answer for the whole group to discuss.

Comprehension Strategies

Directed reading (stop and think) can help reluctant or low-level readers better understand and relate to what they are reading. Frame questions for students that can help them connect the action of the story to their own lives. Questions such as "Have you ever felt like this?" can help students make connections between text and self. These connections will serve to heighten their enjoyment of the reading process.

For additional practice, see the **Comprehension** blackline master on page 175.

Discussion Questions

COMPREHENSION 1. Why are the animals gathered in the pig barn? *(They've come to listen to Major's speech.)*

2. Which animal does most of the speaking? *(Major)*

3. What does this animal look and sound like? *(Encourage students to quote the text directly when describing Major.)*

CRITICAL THINKING 4. What reasons does Major give for the need to revolt? *(Answers will vary. Have students refer to their **Response Notes**.)*

5. Would you say his argument is convincing? Explain your opinion. *(Remind students to support their opinions with facts from the text.)*

Literary Skill

SATIRE Use this opportunity to introduce satire to students. Tell the class that a satire is a work that criticizes through wit or humor. In *Animal Farm*, Orwell satirizes the high-minded supporters of the revolution in Russia. Although the satire is not broad in this excerpt, point out that Major's speech echoes the revolutionary speech of those who desire radical change.

III. GATHER YOUR THOUGHTS

The **problem-solution organizer** on page 133 asks students to list the problems Major describes in his speech. The purpose of the activity is to help students organize the many points that Major makes in his speech. This in turn will prepare them to write about Major, which they are asked to do in Part IV.

Remind the class that their during-reading notes can help them with their organizers. Students have already made notes about the problems that Major discusses. To complete the left side of the organizer, they'll simply need to list the items they've noted in their **Response Notes.** For the right side of the organizer, students will probably note that the only true solution Major suggests is rebellion. At this point in the story, he doesn't offer his "comrades" any alternative.

Prewriting Strategies

WORD WEB As an alternate prewriting strategy, have students do a word web that relates to the word list they complete on page 133. (See pupil page 62 for an example of a word web.) You might ask students to create a word web for a "loaded" or important word from the selection. Words that will work well for this activity include *tyranny, comrade, rebellion, revolt,* and *cruelty.*

For more practice, see the **Prewriting and Writing** blackline master on page 176.

IV. WRITE

On page 134, students are asked to write a **descriptive paragraph** about a character. Before they begin, you might review the characteristics of a descriptive paragraph.

- Sentences work together to present a single, clear picture (description) of a person, place, thing, or idea.

- The best descriptive paragraphs contain sensory language, which makes for more vivid descriptions.

- The paragraph opens with a topic sentence and ends with a concluding sentence.

WRITING RUBRIC Do students' paragraphs

- contain clear descriptions of how Major looks, acts, and feels?

- explain whether Major is or is not a good leader?

- use the correct form of all comparative adjectives?

Grammar, Usage, and Mechanics

After they have finished writing, ask students to revise using the **Writers' Checklist.** At this point, you might also want to teach a mini-lesson on adjectives. Remind the class of the rules for using comparative and superlative adjectives. Review when to use *-er* and *-est* and what to do if the comparison is irregular. For specific examples, see page 134.

V. WRAP-UP

Take a moment at the end of the lesson for students to talk about what they did and did not **understand** about Orwell's "Animals Unite!" What parts did they find particularly difficult? Discuss strategies they can use in the future to help with comprehension problems.

Assessment

For a comprehension check, ask students to complete the **Assesment** blackline master on page 177.

Name _____

VOCABULARY
Words from the Selection

DIRECTIONS Context clues can help you figure out the meaning of a word without looking in the dictionary. Use context clues to figure out what these words mean. Write the meaning of the word on the line.

1. ". . . the very instant that our usefulness has come to an end, we are <u>slaughtered</u> with hideous cruelty."

_____

2. "Remove Man from the scene, and the root cause of hunger and overwork is <u>abolished</u> forever."

_____

3. "At one end of the big barn, on a sort of raised platform, Major was already <u>ensconced</u> on his bed of straw . . ."

_____

4. "Clover was a stout motherly mare approaching middle life, who had never quite got her figure back after her fourth <u>foal</u>."

_____

5. "She took a place near the front and began flirting her white mane, hoping to draw attention to the red ribbons it was <u>plaited</u> with."

_____

Strategy Lesson: Homographs

A homograph is a word having the same pronunciation and often the same spelling as another word but a different meaning. For example, *beam* can mean "a long piece of timber that supports a building" or "a ray of light." Using context can tell you which meaning is appropriate.

DIRECTIONS Use the clues in each sentence to tell you the meaning of the underlined words. Write the letter of that meaning on the blank.

_____ 6. A <u>brood</u> of ducklings filed into the barn.

_____ 7. The white mare drew Mr. Jones's <u>trap</u>.

_____ 8. The tame raven slept on the <u>perch</u>.

_____ 9. Major lived in a <u>stall</u>.

_____ 10. The <u>plain</u> truth is that the life of an animal is misery.

A. division in a stable for one animal

B. come to a stop

C. bar or branch on which a bird can rest

D. freshwater fish

E. young birds hatched one at a time

F. think or worry a long time about something

G. device for catching animals

H. a light, two-wheeled carriage

I. flat stretch of land

J. clear to the senses or mind

Name _____

COMPREHENSION
Graphic Organizer ....

DIRECTIONS Use this character analysis diagram to show what you know about Major.

Character Analysis: Major

How the character acts and feels

How the others feel about the character

Character:
Major

How the character looks

How I feel about the character

Name _____

PREWRITING AND WRITING

Writing a Topic Sentence and Details

DIRECTIONS Your descriptive paragraph about Major (or any other character) should have a topic sentence. Remember the formula for writing a topic sentence:

A specific topic + a specific feeling = a good topic sentence.

A. WRITE A TOPIC SENTENCE. Use the formula to write a topic sentence for your paragraph. First decide: Is Major a good leader or a bad one? Circle how you feel.

Major is a good leader.   **Major is a lousy leader.**

Major + (my opinion of him) = _____

                                    (your topic sentence)

B. GATHER DETAILS. Now think of details or facts that support your opinion of Major. Your support must come from the story, not from your own opinions.

support #1 _____

_____

support #2 _____

_____

support #3 _____

_____

C. WRITE. Write a paragraph about Major here. Start with your topic sentence. Then write your three pieces of support. End with a concluding sentence that restates your opinion of Major.

_____

_____

_____

_____

_____

_____

_____

Name _____

ASSESSMENT

Multiple-Choice Test

DIRECTIONS On the blanks provided, write the letter of the item that best completes each statement or answers each question.

_____ 1. What kind of animal is Major?
   A. a cow   C. a dog
   B. a horse   D. a pig

_____ 2. How old is Major?
   A. 10   C. 15
   B. 12   D. 18

_____ 3. Where do the animals live?
   A. America   C. England
   B. France   D. Germany

_____ 4. Which of the following types of animal did not come to hear Major's speech?
   A. horses   C. rats
   B. cats   D. dogs

_____ 5. Major describes the lives of the animals as . . .
   A. difficult.   C. short.
   B. filled with hunger. D. all of the above

_____ 6. Whom does Major blame for the animals' problems?
   A. themselves   C. human beings
   B. God   D. none of the above

_____ 7. What is the name of the farmer who owns the animals?
   A. Jones   C. Adams
   B. Smith   D. Boxer

_____ 8. What does Major want the animals to do?
   A. run away   C. pray
   B. rebel   D. nothing

_____ 9. How many children does Major have?
   A. 4   C. 100
   B. 25   D. 400

_____ 10. Major predicts that he will soon . . .
   A. have more children. C. die.
   B. retire.   D. run away.

Short-Essay Test

What does Major mean when he says, "Man serves the interests of no creature except himself"?

STUDENT PAGES 136-144

Skills and Strategies Overview

THEME Protest and Revolt

READING LEVEL average

VOCABULARY

◇ flagging ◇ dwindle ◇ grave ◇ cordial ◇ resolute

PREREADING quickwrite

RESPONSE clarify, react, and connect

COMPREHENSION story frame

PREWRITING group discussion

WRITING journal entry / apostrophes in contractions

ASSESSMENT meaning

BACKGROUND

Mohandas Karamchand Gandhi, leader of the Indian nationalist movement who was later known as Mahatma ("great soul"), was one of the most inspirational national leaders of the 20th century. His philosophy of nonviolent confrontation led his country to independence and influenced political activists throughout the world.

Gandhi was repeatedly imprisoned by the British during the first half of the 20th century. He and his followers used widely publicized hunger strikes to draw attention to their cause. Gandhi also fought to improve the status of the lowest classes of society. He believed in manual labor and simple living. In "The Fast," part of his autobiography, Gandhi wrestles with the question of how to shore up the flagging spirits of hundreds of men and women involved in a strike at a textile mill. His idea, to stage a hunger strike, earned him national recognition and gave new meaning to the idea of nonviolent protest.

UNIT THEME Mohandas Gandhi explores the question: Can social protest be completely nonviolent?

GRAPHIC ORGANIZER Some students might benefit by working through an organizer similar to this one.

Sequence of Events: "The Fast"

Bibliography Some students might enjoy reading parts of the following works: *An Autobiography* (1940) by Mohandas K. Gandhi, *Mahatma Gandhi* (1993) by D. Dalton, and *The Book of Gandhi Wisdom* (1995) by Trudy K. Settel.

1. BEFORE YOU READ

Read through the short introduction to "The Fast" on page 136. Ask students whether they know anything about Gandhi. Tell students that this autobiographical excerpt is set in India. Have students complete a one-minute **quickwrite** about social protest.

Motivation Strategy

Explain that this selection is about a man who is determined to stage a nonviolent protest, no matter what the cost. Ask students to think about methods of nonviolent protest they've used in the past. For example: letter writing, town meetings, postings on an Internet bulletin board, and so on. Students might be surprised to see how many times they've made protests without even realizing it.

ENGAGING STUDENTS As an additional motivation strategy, hold a quick debate. Students can debate some form of this question: "Is nonviolent protest preferable to violent upheaval? Why or why not?"

Vocabulary Strategy

Help students use **context clues** as they read to figure out the meaning of difficult or unfamiliar words. Show them the key vocabulary words for this lesson: *flagging, dwindle, grave, cordial,* and *resolute.* Although these words are footnoted at the bottom of the reading pages, students should still try to use context clues to decide what the words mean. For example, tell students that they can figure out what the word *despondency* means just by looking at adjacent words in the sentence, including *despair* and *dwindle.* Clearly the word has something to do with being upset. For additional practice, see the **Vocabulary** blackline master on page 182.

STRATEGY LESSON: HOMOPHONES A homophone is a word having the same pronunciation as another word but a different meaning and often a different spelling. *Eight* and *ate* are homophones. Homophones are really only confusing when one is listening to something read aloud or trying to think how a word is spelled. Help students see that context can help them determine meaning (and spelling). Read the following sentence aloud and ask students how they would spell the second word: "Several knights passed." Then add these words to the sentence: "on horseback." The meaning then becomes clear.

For additional practice with this strategy, see the **Vocabulary** blackline master, page 182.

Prereading Strategies

The purpose of a **quickwrite** is to get students writing almost before they know it. On page 136, students are asked to quickwrite for one minute about the idea of protest. Students should feel free to write about protests they've been involved in, protests that they've read about or seen on TV, or protests they'd like to be a part of in the future. When it comes time to share their writing, have students summarize what they've said and explain their various points of view. Avoid having students read their quickwrites aloud, since this might intimidate those who have chosen to write freely about personal matters.

Spanish-Speaking Students

Mohandas K. Gandhi se conoce a como un hombre honrado y altruísta. Se destacan estas calidades en "El ayuno," una parte de su autobiografía. En esta selección el líder indio describe sus empeños en resolver un conflicto entre los obreros y los dueños de un molino. Después de tres días sin comer, los dos grupos llegaron a un acuerdo, sin recurrir a la violencia que Gandhi rechazaba.

II. READ

Gandhi's method of resolving the strike is unconventional, to say the least. As they are reading, students should think about their reactions to his decision to fast. Do they approve or disapprove? Then have them connect what Gandhi does to their own lives. Could they make the same sacrifices Gandhi made in order to help the strikers? Why or why not? Each time they **react** or **connect**, they should write a comment in their **Response Notes**. These comments will help them feel more involved in the selection.

Response Strategy

QUESTION Readers often ask questions without even knowing it. These questions, such as "What's going on here?" and "What is she talking about?" are the reader's way of talking to himself or herself through a selection. Encourage students to make a note when they catch themselves asking about something they want clarified. Also have them note how they went about answering their question. Questions that remain unresolved at the end of the reading can be addressed by the whole group.

Comprehension Strategies

Story frames, which can be used for fiction or nonfiction, are particularly helpful to students who have trouble seeing how an entire piece holds together. Most story frames ask readers to concentrate on the protagonist and the main problem he or she faces in the story. On page 141, students are asked to fill in a story frame about Gandhi's actions. Their frames will help them explore the problem-solution framework of the article. If you like, use the story frame to help you discuss how even the most complex social protests can be reduced to a simple formula of problem and solution.

RECIPROCAL READING As students take part in reciprocal reading, they should 1. clarify the problem, characters, and setting; 2. predict outcomes; 3. summarize events; and 4. raise questions about the literature. Have them make notes about anything they and their reading partner can't figure out.

For additional comprehension practice, see the **Comprehension** blackline master on page 183.

Discussion Questions

COMPREHENSION 1. Who was Mohandas K. Gandhi? *(He was a Hindu political, social, and religious leader in India.)*

2. Why does he decide to fast? *(He wants to rally the strikers whose spirits are flagging.)*

3. What effect does his fast have? *(It convinces the mill-owners to settle.)*

CRITICAL THINKING 4. How do the strikers feel about Gandhi? *(Answers will vary. Ask students to support what they say with evidence from the selection.)*

5. How do the mill-owners feel about Gandhi? *(Answers will vary. Ask students to support what they say with evidence from the selection.)*

Literary Skill

AUTOBIOGRAPHY If you like, take this opportunity to discuss autobiography with students. Remind the class that an autobiography is a record of a life written by the subject himself or herself. Autobiographies come in many different forms, including letters, memoirs, diaries, and journals. The advantage of reading an autobiography is that it can offer an unparalleled glimpse into the life and thoughts of a person. The disadvantage is that autobiographical writing is highly subjective. The writer offers only the information that he or she wants the reader to know. Remind students that when they are studying the life of a historical figure such as Gandhi, it's important to use a variety of sources, including autobiographical and biographical writing.

III. GATHER YOUR THOUGHTS

Group discussions give students the opportunity to build upon one another's ideas. Remind the class that group members must listen carefully to each other's responses. If they like, they can use someone else's response as a springboard for their own comments and questions. Also reiterate that although disagreement in a discussion is fine, argument is prohibited. In their discussion about Gandhi, students should remember to explore the issue from all sides. They should also be prepared to offer plenty of support from the text for their opinions and ideas.

Prewriting Strategies

CHARACTER CLUSTER As an additional prewriting strategy, students can complete a character cluster that helps solidify their views of Gandhi. Begin by reading aloud portions of his autobiography. After each portion, ask: "What information does this give you about Gandhi? How does it change or enhance your view of him? What questions do you still have about him and his work?" You might keep track of students' comments on a cluster diagram that you draw on the board.

For more practice, see the **Prewriting** blackline master on page 184.

IV. WRITE

Set aside plenty of time for students to write. Remind the class that since they are writing **journal entries**, they will write in the first person and focus primarily on their own thoughts and feelings. After they've finished, ask students to revise using the **Writers' Checklist**.

WRITING RUBRIC Do students' journal entries

- explore a social change?
- clearly explain what the student wants to do and how he/she plans to do it?
- use apostrophes correctly?

Grammar, Usage, and Mechanics

At some point during the revision process, you might want to introduce a mini-lesson on writing contractions. If needed, review with students correct apostrophe placement in contractions.

I can't begin to tell you what's been happening here! It's the most exciting time of my life. I've been elected president of the Student Council and I'll begin working on my cabinet soon.

V. WRAP-UP

Take a moment at the end of the lesson for students to reflect on "The Fast." Encourage students to use the **Readers' Checklist** on page 144 to explore the **meaning** of the selection. Explain that good literature will usually make an impression on readers, be it positive or negative. Ask students to explain the effect Gandhi's words had on them.

Assessment

For a comprehension check, ask students to complete the **Assessment** blackline master on page 185.

Name _____

VOCABULARY

Words from the Selection

DIRECTIONS Draw a line to the situation that best demonstrates the meaning of each vocabulary word.

1. flagging
   a. a runner staggering to the finish line
   b. a coach giving instructions to his players
   c. a player arguing with an umpire

2. dwindle
   a. an ice cream bar melting in the sun
   b. a bottle of milk sitting in the refrigerator
   c. eggs frying in a pan

3. grave
   a. a marching band giving a half-time show
   b. actors rehearsing a comedy
   c. a mayor dedicating a war memorial

4. cordial
   a. a man using an ATM machine
   b. a farmer plowing fields
   c. a president shaking hands with a general

5. resolute
   a. a student taking a nap
   b. a student studying until midnight
   c. a student renting a video

Strategy Lesson: Homophones

A homphone is a word that has the same pronunciation as another word but a different meaning and often a different spelling. For example, *knight* and *night* are homophones.

DIRECTIONS Circle the word that correctly fits in each sentence.

6. Try to eke out a bare / bear existence.

7. The mill-hands showed grate / great courage.

8. They said they would rather die / dye than brake / break their word.

9. The mill-owners had a perfect right / rite to be sarcastic.

10. He could not bare / bear to see his sister in anguish.

Name _____

COMPREHENSION
Retelling

DIRECTIONS On the lines below, retell what happens in "The Fast." Use your own words, not Gandhi's.

_____

_____

_____

_____

_____

_____

_____

_____

Main Idea and Details

DIRECTIONS Now use what you've written to decide: Was Gandhi a good leader? Support your opinion. Use evidence from the selection as support.

my opinion: _____

_____

my support: _____

detail #1 _____

_____

detail #2 _____

_____

detail #3 _____

_____

Name _____

PREWRITING

Writing a Journal Entry

DIRECTIONS **A. CHOOSE A TOPIC.** Think about a change you'd like to see made in your school. Write what you want to change here.

I think this change is needed: _____

B. LIST IDEAS. Now think of ways to make this change. Try to list at least five ideas so that you are sure to explore all different possibilities.

idea #1 _____

idea #2 _____

idea #3 _____

idea #4 _____

idea #5 _____

C. CHOOSE A SOLUTION. Circle the idea from your list that you think is best. Then explain your idea here.

The best idea: _____

_____

_____

_____

_____

_____

_____

_____

_____

Name _____

ASSESSMENT

Multiple-Choice Test

DIRECTIONS On the blanks, write the letter of the best answer for each question.

_____ 1. Where do the strikers work?
   A. in a steel plant   C. at a mill
   B. in an auto plant   D. at a clothing manufacturer

_____ 2. How often do the strikers meet?
   A. daily   C. weekly
   B. hourly   D. twice a week

_____ 3. What does Gandhi fear the strikers will do?
   A. get new jobs   C. lose their self-restraint
   B. move away   D. go back to work

_____ 4. What does Gandhi do to encourage the strikers?
   A. He meets with their bosses.   C. He reorganizes the strike.
   B. He begins a fast.   D. none of the above

_____ 5. What work do the strikers do to earn extra money?
   A. help build a school   C. paint houses
   B. bake cookies   D. baby-sit

_____ 6. What is the mill-owners' first reaction to Gandhi's decision to fast?
   A. They refuse to change their minds.   C. They treat Gandhi with coldness.
   B. They are sarcastic.   D. all of the above

_____ 7. Who is Sheth Ambalal?
   A. a striker   C. a friend of Gandhi's
   B. a mill owner   D. a government official

_____ 8. What is the outcome of the strike?
   A. The two sides settle.   C. The government takes control.
   B. The workers are fired.   D. The mill is shut down.

_____ 9. How long did the strike last?
   A. 14 days   C. 2 months
   B. 21 days   D. 1 year

_____ 10. Where did Gandhi experience a giant strike once before?
   A. China   C. South Africa
   B. France   D. Russia

Short-Essay Test

Was Gandhi's hunger strike effective? Explain why or why not.

Africa

Unit Background   AFRICA (pages 145–160)

The names and boundaries of Africa's many nations have changed often in the 20th century, but climate and topographical features have remained relatively unchanged. This unit focuses on two countries that adjoin—Namibia and South Africa.

A country of more than 300,000 square miles, Namibia is a little bigger than the state of Texas. Formerly administered by South Africa, it became an independent nation in 1990. "A Sea of Dunes" is from a book by Jim Brandenburg called *Sand and Fog: Adventures in Southern Africa*. Brandenburg is an award-winning wildlife photographer. In 1991 the United Nations presented him with a World Achievement Award for "using nature photography to raise public awareness of the environment." His photos are often featured in *National Geographic,* and he has written several books about wolves, all illustrated with his photos. He lives in rural Minnesota near the Canadian border.

Although apartheid has ended in South Africa, economic inequalities remain, as author Phyllis Ntantala shows. Much of the economy is based on mining—not only coal and iron but diamonds and gold. South Africa is the largest producer of gold in the world.

Teaching the Introduction

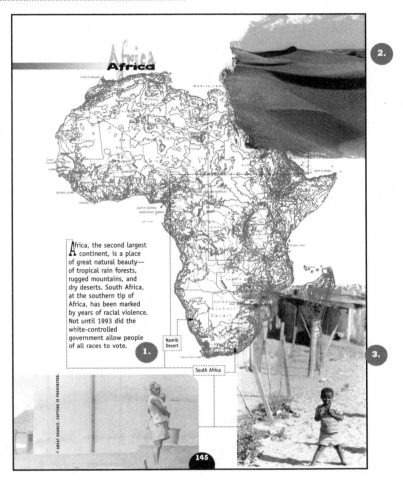

Africa, the second largest continent, is a place of great natural beauty—of tropical rain forests, rugged mountains, and dry deserts. South Africa, at the southern tip of Africa, has been marked by years of racial violence. Not until 1993 did the white-controlled government allow people of all races to vote.

1. Ask students to locate Namibia and South Africa on the map on page 145.

2. Ask what pictures come to mind when students hear the word *desert*.

3. Ask students to tell what they know about apartheid. (The word comes from the Dutch word *apart*, "separate," and the suffix *-heid. Heid* is equivalent to the English word *-hood*. Thus, the word means "separateness.") Even though apartheid has ended, why might much of the population still be poor?

Opening Activity

Ask students to research some aspect of Namibia or South Africa on the Internet. Tell them to focus on one topic and suggest art, music, the economy, the geography, or history. They can then report to the class.

A Sea of Dunes

Skills and Strategies Overview

THEME Africa

READING LEVEL challenging

VOCABULARY

◇cascading ◇precipitation ◇oryx ◇adaptation ◇capillaries

PREREADING picture walk

RESPONSE question

COMPREHENSION graphic organizer

PREWRITING main idea and supporting details

WRITING summary / capitalization

ASSESSMENT ease

BACKGROUND

The Namib Desert extends along the southwest coast of Africa from Angola in the north, through Namibia (a huge, sparsely populated country on the southwestern coast of Africa), and into South Africa. The Namib, whose name means "place of nothing," is approximately eleven hundred miles long and sixty miles wide. The sands of this desert, which vary from red to yellow in color, form dunes that can be as high as eight hundred feet. Although the Namib is one of the driest places on earth (its rainfall is less than one inch a year), it is a place of high humidity. As a result, there is a fair amount of fog and dew. Animals such as antelopes, zebras, ostriches, and flamingos live in the Namib. The Khoikhoi people also make their home in the desert. Many work in the desert's huge diamond, salt, and tungsten mines.

UNIT THEME Learning about faraway places and new customs helps broaden students' understanding of the world. Understanding how other cultures work can shed light on students' understanding of their own cultures.

GRAPHIC ORGANIZER A topic net such as the one below can help readers and writers break large topics into smaller, more manageable chunks.

Topic Net: The Namib Desert

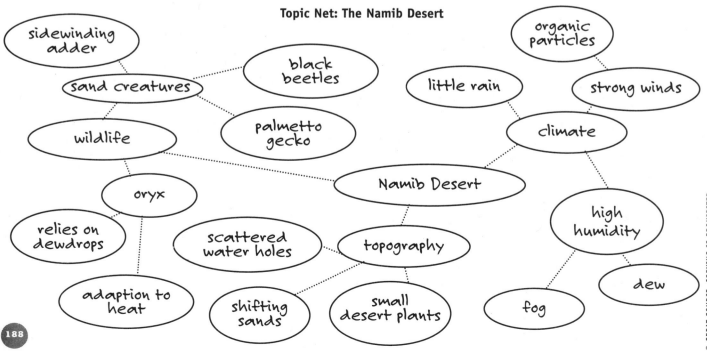

BEFORE YOU READ

> Review with students the introduction to the lesson. Check to be sure they understand the "ingredients" for nonfiction: title, headings, pictures, and captions. Remind students that they'll be examining these ingredients during their **picture walks**.

Motivation Strategy

Explain that "Sea of Dunes" is about a place that very few people have ever seen. Ask students: "What's the most exotic or isolated or incredible place you've ever visited?" Have them describe what they saw, heard, and felt there.

ENGAGING STUDENTS To further engage students, explain that in many parts of the world, life is a daily struggle for survival. What skills and qualities do students have that make them "survivors"? Students can think about their skills as they read the selection.

Vocabulary Building

As students read, point out words that require some technical knowledge of science and the environment. You might begin by showing them these key vocabulary words: *cascading, precipitation, oryx, adaptation,* and *capillaries*. Explain that some of these words can be defined in context, and others will require some dictionary work. When they read expository nonfiction, students should do so with a pencil in hand and a dictionary at their side. Any words that cannot be defined in context should be underlined and researched later. Tell students that they should interrupt the rhythm of their reading (to check a definition) only if the word is essential to understanding the sentence or paragraph.

For additional practice with these words, see the **Vocabulary** blackline master, page 192.

STRATEGY LESSON: PREFIXES Tell students that *anti-* is a common prefix meaning "against, opposed to, preventing," or "the opposite of." Ask what they can guess about the meaning of *antarctic* ("opposite the arctic"). Then ask them to suggest other words with the prefix *anti-* or *ant-* (before a vowel). They might suggest *antihistamine* or *antibiotic*, for example.

For additional practice with this strategy, see the **Vocabulary** blackline master, page 192.

Prereading Strategies

Doing a **picture walk** before reading can help familiarize students with the topic of the selection. This is a particularly valuable strategy to use when you know that the topic will be an unfamiliar one, such as life in the Namib Desert. Remind students to look at each photo and caption carefully. Have them record their individual responses on the chart on page 146.

Spanish-Speaking Students

El desierto de Namibia cubre un extenso vasto de tierra. Es árido, hace calor, hace viento, y está cubierto de arena. A pesar de estas condiciones, ciertos animales y plantas florecen allí. Los animales en particular han adaptado al clima del desierto, guiando sus vidas según la dirección del viento y el sumo de la precipitación. Han aprendido evitar a otros animales, usando la arena como un refugio del peligro.

READ

As they read, students will record details that they find interesting or important in the **graphic organizer** on page 147. Encourage students to pause at the end of each page so that they can record their ideas. In addition to recording details, students should also make notes about any **questions** they have. Have them write their questions in the **Response Notes** columns. When they've finished reading, give them time to go back to their questions to see which they can answer. Questions that they can't answer should be discussed by the group.

Response Strategy

REACT AND CONNECT As an additional response, have students react and connect to the descriptions in the selection.

Comprehension Strategies

The **graphic organizer** on page 147 can help students keep track of the details Brandenburg uses to support his main idea that animals have different ways to adapt in the Namib Desert. In addition, the organizer will give them practice using some of the specialized vocabulary the author uses in the article. When they've finished reading, students can share their organizers with the rest of the class. Did some students find information that the rest of the class missed?

DIRECTED READING As an alternate comprehension strategy, you might do a directed reading of the text. This strategy is particularly useful when students are reading texts that contain unfamiliar or specialized vocabulary. Read the article aloud to the class or have students read it aloud to you. Stop at various points and ask: "What's the author talking about here?" or "What type of animal is this and why is it able to survive in the Namib?" These questions will also help students with the graphic organizer on page 147.

For additional comprehension practice, see the **Comprehension** blackline master on page 193.

Discussion Questions

COMPREHENSION 1. Where is the Namib Desert? *(It is along the southwest coast of Africa.)*

2. What makes life so difficult in the Namib? *(It is extremely dry.)*

3. What kinds of animals live in this desert? *(Only those that can adapt to the climate, such as the gecko and the sidewinding adder.)*

4. What are some of the adaptation methods Brandenburg describes? *(Review with students the ways the creatures of the Namib have adapted to survive. Pages 148–150 contain a great deal of information.)*

CRITICAL THINKING 5. What is the "sea of dunes"? *(The high winds create sand dunes that resemble the waves of an ocean.)*

6. Does Brandenburg admire the creatures he describes? How do you know? *(Have students point to particular words and phrases such as* "incredible" *and* "remarkable" *that show the author's enthusiasm and admiration.)*

Literary Skill

METAPHOR The title of Brandenburg's article provides an excellent opportunity to discuss metaphor with students. Remind the class that a metaphor is a figurative comparison between two unlike things. With his title, Brandenburg makes a comparison between a desert and the ocean. The key to the comparison is, of course, the "waves" the wind creates in the sand. On a more subtle level, though, Brandenburg uses the metaphor to give readers a sense of the vastness of the desert. It is as large or larger than some oceans of the earth and can be equally inhospitable to human life.

III. GATHER YOUR THOUGHTS

The goal of these prewriting activities is to help students collect what they learned and then build a topic of their own to write about. Have students begin by finding the **main idea** of the article. Explain that the Namib Desert is the topic of the piece and that the main idea focuses on the necessity of creature adaptation. Show students that in the very beginning of the article, Brandenburg poses the question that is at the heart of his main idea: "How does life exist in the Namib Desert?" He uses the rest of the article to answer this question, providing one **detail** after another.

Prewriting Strategies

GATHERING DETAILS As an additional prewriting activity, work with students to find the details Brandenburg uses to support his main idea. This strategy will be particularly helpful to those students who have trouble understanding the point that Brandenburg makes. As a class, work through the article paragraph by paragraph, searching for details that help illuminate the point the author is trying to make.

For more practice, see the **Prewriting and Writing** blackline master on page 194.

IV. WRITE

On page 152, students are asked to write a **summary** of "A Sea of Dunes." In their summaries, students will need to state Brandenburg's main idea and then explain how he supports it. Remind them that a summary should be approximately one-third the length of the original and should contain only the most essential facts and details. After they've finished writing, have students revise their work using the **Writers' Checklist**.

WRITING RUBRIC Use this writing rubric to help students focus on the assignment requirements and for help with a quick assessment of their writing.

Do students' summaries

- clearly state the main idea of the article?

- include an explanation of the most important details?

- begin with a topic sentence and end with a concluding sentence?

Grammar, Usage, and Mechanics

Before they revise, you might teach a mini-lesson on rules for capitalization. In addition to capitalizing place names, students should remember to capitalize the names of ethnic groups, national groups, and all languages.

Incorrect: The khoikhoi live in the namib desert and in parts of south africa.

Correct: The Khoikhoi live in the Namib Desert and in parts of South Africa.

V. WRAP-UP

Finish the lesson by inviting students to tell what they found **easy** or difficult about the article. Their comments can help you decide which reading strategies they might use with future expository nonfiction assignments.

Assessment

For a comprehension check, ask students to complete the **Assessment** test on page 195.

Name _____

VOCABULARY

Words from the Selection

DIRECTIONS Draw a line between the terms in column A and their proper definition in Column B.

A. terms

1. cascading
2. precipitation
3. adaptation
4. capillaries
5. oryx

B. definitions

tiny blood vessels

an African antelope

water or moisture

falling in a series of stages, like a waterfall

change in an animal that allows it to fit in with and live longer in its environment

Strategy Lesson: Prefixes

The words in the second column all contain the prefix *anti-,* meaning "against, opposed to, preventing," or "the opposite of."

DIRECTIONS Draw a line to the word that best answers each question in the first column.

6. What does one put in a car in very cold weather?

antisocial

7. What does one take to relieve or prevent depression?

anti-inflammatory

8. What might one buy to relieve or prevent inflammation?

antifreeze

9. What might an unfriendly person be called?

antidepressant

10. What would someone who dislikes the United States be called?

anti-American

Name _____

COMPREHENSION
Graphic Organizer

DIRECTIONS Use this chart to organize information from "A Sea of Dunes." Consult your book if you need to. You will not fill in all the boxes for all the desert creatures.

	Lives where in the desert?	Eats what?	Gets water from where?	Adapts how?
oryx				
black beetles				
sidewinding adder				
sand grouse				

Name _____

PREWRITING AND WRITING

Writing a Summary

DIRECTIONS Remember that when you write a summary, you need to use your own words and not the author's words. Use this page to plan what you will write about Brandenburg's article.

A. BRAINSTORM DESCRIPTIVE WORDS. Think of words that describe the Namib Desert. Don't look at your book. Come up with your own descriptive words.

Descriptive words: The Namib Desert

barren
dry

B. WRITE AN INTRODUCTION. Next write an introduction for your summary. Use words from your word box above. In your introduction, tell

→ your topic (what you're writing about)

→ some information about the topic (location of the Namib desert, what it looks like, and so on)

→ Brandenburg's main idea

_____

_____

_____

C. INCLUDE SOME SUPPORTING DETAILS.

_____

_____

D. WRITE A CONCLUSION. On these lines, write a conclusion for your summary. In your conclusion, you should

→ restate your topic sentence

→ explain why your topic is important

_____

_____

_____

Name _____

ASSESSMENT

Multiple-Choice Test

DIRECTIONS On the blanks provided, write the letter of the best answer for each question.

_____ 1. What does life in the Namib Desert ultimately depend on?
   A. the sea
   B. the winds
   C. the sand
   D. the fog

_____ 2. What does the powerful wind do in the Namib Desert?
   A. sculpts the sands
   B. scatters organic particles
   C. brings in moisture in the form of fog
   D. all of the above

_____ 3. About how often does the dense fog appear in this region?
   A. one morning in every five
   B. one morning in every thirty
   C. one morning in every fifteen
   D. one night in every fifteen

_____ 4. Where does the oryx get its nourishment and water from?
   A. other animals
   B. the desert grass
   C. small water holes
   D. none of the above

_____ 5. What allows the oryx to live in the intense heat of the desert?
   A. It can go months without water.
   B. It stores sweat under its tongue.
   C. It hibernates through the hottest months.
   D. It has developed a cooling system in its nasal passages.

_____ 6. From where does the palmetto gecko get its water?
   A. from the sand
   B. from its eyes
   C. from underground streams
   D. all of the above

_____ 7. Which animal gets moisture by standing almost on its head?
   A. the palmetto gecko
   B. the oryx
   C. the sand grouse
   D. the black beetle

_____ 8. What does the sidewinding adder find in the sand?
   A. coolness and water
   B. coolness and camouflage
   C. water and camouflage
   D. all of the above

_____ 9. Why is the male sand grouse willing to fly up to fifty miles to a water hole?
   A. to get water for himself
   B. to get water for his mate
   C. to get water for his chicks
   D. none of the above

_____ 10. What "daily miracles" occur in the Namib Desert?
   A. The wind brings food.
   B. The fog brings water.
   C. The creatures survive.
   D. all of the above

Short-Essay Test

What makes life in the Namib Desert so challenging?

The Widows of the Reserves

STUDENT PAGES 153–160

Skills and Strategies Overview

THEME	Africa
READING LEVEL	easy
VOCABULARY	◇ strenuous ◇ bewildered ◇ starvation ◇ scraggy ◇ emaciated
PREREADING	think-pair-and-share
RESPONSE	mark and highlight
COMPREHENSION	directed reading
PREWRITING	compare and contrast
WRITING	article / commas
ASSESSMENT	depth

BACKGROUND

The Republic of South Africa is the southernmost country on the African continent. The country extends for about one thousand miles (1,600 km) from north to south and from east to west. From 1948 to 1993–94, South Africa's political and social structure was based on apartheid, a system of legalized discrimination that allowed for political and economic dominance of the white minority.

Under the leadership of President F. W. de Klerk, the South African government slowly began to dismantle the apartheid system in 1990. Even so, most South African blacks continued to struggle with poverty, inadequate health care, and an inferior education system that was put into place under apartheid leadership. Today, the majority of blacks in South Africa lead lives of hunger and privation, although improvements in the school systems across the country have offered hope for new generations of South African children.

UNIT THEME Learning about life in faraway places helps broaden students' understanding of the world. Understanding the struggles others endure helps students gain insight into their own problems.

GRAPHIC ORGANIZER The Venn diagram students complete on page 158 might look something like this one.

Venn Diagram: "The Widows of the Reserves"

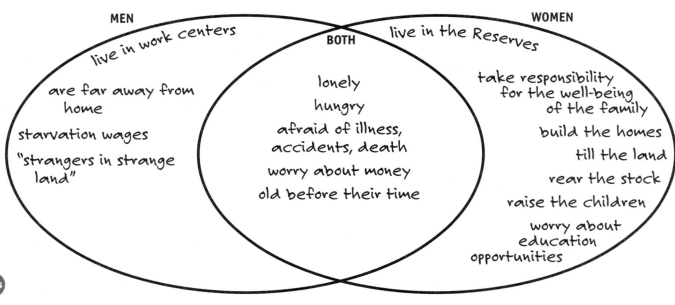

MEN — live in work centers

- are far away from home
- starvation wages
- "strangers in strange land"

BOTH
- lonely
- hungry
- afraid of illness, accidents, death
- worry about money
- old before their time

WOMEN — live in the Reserves

- take responsibility for the well-being of the family
- build the homes
- till the land
- rear the stock
- raise the children
- worry about education opportunities

BEFORE YOU READ

Help students understand that reading is an active and not a passive activity. Read through the introduction to the lesson with students. Divide the class into small groups and then have them begin the **think-pair-and-share** on page 153. (Refer to the **Strategy Handbook**, page 40, for more information.)

Motivation Strategy

Tell students that this article is about men and women in South Africa who live lives of extreme hardship.

ENGAGING STUDENTS Ask students about the hardships their families have faced in the past. What problems have their families endured? What did they do to cope? Questions like these can help students connect the topic of the article to their own lives.

Vocabulary Building

Learning the **synonym** of an unfamiliar word is a shortcut for those who don't have the time or memory skills to learn the full definition. (As an added advantage, learning synonyms is an especially helpful strategy for students preparing to take standardized tests.) Ask the class for synonyms for these words from the selection: *bewildered* and *scraggy*. The other three vocabulary words, *strenuous, starvation*, and *emaciated*, do not have one-word synonyms. Students should learn the definitions for these words. For more practice, see the **Vocabulary** blackline master, page 200.

STRATEGY LESSON: SUFFIXES Knowing the meaning of some common English suffixes can help students learn new words. Two common suffixes from Old English are *-hood* and *-dom*. In "The Widows of the Reserves," Ntantala writes of widowhood, womanhood, adulthood, and childhood. In each case *-hood* means "a group sharing a quality of." The suffix *-dom* can mean "state or condition" (stardom), as well as "position or rank" (dukedom) and "realm or area of" (kingdom). Ask students to come up with other words with the suffix *-hood*. For additional practice, see the **Vocabulary** blackline master, page 200.

Prereading Strategies

The **think-pair-and-share** sentences on page 153 give students an introduction to the topic of "The Widows of the Reserves." Remember that the purpose of a think-pair-and-share is to get students thinking about and discussing the selection. The actual ordering of the sentences is of secondary importance. The value of this activity comes from students talking about—and perhaps even debating—what the sentences mean.

PREDICTION As an alternate prereading strategy, have each student make a brief prediction about the topic of the article. To help them get started, ask the class: "What is a widow?" "Who are the widows?" "What are the Reserves?" "What does the one have to do with the other?" These questions may help struggling students think more clearly about the topic of the piece.

Spanish-Speaking Students

"Las viudas de las reservaciones" pinta un retrato desgarrador del sistema social de Sud Africa. La mayoría de la población negra vive en condiciones horribles e injustas. Para ganar bastante dinero los hombres tienen que trabajar muy duros y muy lejos de sus familias. Por eso, las mujeres viven como si fueran viudas, esforzándose diariamente a sobrevivir, y siempre esperando mejorar el futuro para los hijos.

READ

As they read, students should use their pens to **mark** and **highlight** ideas that seem important. Having students annotate as they read shows them how important it is to interact with a text. Good readers are constantly looking for information, taking notes about their ideas, and asking questions to clarify things they don't understand. Their during-reading notes will also come in handy later, when they need to respond to certain sections of the text.

Response Strategy

REACT AND CONNECT As an additional response strategy, have students react and connect to what they are reading. Many of your students will want to respond to the injustices that Ntantala describes. Comments such as "This is awful!" and "Maybe they should . . ." give students a chance to air their own opinions and help them stay involved in what they are reading.

Comprehension Strategies

In a **directed reading**, the teacher sets the pace of the reading. This is an especially effective strategy to use with low-level readers. During your directed reading of "The Widows of the Reserves," you'll want to stop occasionally and ask questions that can help improve students' understanding of the selection. In addition to the **stop and think** questions scattered throughout the selection, you might ask students to pause at the end of page 155 and retell what Ntantala has described up to that point. When they've finished the entire article, have students summarize what they've learned.

For additional practice, see the **Comprehension** blackline master on page 201.

Discussion Questions

COMPREHENSION 1. Why are these women in South Africa called "widows"? *(They have to live separate from their husbands, who have traveled to the city in order to find work.)*

2. What are some of the difficulties the widows face on a day-to-day basis? *(With little or no help from their husbands, the "widows" take care of the land, the children, the house, and so on.)*

3. What do these men and women want most for their children? *(a good education)*

CRITICAL THINKING 4. What is the tone of Ntantala's article? Is she angry or sad? *(Answers will vary. Ask students to support their interpretations with evidence from the text. For more information about tone, see the Literary Skill section below.)*

5. How did you feel as you were reading "The Widows of the Reserves"? *(Answers will vary.)*

Literary Skill

TONE You might use this article as a springboard for discussion about tone and how tone can affect the reader's understanding of the piece as a whole. Point out to students that tone is an important aspect of Ntantala's style. Although she writes in the third person, she is clearly quite involved in the story she tells. Ntantala is outraged by the plight of these women and she conveys her outrage through word choice. Throughout the article she uses strong, sometimes "loaded" words that help the reader share in her anger. Words such as *void, snatched, torn, riddled*, and *emaciated* play on our emotions and emphasize the terrible lives of these men, women, and children.

III. GATHER YOUR THOUGHTS

On page 158, students are asked to create a Venn diagram that **compares and contrasts** the lives of the men and women of the Reserves. Remind students that when they compare and contrast, they say how two people, places, or things are the same and different. Comparing and contrasting is a critical thinking activity that can help sharpen and refine students' understanding of a selection. It forces students to return to the text for specific facts and details.

Prewriting Strategies

GRAPHIC ORGANIZER To further sharpen students' critical thinking skills, you might have them create a Venn diagram that explores how the women of the Reserves are similar to and different from women they know. (Question 2 on student's page 158 can get them thinking about this topic.) Ask students to have their diagrams look the same as the one in the book.

For more practice, see the **Prewriting and Writing** blackline master on page 202.

IV. WRITE

On page 159, students are asked to write an **article** about the women of the Reserves. Tell the class that the article's lead (its opening paragraph) should answer the questions who? what? where? when? why? and how?

When students have finished their articles, use the writing rubric below.

WRITING RUBRIC Do students' articles

- describe the women of the Reserves and their roles in their families?
- explain why the lives of these women are so difficult?
- stay focused on the topic of South Africa and its "widows"?

Grammar, Usage, and Mechanics

At this point, you also may want to introduce a mini-lesson on commas. You might review with students the rules for commas with coordinate adjectives, parenthetical expressions, and transition words. Your more sophisticated writers will want to use these grammatical structures in their writing.

Incorrect: However the letter contained upsetting frightening news.

Correct: However, the letter contained upsetting, frightening news.

V. WRAP-UP

To measure the **depth** of students' connections to the article, ask: "How has Ntantala's writing changed your view of life in South Africa?" Or "How has this affected your perception of your own day-to-day problems and grievances?" These questions will show students that what they read can greatly affect the way they see themselves and the way they see the world.

Assessment

For a comprehension check, ask students to complete the **Assessment** on page 203.

Name _____

VOCABULARY

Words from the Selection

DIRECTIONS The list on the left contains definitions or synonyms for the vocabulary words on the right. Write each vocabulary word beside its proper synonym or definition.

1. confused _____   starvation

2. suffering severely from hunger _____   scraggy

3. requiring great effort _____   bewildered

4. bony and lean _____   emaciated

5. extremely thin and underfed _____   strenuous

Strategy Lesson: Suffixes

The suffix –*hood* means "a group sharing a quality of" (adulthood). The suffix –*dom* can mean "position or rank" (serfdom) and "realm or area of." Both suffixes can be added to nouns to form new nouns.

DIRECTIONS On the blanks, add the suffix –*hood* or –*dom* to each of the underlined words, depending on which suffix you think fits.

6. Everyone in the neighbor_____ came to the picnic.

7. Union members became part of the brother_____ of engineers.

8. The animal king_____ is large and varied.

9. Hollywood is the capital of U.S. film_____.

10. Some people are not suited for parent_____.

Name _____

COMPREHENSION

Reader Response

DIRECTIONS On the lines below, write a brief journal entry about how "The Widows of the Reserves" made you feel. Choose one of these three phrases as the opening for your entry:

I know the feeling . . .

I can't really understand . . .

If I had been . . .

My Journal Entry

_____

_____

_____

_____

_____

_____

_____

_____

Group Discussion

DIRECTIONS Work with a partner or a small group to answer these questions about Ntantala's article. Be ready to share your answers with the rest of the class.

• What—if anything—might the women of the Reserves do to improve their lives?

_____

_____

• If you had one piece of advice for these women, what would it be?

_____

_____

• What do you think Ntantala's advice would be?

_____

_____

_____

Name _____

PREWRITING AND WRITING
Writing an Article

DIRECTIONS To write an article, follow these steps.

STEP 1. DECIDE ON A TOPIC. On the lines below, write the topic for your article. (Your book asks you to write an article about the women of the Reserves.)

_____

_____

STEP 2. MAKE NOTES. Next, make notes about the who, what, where, when, why, and how of your topic. Use this organizer.

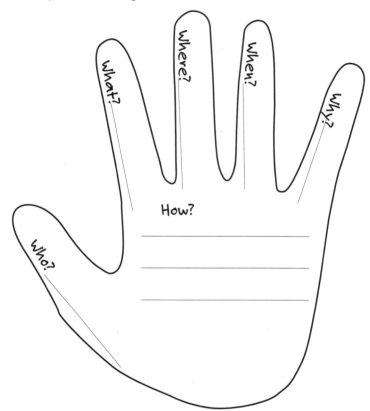

STEP 3. WRITE A LEAD. The lead of an article tells what the article is going to be about. In the lead, you explain who, what, where, when, why, and how. Write your lead here.

_____

_____

_____

STEP 4. WRITE AN ARTICLE. Write your complete article in your book, on page 159.

Name _____

ASSESSMENT

Multiple-Choice Test

DIRECTIONS On the blanks provided, write the letter of the item that best completes each statement or answers each question.

_____ 1. Why are these women known as "the widows" of the Reserves?
   A. Their husbands have died.   C. both A. and B.
   B. Their husbands live far away.   D. none of the above

_____ 2. Thousands of South African women have husbands who are torn away because . . .

   A. they must find work far away.   C. they are sent to prison.
   B. this is the custom.   D. none of the above

_____ 3. What jobs are the "widows" forced to do on their own?
   A. build their homes   C. take care of the stock
   B. bring up the children   D. all of the above

_____ 4. What weather disaster do these women fear?
   A. tornadoes   C. droughts
   B. monsoons   D. floods

_____ 5. What diseases do these men die from in their work place?
   A. flu and t.b.   C. miner's phthisis and t.b.
   B. pneumonia and miner's phthisis   D. cancer and the flu

_____ 6. Many in South Africa feel these women bring in a poor harvest because . . .
   A. they are weaker than men.   C. they use bad farming methods.
   B. they aren't as smart as men.   D. they have too many jobs.

_____ 7. How do the "widows" feel about education?
   A. It is important only for boys.   C. It is a waste of time.
   B. It will free them from poverty.   D. It is important only for girls.

_____ 8. The author says these women are lucky if they have . . .
   A. shelter.   C. some kind of transportation.
   B. the ability to read and write.   D. a cow from which to get milk.

_____ 9. How do the men communicate with the women?
   A. They call on the phone.   C. They write letters.
   B. Friends bring messages back and forth. D. none of the above

_____ 10. What is the tone of this article?
   A. sort of hopeless   C. sort of hopeful
   B. sort of promising   D. none of the above

Short-Essay Test

Why are most of these women "old" by the time they are thirty?

Luis Rodriguez

Unit Background   **LUIS RODRIGUEZ** (pages 161–176)

Luis J. Rodriguez was born in 1954 in El Paso, Texas. In *Always Running: la vida loca, gang days in L.A.* (1993), which Gary Soto called "fierce and fearless," Rodriguez recounts his days as a gang member. The book is dedicated to twenty-five friends who died as a result of gang violence. Rodriguez is a journalist and a poet, and two of his early poetry collections are *Poems Across the Pavement* (1989) and *The Concrete River* (1991). He won an Illinois Arts Council Poetry Fellowship and a Lannan Fellowship in Poetry in 1992. A recent book for young people is titled *It Doesn't Have to Be This Way: A Barrio Story* (1999).

The two excerpts from *Always Running* deal with Rodriguez's past as a gang member and with his efforts to keep his son Ramiro from following in his footsteps.

Teaching the Introduction

Chicago, the immediate setting of the two excerpts, is home to many Hispanics. The photo at left center shows a Mexican flag above the heads of a crowd at a celebration, perhaps a parade in Chicago honoring Mexican Independence Day.

1. Ask students why people join gangs. What do gangs provide that other organizations or families do not? Why are gangs violent?

2. Ask students to discuss what they would do if one of their children wanted to join a gang, which is the subject of *Always Running*.

Opening Activity

Ask students to compose a short letter to someone who wants to join a gang. What would they say to this person? Alternatively, ask students to give a three-minute impromptu talk on the same topic.

STUDENT PAGES 162–170

Skills and Strategies Overview

THEME Luis Rodriguez

READING LEVEL easy

VOCABULARY
◇ scum ◇ icicles ◇ imminent ◇ beleaguered ◇ personnel

PREREADING walk-through

RESPONSE react and connect

COMPREHENSION directed reading

PREWRITING narrowing a topic

WRITING autobiographical paragraph / commas

ASSESSMENT style

BACKGROUND

In his explosive autobiography, *Always Running,* Luis J. Rodriguez, who is a former Los Angeles gang member, describes how joining a gang made him feel a sense of security and power that he was otherwise unable to find in a life marked by poverty and despair.

Unlike many of his fellow gang members, however, Rodriguez abhorred the violence of gang life. Eventually he was able to extricate himself from his gang. After finishing school, he began writing about his experiences, hoping to share what he learned with today's children. Rodriguez has published many books for children and an award-winning book of poetry.

UNIT THEME Luis Rodriguez reveals the ugliness and violence of street-gang life in the United States.

GRAPHIC ORGANIZER A web similar to this one will help students understand Rodriguez's story-within-a-story narrative style.

Story Map: "Ramiro," part 1

Late 1960s, early 1970s: Luis Rodriguez is involved in a Los Angeles gang.
His teen years: drugs, shootings, beatings, arrests.
In his twenties, he sneaks away and removes himself from "La Vida Loca."

1.

EVENTS BEFORE THE STORY IS TOLD

2.

STORY EVENTS
Ramiro is on restriction. His parents worry that he is sliding into street-gang habits.
Ramiro is fascinated by gangs.
He is suspended for gang fighting.
An S.O.S. contract is issued on Ramiro.
Luis decides he will do anything to keep Ramiro off the streets.

After enduring the death-fires of gang life, Luis feels ready to make a new start.
He becomes a journalist, publisher, critic, and poet.
He marries and has children. His oldest son is Ramiro.

⫶. BEFORE YOU READ

Ask students to read the information about Luis Rodriguez on page 161 and the introduction to the lesson on page 162. The purpose of these two pages is to motivate and focus students. Next introduce the prereading activity, which is a **walk-through** of the selection.

Motivation Strategy

Start out by explaining to students that *Always Running* is about street gangs. Discuss what students already know about this topic. Have them share stories they've heard about or read.

ENGAGING STUDENTS You might further engage students by telling them that a character in *Always Running* is becoming increasingly more involved in gang life. Ask students: "What can parents do to protect their children from gangs?"

Vocabulary Building

Point out the key vocabulary words for the lesson: *scum, icicles, imminent, beleaguered,* and *personnel.* Help students use **context** as they read to figure out the meanings of difficult words. The footnotes define some of these words for students. Model using context and then checking your ideas against the footnote: "I don't know the word *scum.* I see, though, that it appears in a sentence with "dark," "car oil," and "decay." This tells me that *scum* must mean something like "dirty" or "disgusting." For more practice, see the **Vocabulary** blackline master, page 210.

STRATEGY LESSON: PREFIXES Remind the class that prefixes are word parts that come before the root word (*pre-* = before). Prefixes can change the meaning of a word. For example, when you add the prefix *mal-* (which means "badly" or "poorly") to the word *adjusted,* you end up with a completely new word: *maladjusted.* Ask students to circle the prefix in the word *intolerable* (page 163) and in *displacement* (page 164). Tell them that *in-* means "into" or "not" and that the *dis-* means "apart, away," or "reverse."

For additional practice with this strategy, see **Vocabulary** blackline master, page 210.

Prereading Strategies

As a prereading exercise, students will complete a **walk-through** of the selection. Have students do their walk-throughs with a highlighter in hand. Ask them to **highlight** headlines, words, and pictures that grab their attention. Having them highlight or mark the text during their walk-throughs will slow them down a bit and encourage them to pay more attention to what they're seeing. When they've finished their walk-throughs, students can complete the web on page 162.

Spanish-Speaking Students

En esta selección, sacada de su autobiografía, *Always Running,* Luis Rodriguez escribe de su hijo, Ramiro. Un adolescente de quince años, Ramiro está en peligro de sucumbir a la vida loca de la calle. Rodriguez no quiere que su hijo pertenezca a una banda y abandone las oportunidades de tener un buen futuro. Rodriguez está determinado a proteger a su hijo, pero no quiere estropear su relación.

II. READ

Rodriguez includes some very graphic details about street-gang life. Students will want to **react** to his descriptions and his story. Encourage them to note parts of the story that surprise or dismay them. Their notations will be helpful to them when they are asked to respond in some detail to the memoir.

Response Strategy

QUESTION As an additional response strategy, have students keep a running list of the questions they'd like to ask Luis and Ramiro. They might find answers to some of these questions in the continuation of the excerpt, so you may want to save what they've written for later.

Comprehension Strategies

Directed reading is a particularly useful strategy when you have a selection that you know will provoke discussion or debate. Also, struggling students will probably appreciate your helping them make the leap back and forth between story and flashback, which they'll need to do a couple of times in order to understand the story Rodriguez is telling. Each time something new happens in the story, or the setting changes, have students stop and think. Ask: "What just happened? Who is Luis describing here? What does this have to do with the story about Ramiro?"

GRAPHIC ORGANIZER Another comprehension strategy that will work well with this excerpt is a sequence chart that shows what happens first, what happens next, and so on. This will help students keep track of what is happening in the present and what happened in the past. Draw a chart on the board. Then stop each time something new happens and ask a student to record the event on the chart. You might add a second section to the chart when it comes time to read the continuation of Rodriguez's story.

For additional practice, see the **Comprehension** blackline master on page 211.

Discussion Questions

COMPREHENSION 1. Why is Ramiro suspended from high school? *(for fighting)*

2. What happens after he is suspended? *(His father moves him to a new school.)*

3. How does Luis feel about his son's gang involvement? *(He is horrified.)*

CRITICAL THINKING 4. In what ways is Ramiro repeating his father's mistakes? *(His father also joined a gang when he was a teenager.)*

5. Do you predict that Luis will succeed in protecting Ramiro? Explain your prediction. *(Ask students to support what they say with evidence from the selection.)*

Literary Skill

FLASHBACK The first part of "Ramiro" provides an excellent opportunity to review the characteristics of—and purpose for—a flashback. Explain that a flashback is an interruption in the narrative. A flashback shows an episode that happened before the interrupted point in the story. Writers use flashback for essentially one reason: to shed light on the story they are telling. Rodriguez's flashback, which begins on page 165, helps explain why he is so opposed to his son Ramiro's gang involvement. The reader is able to understand that Luis speaks from experience. He too had a series of dangerous run-ins with street gangs when he was a boy.

III. GATHER YOUR THOUGHTS

On page 167, students are asked to recall the events of "Ramiro" and then practice **narrowing** their own autobiographical **topics**. To complete the first half of the page, students will need to return to the text to make sure they retell the story in the proper order. Since there are only six frames on the strip, students will have to decide which events are most important. This exercise will further strengthen their understanding of the story.

Prewriting Strategies

NARROWING THE FOCUS The second part of page 167 shows students how to take a broad topic and break it apart into more manageable chunks. Sometimes young writers try to cover too much in their writing. This is particularly true when the assignment is to write an autobiographical piece. Students try to cover their entire lives in just three paragraphs. Ask students to examine the example on the left side of the page. Then have them try narrowing an autobiographical topic of their own. Check their work before asking them to move on to page 168.

On page 168, students are asked to create a story star that tells who, what, where, when, and how of the topic they wrote about on the previous page. Remind students to be specific when they answer each question.

For additional help, see the **Prewriting and Writing** blackline master, page 212.

IV. WRITE

Remind students to refer to the organizer on page 168 as they write their **autobiographical paragraphs**. Their organizers will help them stay focused on the most essential questions. When they've finished writing, ask them to revise using the **Writers' Checklist**.

Use the writing rubric to help students zero in on the assignment requirements and for help with a quick assessment of their writing.

WRITING RUBRIC Do students' autobiographical paragraphs

- stay focused on one event or experience?

- contain information about who, what, where, when, and how?

- use commas around appositives?

Grammar, Usage, and Mechanics

You might also use this opportunity to introduce a mini-lesson on commas. Remind students to use commas in dates between the day and the year. Also review how to use commas with appositives and explanatory words and phrases.

Incorrect: Ramiro who is my son was in terrible trouble.

Corrected: Ramiro, who is my son, was in terrible trouble.

V. WRAP-UP

Have students take a moment at the end of the lesson to think about their reaction to Rodriguez's writing **style**. Did students enjoy Rodriguez's straightforward, unadorned style? Did they find it easy to read? Ask students to explain what they did and did not like about Rodriguez's writing. Then see if they change their minds after reading the second part of "Ramiro."

Assessment

For a comprehension check, ask students to complete the **Assessment** blackline master on page 213.

Name _____

VOCABULARY

Words from the Selection

DIRECTIONS Answer these questions that use words from the selection. Explain your answers.

1. If there is <u>scum</u> on a pond, does it mean the pond is dirty or clean?

_____

2. If an event is <u>imminent</u>, does it mean that it will or won't occur?

_____

3. When my mother has a <u>beleaguered</u> expression, should I leave her alone or join in her fun?

_____

4. Is a <u>personnel</u> office meant for people or products?

_____

5. Are <u>icicles</u> formed in the winter or in the summer?

_____

Strategy Lesson: Prefixes

DIRECTIONS Read this list of prefixes and what they mean. Then decide what the five words on the lines below mean. Write the definitions on the lines.

in- = into, not	dis- = apart, away, reverse	un- = not, opposite of

6. intolerable _____

7. unexpected _____

8. displacement _____

9. unlikely _____

10. disobedience _____

Name _____

COMPREHENSION
Graphic Organizer

DIRECTIONS Use these character trait organizers to show what you know about Luis and Ramiro. Name four traits (characteristics) for each character. Then give examples from the story that support what you've said.

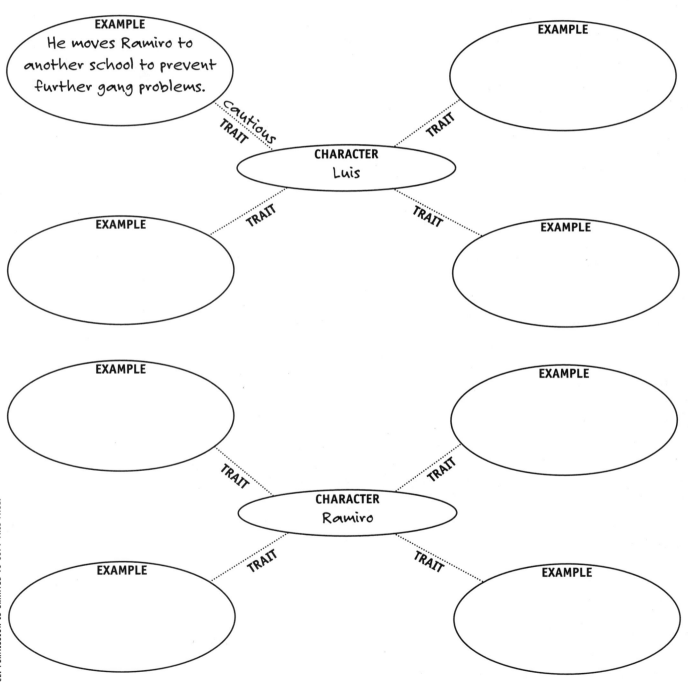

EXAMPLE
He moves Ramiro to another school to prevent further gang problems.

Cautious **TRAIT**

EXAMPLE

TRAIT

CHARACTER
Luis

EXAMPLE

TRAIT

TRAIT

EXAMPLE

EXAMPLE

EXAMPLE

TRAIT

TRAIT

CHARACTER
Ramiro

EXAMPLE

TRAIT

TRAIT

EXAMPLE

Name _____

PREWRITING AND WRITING
Writing an Autobiographical Paragraph

DIRECTIONS **A. CHOOSE A TOPIC.** Before you can write about yourself, you need to decide what you want to say. First think of a topic. Tell about something important or interesting that happened to you.

My topic _____

B. GATHER DETAILS. Then gather details about the event. These questions can help you think about the most important details of your event:

What happened? _____

_____

Where were you? _____

_____

Who else was there? _____

_____

When did it happen? _____

_____

How did it end? _____

_____

How did you feel once the whole thing was over? _____

_____

_____

C. WRITE A TOPIC SENTENCE. Write a topic sentence that introduces the story you're going to tell. Use this formula:

What happened + how I felt = my topic sentence.

My topic sentence _____

_____

_____

D. WRITE. Write an autobiographical paragraph in your book on page 169. Be sure to use plenty of details. Help your readers see, hear, smell, taste, and feel the event you are describing.

Name _____

ASSESSMENT

Multiple-Choice Test

DIRECTIONS On the blanks provided, write the letter of the answer for each question.

_____ 1. Who narrates "Ramiro"?
A. Ramiro
B. Luis
C. Trini
D. Rubén

_____ 2. Where does the Rodriguez family live?
A. Miami
B. Los Angeles
C. Chicago
D. New York

_____ 3. Why is Ramiro being punished by his father?
A. for shoplifting
B. for skipping school
C. for associating with gangs
D. for missing his curfew

_____ 4. What is "the bone-chilling hawk"?
A. the police
B. the weather
C. school officials
D. the landlord

_____ 5. How does Luis feel about his son?
A. He's tired of hassling and wants to send Ramiro away.
B. He's proud and hopes Ramiro continues to do well.
C. Ramiro can do no wrong.
D. He loves Ramiro, but he is worried.

_____ 6. What jobs has Luis Rodriguez had?
A. journalist
B. critic
C. poet
D. all of the above

_____ 7. What is the Rodriguez neighborhood like?
A. beautiful
B. gang-infested
C. quiet
D. none of the above

_____ 8. What nationalities live in the neighborhood?
A. Puerto Ricans
B. Mexicans
C. Poles
D. all of the above

_____ 9. What does S.O.S. mean to the gangs?
A. save our school
B. sink or swim
C. help
D. smash on sight

_____ 10. How many friends did Luis lose to gang violence during his teen years?
A. 60
B. 21
C. 25
D. 10

Short-Essay Test

Rodriguez describes Humboldt Park as a "changing neighborhood." What does he mean? What do the changes mean to the people who live there?

Ramiro (continued)

Skills and Strategies Overview

THEME Luis Rodriguez

READING LEVEL easy

VOCABULARY
◇ultimatum   ◇dissipating   ◇scurried   ◇hysteria   ◇frigid

PREREADING preview

RESPONSE predict and visualize

COMPREHENSION reciprocal reading

PREWRITING graphic organizer

WRITING character description / commas

ASSESSMENT depth

BACKGROUND

In this section of his autobiography, Luis Rodriguez describes how his disagreements with Ramiro escalate until they are at all-out war. Although Luis has moved Ramiro to a new school and has restricted him to the house during his free time, street gangs are still very much a part of the boy's life. Tensions mount when Rodriguez delivers an ultimatum. Unable to listen to his father's angry pleading for another second, Ramiro runs away and refuses to return home.

UNIT THEME Luis Rodriguez reveals the ugliness and violence of street-gang life in the United States. When his son, Ramiro, becomes involved in a gang, Rodriguez is forced to come to terms with his own difficult past.

GRAPHIC ORGANIZER Students might benefit from making a sequence map similar to this one.

Sequence Map: "Ramiro," parts 1 and 2

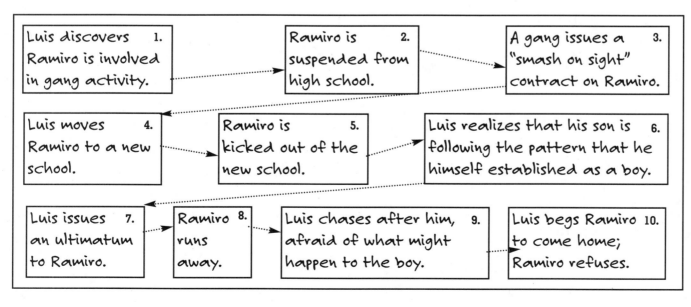

Luis discovers 1. Ramiro is involved in gang activity.

Ramiro is 2. suspended from high school.

A gang issues a 3. "smash on sight" contract on Ramiro.

Luis moves 4. Ramiro to a new school.

Ramiro is 5. kicked out of the new school.

Luis realizes that his son is 6. following the pattern that he himself established as a boy.

Luis issues 7. an ultimatum to Ramiro.

Ramiro 8. runs away.

Luis chases after him, 9. afraid of what might happen to the boy.

Luis begs Ramiro 10. to come home; Ramiro refuses.

⊥. BEFORE YOU READ

Before beginning this lesson, you might have a volunteer **summarize** what happened in the first part of Rodriguez's story. Then ask students to read through the introduction on page 171. When they're ready, students should begin their **preview** of the second part of "Ramiro."

Motivation Strategy

In this part of "Ramiro," Rodriguez describes a terrible argument with his son. Ask students to discuss arguments that they've had at home. What did they do to ease the tension? What did their family members do?

ENGAGING STUDENTS You might also take this opportunity to ask students to discuss street-gang problems where they live. Does the problem exist? Why or why not?

Vocabulary Building

Help students use **context clues** as they read to figure out the meanings of difficult words. For the most part, Rodriguez's word choices are simple in "Ramiro," yet he occasionally uses simple words in unfamiliar ways. (For example, he talks about "the mouth of darkness.") Remind students that they can look for clues in surrounding sentences to help them figure out the meaning of a word they don't know. For practice, have students use context clues to figure out the meaning of these key vocabulary words: *ultimatum, scurried, hysteria, frigid,* and *dissipating.* For additional practice, see the **Vocabulary** blackline master, page 218.

STRATEGY LESSON: SUFFIXES Knowing the meaning of some common English suffixes can help students understand how words are formed. Two common suffixes are *–ness* meaning "state, quality" or "condition" and *–ion* which can mean "act of, result of," or "condition of." The suffix *–ness* can be added to adjectives to form nouns (darkness). The suffix *–ion* can be added to verbs to form nouns. Ask students to come up with some additional words with the suffix *–ness.*

For additional practice with suffixes, see the **Vocabulary** blackline master on page 218.

Prereading Strategies

Before they read the continuation of "Ramiro," students are asked to do a **preview.** A preview gives readers the chance to make predictions about how things will turn out. During a preview, which should be quick but thorough, readers watch for clues about outcomes. Headers, vocabulary words, art, and the **stop and think** questions will give students clues about what happens in this part of the story. Students can use these clues to help them answer the questions on the **preview card.**

RETELLING As an additional prereading activity, you might ask a student or group of students to briefly retell the events of the first part of "Ramiro." (If you like, have them refer to the charts they created on page 167.) The rest of the students can listen to the retelling, offering suggestions and corrections as needed. This way the whole class is involved in reviewing what has already happened. After the retelling, students will be better prepared to move on to the next part of the story.

Spanish-Speaking Students

En la segunda parte de "Ramiro" Rodriguez y Ramiro acaban de pelear. Ramiro se huye de la casa y Rodriguez le persigue. Anda por unas calles oscuras y amenazantes, pidiendo información sobre su hijo. Quiere encontrarle y llevarle a casa, pero sabe que tiene que estar cuidadoso. Si hace un error y le inquieta a Ramiro, puede perderlo para simepre.

II. READ

As they read, students should **visualize** the characters and events described. Each time they "see" something new or interesting, students should make a quick sketch in the **Response Notes**. They can refer to their sketches later, when it comes time to remember key events of the story.

Response Strategy

REACT AND CONNECT As they were reading the first part of "Ramiro," students made notes about their reactions and connections to Luis's story. Encourage them to do the same here. Also remind them to note events or people that remind them of their own lives. Students' reaction and connection comments can help them feel more involved in the story.

Comprehension Strategies

Reciprocal reading is a strategy you can use to gently prod students into thinking critically about a selection. During a reciprocal reading, readers respond to a text in four different ways: 1. they clarify the action; 2. they make predictions; 3. they ask questions; and 4. they summarize what the author has said. These four different types of responses can help students make inferential responses about main idea, theme, character, style, and so on.

GRAPHIC ORGANIZER Another comprehension strategy that will work well with this part of "Ramiro" is a sequence organizer designed to reveal the chain of events Rodriguez describes. (See page 214 for an example of a sequence organizer.) This activity will be particularly valuable to students who are struggling to understand the action of the story.

For additional practice, see the **Comprehension** blackline master on page 219.

Discussion Questions

COMPREHENSION 1. Why does Luis issue an ultimatum to his son? *(He thinks that this will force Ramiro into leaving the gang.)*

2. What is Ramiro's response? *(He runs away.)*

3. Where does Ramiro go when he leaves the house? *(He hides in the streets.)*

CRITICAL THINKING 4. Is Luis angry with his son? Explain. *(Ask students to support their ideas with evidence from the selection.)*

5. What does Luis mean when he says, "it was my voice cracking open the winter sky"? *(Have students focus on the verb "cracking." Does it imply anguish or anger?)*

Literary Skill

PERSONIFICATION This last half of "Ramiro" provides an opportunity to discuss personification, a figure of speech in which human characteristics are given to nonhuman things. Personification can make events more vivid. In this excerpt Rodriguez writes that Ramiro "veered into a building that swallowed him up and spit him out the other side." Here, a building is given human characteristics that help the reader see not only the speed with which Ramiro is moving but also the harshness and indifference of his environment.

III. GATHER YOUR THOUGHTS

A **graphic organizer** like the one on page 174 will help students understand Ramiro and explore character motivation. Once they understand what motivates him, they can begin to think more interpretively about the text. If you like, do the character organizer as a whole-class activity. Then ask students to work with you to complete the same organizer for Luis. What do the two characters have in common? How are they different?

Prewriting Strategies

STORY FRAME If you're not certain that students have completely understood the action of "Ramiro," you might have them complete a story frame that explores the events of Rodriguez's memoir. Your more-advanced readers and writers may want to do one large frame that takes into account both parts of the excerpt.

For more practice, see the **Prewriting** blackline master on page 220.

IV. WRITE

Set aside plenty of time for students to write their **character descriptions**. When they've finished, have them share their work with a writing partner. Writing partners should read and then comment on the cohesiveness of the paragraph in addition to the mechanics and spelling. Have them keep the questions in this writing rubric in mind as they read their partner's work.

WRITING RUBRIC Do students' paragraphs

• describe how Ramiro feels and what his situation is?

• open with a clear topic sentence?

• contain three or more details to support the topic sentence?

• stay focused on Ramiro throughout?

Grammar, Usage, and Mechanics

You might also take this opportunity to teach a brief mini-lesson on commas. Remind the class that commas are used to set off introductory phrases and direct quotations. For example:

Incorrect: Later that evening Luis told Trini "Our boy is gone."

Correct: Later that evening, Luis told Trini, "Our boy is gone."

V. WRAP-UP

To measure the **depth** of students' connections to this selection, take a moment at the end of the lesson for students to discuss what "Ramiro" made them think about. Did it affect them in some way? Did it make them want to rethink some of their ideas and beliefs? As students answer the questions on the **Readers' Checklist,** encourage them to make connections between what they've read and their own lives.

Assessment

For a comprehension check, ask students to complete the **Assessment** blackline master on page 221.

Name _____

VOCABULARY

Words from the Selection

DIRECTIONS Read these sentences from "Ramiro." Use context clues to help you figure out what the underlined words mean. Then write the meaning of each word on the lines.

1. "One evening that winter, after Ramiro had come in late following weeks of trouble at school, I gave him an <u>ultimatum</u>. Yelling burst back and forth. . . ."

2. "He flew over brick walls, <u>scurried</u> down another alley. . . ."

3. "I saw Ramiro's fleeing figure, his breath rising above him in quickly-<u>dissipating</u> clouds.

4. "As I watched his escape, it was like looking back into a distant time, back to my own youth, when I ran and ran, when I jumped over peeling fences, fleeing *vatos locos*, the police or my own shadow in some drug-induced <u>hysteria</u>."

5. "I saw Ramiro run off and then saw *my* body entering the mouth of darkness, my breath cutting the <u>frigid</u> flesh of night; it was my voice cracking open the winter sky."

ultimatum _____

scurried _____

dissipating _____

hysteria _____

frigid _____

Strategy Lesson: Suffixes

The suffix *–ness* means "state, quality," or "condition." The suffix *-ion* can mean "act of, result of," or "condition of." The suffix *-ness* can be added to adjectives to form nouns. *Pale* (adjective) + *-ness* = paleness (noun). The suffix *-ion* can be added to verbs to form nouns. *Evict* (verb) + *-ion* = eviction (noun).

DIRECTIONS In the blanks, add the suffix *–ness* or *–ion* to each of the underlined words, depending on which suffix you think fits.

6. We gasped at the <u>vast</u> _____ of the ocean.

7. The <u>elect</u> _____ will be held in November.

8. Can you make a <u>predict</u> _____ about the World Series?

9. Extreme <u>shy</u> _____ prevented her from making many friends.

10. <u>Ill</u> _____ caused him to miss school.

Name _____

COMPREHENSION
Story Frame

DIRECTIONS Fill in this story frame about "Ramiro." Add lines if you need to.

The story takes place _____
_____
_____

_____ is a character in the story who
_____
_____

_____ is another character in the story who
_____
_____

A problem occurs when _____
_____
_____

After that, _____.

And, _____
_____

The problem is solved when _____
_____
_____

The story ends with _____
_____
_____

Name _____

PREWRITING
Writing About a Character

DIRECTIONS How do you write about a character? Follow these steps.

STEP 1. GATHER CHARACTER TRAITS. List four traits that describe Ramiro. (Traits tell what type of person the character is. For example, he is *intelligent, funny,* and *quick-to-anger.*) Along with each trait, give some "proof" or evidence from the selection.

• trait 1 _____

proof: _____

• trait 2 _____

proof: _____

• trait 3 _____

proof: _____

• trait 4 _____

proof: _____

STEP 2. WRITE A TOPIC SENTENCE. Look at your list of character traits. Choose the three most interesting ones and use them in a topic sentence about the character.

Ramiro is _____ ,

_____ , and _____ .

Name _____

ASSESSMENT

Multiple-Choice Test

DIRECTIONS On the blanks provided, write the letter of the best answer for each question.

_____ 1. Why does Ramiro run out into the street?
   A. He is chasing a friend.   C. He had a fight with his mother.
   B. He left his jacket at school.   D. He had a fight with his father.

_____ 2. What did Luis do after Ramiro ran out?
   A. He called the police.   C. He ran after him.
   B. He sent his brother after him. D. He phoned Ramiro's friends.

_____ 3. Who tries to help Luis find his son?
   A. friends   C. neighbors
   B. family   D. the police

_____ 4. What does Luis say when he catches up with Ramiro?
   A. "You're grounded."   C. "Come home."
   B. "I love you."   D. "I'm telling your mother."

_____ 5. What is Ramiro's reaction?
   A. He comes home.   C. He takes off again.
   B. He hugs his father.   D. He cries.

_____ 6. How does Ramiro's reaction make Luis feel?
   A. very upset   C. pleased
   B. hopeful   D. unsure

_____ 7. Which adjective best describes Ramiro?
   A. loving   C. fun-loving
   B. gentle   D. rebellious

_____ 8. What did Ramiro's flight remind Luis of?
   A. a TV show   C. a movie
   B. a book   D. his past

_____ 9. What is an ultimatum?
   A. an outburst   C. a compliment
   B. a final statement   D. a plot summary

_____ 10. Did Luis use drugs when he was a teenager?
   A. no   C. yes
   B. No, but he sold them.   D. He doesn't say.

Short-Essay Test

In what ways does Ramiro remind Luis of himself and his past?

Conflict

Unit Background   CONFLICT (pages 177–196)

The selections in this grouping focus on racial and religious conflict. The first selection is an excerpt from Zora Neale Hurston's autobiography *Dust Tracks on a Road* (1942). She writes of an incident when a black man goes into a barber shop in which black men and women, including Hurston, are employed. When the potential customer asks for a haircut and shave, he is directed instead to a shop that caters to Negro customers. Hurston ponders the ironies of the situation. In fact, the customer should probably have been served, but doing so would have deprived the Negro owner of the shop of business.

The second selection is an autobiographical account by an Arab and Muslim writer about the discrimination she has faced and her reactions to it.

Teaching the Introduction

The top photo shows violent conflict; the right photo is of writer Zora Neale Hurston. The bottom-left photo shows a Muslim woman wearing a *hejab* that covers her head and part of her face.

"As Americans we need to take a little time to look and listen carefully to what is around us. . . ."

1.

"Education is the key to understanding."

"My business was threatened." 2.

". . . self-interest rides over all sorts of lines."

Zora Neale Hurston

177

1. Ask students to discuss the quotation on this page: "Education is the key to understanding." Does religious and racial conflict result from lack of understanding?

2. Ask what the word *discrimination* means. If you think the following question is suitable for your class, ask whether students feel they have ever consciously or unconsciously discriminated against someone in school or in the community.

Opening Activity

Assign students to small groups and have each group design a poster that makes a statement about the unfairness of discrimination. Their work can be displayed in the classroom.

STUDENT PAGES 178–186

Skills and Strategies Overview

THEME Conflict

READING LEVEL easy

VOCABULARY

◆belligerently   ◆crusader   ◆snarled   ◆sanction   ◆militant

PREREADING anticipation guide

RESPONSE question

COMPREHENSION story frame

PREWRITING fact and opinion

WRITING opinion paragraph / capitalization

ASSESSMENT meaning

BACKGROUND

Zora Neale Hurston (1891–1960) is recognized today as one of the true literary geniuses of the 20th century. During her lifetime, however, she found it impossible to make a living as a writer and was forced to support herself as a ladies' maid and field hand.

Dust Tracks on a Road is Hurston's 1942 memoir of her life. In it, she recalls her childhood, the years she spent in the fields picking crops, and her life as a fledgling writer and researcher. Hurston's goal as a writer, she said, was to document the true voice of African Americans, which could be heard only in the folk tales, spirituals, and poems shared on front porches and street corners across the country. Although she was deeply proud of her heritage, Hurston was nevertheless ambivalent about the growing movement for African-American civil rights. She often wondered who would benefit most from desegregation laws. Would it be blacks who were suddenly able to have their hair cut in "whites-only" barbershops, or would it be whites who would end up with the lion's share of the business?

UNIT THEME In this unit, students explore the two sides of a conflict and then ask themselves: *Who was right?* and *What would I have done?*

GRAPHIC ORGANIZER When filled in, the diagram on the **Comprehension** blackline master on page 229 might look something like this.

Herringbone Diagram: "Refusing Service"

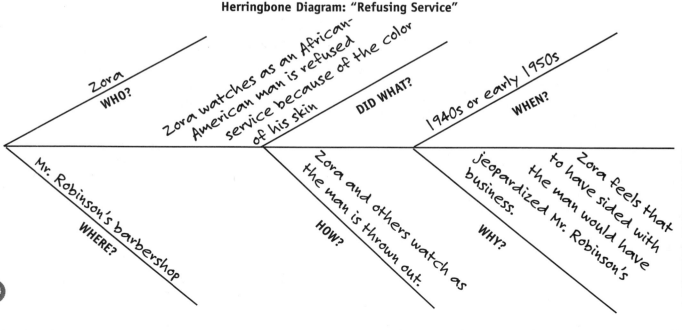

Zora
WHO?

Zora watches as an African-American man is refused service because of the color of his skin
DID WHAT?

1940s or early 1950s
WHEN?

Mr. Robinson's barbershop
WHERE?

Zora and others watch as the man is thrown out.
HOW?

Zora feels that to have sided with the man would have jeopardized Mr. Robinson's business.
WHY?

BEFORE YOU READ

Review with students the introduction to the lesson and provide some information about Zora Neale Hurston. Then introduce the prereading activity—an **anticipation guide**—on page 178.

Motivation Strategy

Explain that "Refusing Service" is the true story of an African-American man who is refused service in a barbershop because of the color of his skin. Ask students to discuss how they think the man might have felt.

ENGAGING STUDENTS To further motivate students, tell the class that Hurston's essay is about a woman who questions whether it is preferable to remain silent (and safe) or to speak your mind when you see something has gone badly wrong. What are students' opinions on this topic?

Vocabulary Building

Help students use **context clues** to figure out the meaning of at least two of the key vocabulary words, which are *belligerently*, *crusader*, *snarled*, *sanction*, and *militant*. Students can figure out the meaning of *snarled* (page 179) by looking at surrounding sentences. It's clear that the "crusader" is angry, for he insults and threatens the barber. Readers can assume that *snarled* is an angry way of speaking. Students can probably figure out the meaning of *militant* by the same method. Urge them to check the footnote definitions for the other three words.

For more practice with these key vocabulary words, see the **Vocabulary** blackline master, page 228.

STRATEGY LESSON: LATIN AND GREEK WORD PARTS As an alternate strategy, tell students that knowing some Latin words can help them understand the meaning of various words. For example, *manicure* (or *manicurist*) is made up of two Latin words: *manus* (hand) and *cura* (care). Some other words that come from these Latin words are *secure*, *curator*, and *manufacture*.

For more practice with this strategy, see the **Vocabulary** blackline master, page 228.

Prereading Strategies

ANTICIPATION GUIDE An anticipation guide asks students to activate prior knowledge about a topic or idea and then has them apply that knowledge to a set of statements about the story. Usually an anticipation guide can help arouse students' interest in the selection. Encourage your students to revisit the anticipation guide on page 178 as they are reading and later, when the reading is completed. Students can observe how their responses changed or stayed the same based on the information provided.

Spanish-Speaking Students

Zora Neale Hurston escribe de un incidente que la ha afectado mucho. Hace años un dueño negro de una peluquería para gente blanca rehusó cortarse el pelo de un hombre negro. Simpatizaba con la lucha de justicia para la población negra, y había trabajado duro para obtener su puesto como peluquero. Por eso, no quería correr el riesgo de perder su peluquería para que un hombre pudiera hacer un comentario sobre los derechos civiles. Hurston analiza dos lados de este conflicto, sin saber cuál hombre fue mas justificado en su comportamiento.

II. READ

Remind students to write any **questions** they have for Zora Neale Hurston in the **Response Notes.** Be prepared for some provocative questions, since the choice Hurston makes (to keep quiet) might be criticized by some students. You can use their questions and comments as a basis for discussion about equal rights and equality.

Response Strategy

PREDICT   As an alternate response strategy, ask students to note their during-reading predictions as they read. They can predict what will happen to the man who is insisting on service, and they can predict whether or not Hurston will speak up in his defense. Their predictions will make them feel more involved in the story and help hold their interest until the end.

Comprehension Strategies

Students are asked to fill in a set of **story frames** as they are reading "Refusing Service." Story frames can help students understand the sequence of events in a story. Rather than simply asking students to "tell what happens," story frames give a framework for response that prods the reader into thinking carefully about elements of setting, character, and plot. Encourage students to reread their story frame notes once they've finished the selection. They may want to make some small revisions to their thoughts and ideas.

DIRECTED READING   As an alternate comprehension strategy, try doing a directed reading of the selection. In a directed reading, you or a group leader reads the selection aloud, pausing every once in a while to pose **stop and think** questions that can help students make factual and inferential responses. A directed reading allows the teacher to see what, if anything, is causing problems in the selection. Using students' comments as a guide, you might want to speed up or slow down the pace of the reading, depending on how well students are comprehending the selection.

For additional practice, see the **Comprehension** blackline master on page 229.

Discussion Questions

COMPREHENSION   1. What kind of "service" does the African-American man ask for? *(a haircut and shave)*

2. Why does the barber say no? *(because the man is African American)*

3. Does anyone speak up in the man's defense? *(no)*

4. What happens to the man eventually? *(He's forced to leave the shop.)*

CRITICAL THINKING   5. Why don't Hurston and the others defend the man? *(Hurston, who works at the shop, is afraid for her job. She is particularly afraid that Banks's business will suffer if people make an issue of the man's complaint.)*

6. Did Hurston make the right choice by staying silent? Explain your opinion. *(Remind students to fully explain their ideas.)*

Literary Skill

CHRONOLOGICAL ORDER   Hurston uses chronological order to tell her story of the man in the barber shop. This makes her narrative easy to read and follow. You might take this opportunity to teach a brief lesson on time-order and the use of transitions in a narrative. Remind students that when writers use chronological order, they usually use time-order transitional words and phrases to help their narrative read smoothly. Words and phrases such as *first, last, later, after that, the next day,* and *a week later* cue readers as to where they are in the story. You might want to keep a list of transitional words and phrases posted on the board. Students can refer to the list as they write their paragraphs, articles, and essays.

III. GATHER YOUR THOUGHTS

The activities on page 183 are designed to help students differentiate between **fact** and **opinion** in a piece of writing. Before they begin, remind students that an opinion is what someone believes is true. Opinions state personal beliefs. A fact is a statement that can be proven to be true. Facts are used to support opinions. Also tell students that when they write a persuasive paragraph, letter, or essay, they must support their opinions with known facts. Otherwise, the opinion might be considered invalid. When they form their opinions about "Refusing Service," they'll use facts (characters, events, details, and quotations) from the selection to support what they say.

Prewriting Strategies

OPINION STATEMENT For an additional prewriting activity, you might want to have students practice writing opinion statements for "Refusing Service." Show students this formula:

A specific topic   +   a specific opinion   =   a good opinion statement.

Opinion statements must be clear and succinct. In general, writers should avoid using strong words such as *all, best, every, never*, or *worst* because they are difficult to prove, no matter how reliable the facts.

For more practice, see the **Prewriting and Writing** blackline master on page 230.

IV. WRITE

Ask students to give their **opinion paragraphs** to a writing partner for review. Writing partners should check to make sure that the opinion statement is supported with three strong facts from the text. Use the questions below in the writing rubric to help with a quick assessment of students' work.

WRITING RUBRIC Do students' opinion paragraphs

- begin with a clear opinion statement?

- include three or more facts from the selection to support the opinion statement?

- stay focused on the topic of people and how they treat each other?

Grammar, Usage, and Mechanics

When students are at the revision stage, you might teach a brief lesson on capitalization. Start by reminding students of the rules for capitalization. The first word of every sentence, direct quotation, and indirect quotation must be capitalized.

Incorrect: she says, "self-interest is often more important than any other loyalties."

Correct: She says, "Self-interest is often more important than any other loyalties."

V. WRAP-UP

Give students the chance to discuss the **meaning** of Hurston's piece. What did it mean to them personally? Did it affect their outlook on the world? If so, how? Their comments will help them identify what they've learned from Hurston's story.

Assessment

For a comprehension check, ask students to complete the **Assessment** blackline master on page 231.

Name _____

VOCABULARY

Words from the Selection

DIRECTIONS Use context clues to decide which word from the list belongs in each sentence. Write that word on the blank.

◇belligerently ◇crusader ◇snarled ◇sanction ◇militant

1. A man in the subway angered people by _____ demanding money.

2. Several people _____ at him, but they gave him some loose change.

3. Although most passengers didn't _____ begging for money, they felt sorry for the man.

4. One very _____ passenger picked up his phone to call police.

5. Another passenger, a sort of _____, argued that the man had a right to ask for money.

Strategy Lesson: Latin and Greek Word Parts

DIRECTIONS Study the word parts and their meanings in the left-hand box. Then answer the questions below by writing the correct answers from the right-hand box on the blanks. You will not use one word.

manus	=	hand
pedem	=	foot
cura	=	care
meter	=	device for measuring
scribere	=	to write

manuscript
curator
pedometer
scribble
pedicure
speedometer

6. Which word means an instrument for measuring the distance traveled in walking?

_____

7. Which word means "care or treatment of the feet"?

_____

8. Which word originally meant "written by hand"?

_____

9. Which is the word for a person in charge of a museum or art gallery?

_____

10. Which word means to write or scrawl carelessly?

_____

Name _____

COMPREHENSION
Graphic Organizer

DIRECTIONS Use this herringbone diagram to show the who, what, where, when, why, and how of "Refusing Service." Then answer two questions about the selection.

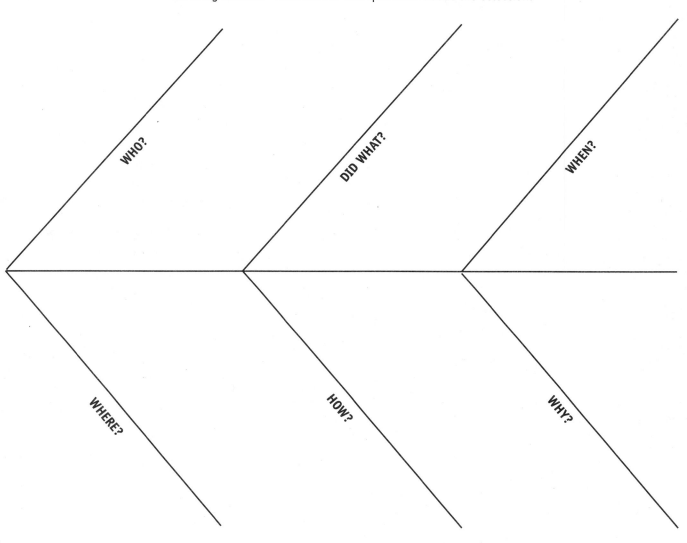

1. What three adjectives (descriptive words) would you use to describe Hurston?

_____ _____ _____

2. What three adjectives would you use to describe the African-American man who sits in the barber chair?

_____ _____ _____

Name _____

PREWRITING AND WRITING
Writing an Opinion Paragraph

DIRECTIONS Follow these steps as you are writing your opinion paragraph.

STEP 1. WRITE AN OPINION STATEMENT. An opinion statement is the same as a topic sentence. Use it as the first sentence of your paragraph.

A specific topic + a specific opinion = a good opinion statement.

"Refusing Service" + how people treat each other = your opinion statement.

In "Refusing Service," people treat each other

_____

_____

> **TIP**
> Opinion statements must be clear and brief. Avoid using strong words such as <u>all</u>, <u>best</u>, <u>every</u>, <u>never</u>, or <u>worst</u> because they are usually hard to prove, no matter how good your facts are.

STEP 2. SUPPORT YOUR OPINION. An opinion must be supported by facts. Find three facts from "Refusing Service" that support your opinion. Each fact should have something to do with how people treat each other.

fact #1 _____

fact #2 _____

fact #3 _____

STEP 3. WRITE. Write your opinion paragraph here. Begin with your opinion statement. Then offer your facts. Close with a sentence that ties everything together.

_____

_____

_____

_____

Name _____

ASSESSMENT

Multiple-Choice Test

DIRECTIONS On the blanks provided, write the letter of the best answer for each question.

_____ 1. What does the man say he wants when he walks into Banks's shop?
   A. a haircut and shave
   B. a meeting with the owner
   C. a new suit
   D. Zora's help

_____ 2. Why does Banks refuse to serve the man?
   A. because the shop is busy
   B. because the shop is for whites only
   C. because the man is rude
   D. because the man is dirty

_____ 3. What threat does the man make?
   A. that he'll kill Banks
   B. that he'll kidnap Zora
   C. that he'll steal Banks's business
   D. that he'll sue

_____ 4. What is Zora doing while the action is going on?
   A. She's not even there.
   B. She's watching quietly.
   C. She's talking with her friends.
   D. She's arguing with Banks.

_____ 5. Why doesn't Zora speak up and side with the man?
   A. She thinks he's an idiot.
   B. She doesn't understand what he's saying.
   C. Banks is her husband.
   D. She worries the shop business will be hurt.

_____ 6. How does the incident end?
   A. Zora tells the man to come back later.
   B. The man's wife pulls him out of the shop.
   C. The man is thrown out of the shop.
   D. Banks agrees to serve him.

_____ 7. Why does Hurston say that wrecking George Robinson on a "race angle" would have been wrong?
   A. George Robinson is the only nice white man in town.
   B. George Robinson, who is black, helps other blacks get ahead.
   C. George Robinson is her husband.
   D. none of the above

_____ 8. What does Hurston mean when she says the man was "one of us"?
   A. He's a barber also.
   B. He's African American also.
   C. He struggles to make a living also.
   D. all of the above

_____ 9. Where do you think this story take place?
   A. somewhere in Canada
   B. somewhere in Europe
   C. somewhere in the United States
   D. somewhere in the Caribbean

_____ 10. How does Hurston feel about the incident?
   A. confused
   B. angry
   C. regretful
   D. all of the above

Short-Essay Test

Do you think Hurston made the right choice in staying silent? Explain your opinion.

Time to Look and Listen

Skills and Strategies Overview

THEME	Conflict
READING LEVEL	average
VOCABULARY	✧discrimination ✧incompatible ✧ethnicity ✧uncivilized ✧monotheistic
PREREADING	skimming
RESPONSE	react and connect
COMPREHENSION	graphic organizer
PREWRITING	supporting an opinion
WRITING	opinion article / apostrophes
ASSESSMENT	understanding

BACKGROUND

In her essay "Time to Look and Listen," Magdoline Asfahani explains how it feels to be discriminated against. Asfahani's essay should be eye-opening for students because it concerns the here and now, rather than events that took place years before they were born. Each day, Asfahani is reminded by others that she doesn't "fit in" because she is of Arab descent. She and her brother are taunted and teased and become the butt of their classmates' jokes. And, since anti–Middle East sentiments continue to run strong, Asfahani sees no end in sight to the blatant discrimination she and her family are forced to endure. Determined to be silent no longer, Asfahani shares her views. It is time, she tells readers, "to look and listen" and be tolerant of people of all races. Only then will young children be free of the terrible taunting that marred her childhood.

UNIT THEME Magdoline Asfahani asks readers to judge people on the basis of how they act, rather than how they look.

GRAPHIC ORGANIZER **Episode Analysis: "Time to Look and Listen"**

EPISODE #	PROBLEM	RESPONSE	ACTION	OUTCOME
1	7th grade: TWA plane hijacked to Beirut	Magdoline is "blamed" for incident.	She tries to defend herself and her heritage.	Magdoline becomes an "outcast."
2	7th–11th grade: violence and bloodshed in the Middle East	Magdoline is "blamed" and treated as an outcast.	She tries to hide her cultural identity.	She hurts her parents and herself by pretending to be something she is not.
3	11th grade: must go to Middle East to visit a sick grandmother	Chemistry teacher makes a nasty joke—Magdoline is outraged.	She decides to learn all she can about her heritage.	She begins to accept herself for who she is and is no longer ashamed of her heritage.

BIBLIOGRAPHY Consider inviting students to read other books about the immigrant experience:

It's Only Goodbye by Virginia T. Gross (easy)
Dreams in the Golden Country by Katherine Lasky (easy)
Home Child by Barbara Haworth-Attard (average)
In a New Land: An Anthology of Immigrant Literature edited by Sari Grossman (average)
American Mosaic: The Immigrant Experience in the Words of Those Who Lived It ed. by Jean Morrison (challenging)

1. BEFORE YOU READ

Read through the introduction with students. Be sure they understand why a reader might skim or scan a text before reading it. Then ask students to do the prereading activity, a **skim** of "Time to Look and Listen."

Motivation Strategy

To help students become thematically involved in the essay, ask: "What examples of prejudice have you seen at school? What examples of prejudice have you seen in your town? Is there anything we can do to stop people from being prejudiced?"

ENGAGING STUDENTS To motivate students, tell the class this essay is about a girl their own age who is taunted by her classmates because of her heritage. Ask them how she might have felt.

Vocabulary Building

Write the vocabulary words on the board: *discrimination, incompatible, ethnicity, uncivilized,* and *monotheistic*. Be sure the students can pronounce the words. Then ask them to use their knowledge of **prefixes**, **suffixes**, **roots**, and their past reading to make some inferences about the meanings of the words. Ask which word or words students would have to define with the help of a footnote or dictionary.

For additional practice with these words, see the **Vocabulary** blackline master on page 236.

STRATEGY LESSON: GREEK PREFIXES AND SUFFIXES As an alternate strategy, tell students that knowing the meaning of some common word parts from the Greek can help them understand the meaning of many words. For example, the word *monotheistic* (page 190) comes from *mono-* (single) and *theo-* (god). Other words beginning with *mono-* include *monorail, monoplane*, and *monogram*.

See the **Vocabulary** blackline master on page 236 for additional work with Greek prefixes and suffixes.

Prereading Strategies

Skimming gives readers the chance to glance over a selection before they begin reading. Skimming introduces readers to the selection topic and at the same time alerts them to any problems they might have (such as challenging vocabulary) during their close readings. When they skim, students should look quickly at the first sentence of every paragraph. They should pay particular attention to key words and phrases and watch for repeated or unfamiliar words.

READ-ALOUD As an alternate prereading strategy, have students take turns reading aloud the first several paragraphs of the essay. Listen carefully for hesitations in the reading. If students seem to have no trouble, have them continue reading on their own. If they appear to be struggling, do a small-group or whole-class read-aloud of the rest of the selection.

Spanish-Speaking Students

En "Es la hora de ver y escuchar" autora Magdoline Asfahani describe su juventud dolorosa, cuando se sentía avergonzada de ser árabe en un mundo de americanos. Ella era diferente de sus compañeros de clase y tenía que aguantar mucho prejuicio. Luego en su vida, ella aprendió abrazar su patria. Se dio cuenta de que el futuro dependía de un entendimiento y apreciación mutual entre los seres humanos.

II. READ

When students **react** and **connect** to a selection, they explain how the selection makes them feel. This response strategy helps students see that their individual responses to a reading can help them better understand the author's message. Encourage students to make detailed notes about their reactions to Asfahani's article. Do they agree with her ideas? Do they have the same views on discrimination? Also remind students to make connections between what Asfahani describes and their own lives. Have they ever experienced some of the same emotions that Asfahani writes about? Later, they can use their notes to help them write their opinion statements.

Response Strategy

VISUALIZE As an alternate response strategy, have students complete an "Episode Analysis" form like the one on the first page of this lesson.

Comprehension Strategies

As they read the article, students will fill out some problem-solution **graphic organizers** that will help them keep track of the difficulties Asfahani experiences because she is of Middle-Eastern descent. Before they begin reading, you might point out to students that they'll be building toward a completed chart that looks like the one on the right-hand side of page 189. If you like, post this chart on the board for students to refer to as they read. When the class has finished the article, ask for volunteers to come up to the board and fill out small sections of the organizer. Work together to understand the issues Asfahani raises.

For additional practice, see the **Comprehension** blackline master on page 237.

Discussion Questions

COMPREHENSION 1. Where did Asfahani's parents emigrate from? *(the Middle East)*

2. What happened to Asfahani in seventh grade that caused her to change her feelings about herself? *(Students began taunting her because of her Middle-Eastern heritage.)*

3. What does she do to try and "hide" her heritage? *(She tries to forget the Arabic language; she lies about her parents; she no longer invites friends to her home.)*

CRITICAL THINKING 4. What is the tone of Asfahani's essay? *(Answers will vary. Remind students that tone is the overall feeling, or effect, created by a writer's use of words. See below.)*

5. Do you agree with Asfahani's opinion that people nowadays are showing a "greater sensitivity" to cultural issues? *(Ask students to support their opinions by discussing their own experiences.)*

Literary Skill

TONE As you know, tone is the author's attitude or feeling about a subject or the audience. An author's tone can be serious, humorous, satiric, and so on. In "Time to Look and Listen," Asfahani's tone reveals the depth of her feelings about the subject. She is angry and hurt and is not afraid to show it. Work with students to understand the tone of the article. Since the easiest place to find clues about tone is in the author's word choices, ask students to find words in the essay that show Asfahani's outrage. They might suggest words such as *cruel, attacked, uncivilized, brutal, humiliated, excluded,* and *mocked.*

GATHER YOUR THOUGHTS

The goal of these prewriting activities is to help students understand how an author formulates and then supports an opinion. Remind students that an **opinion** is a statement of one's personal beliefs. Opinions are supported by facts—statements that can be proven true. In her essay, Asfahani uses facts from her own life and observations of the people and places she has seen to support her opinion that Americans need to stop rushing to judgment. Because Asfahani is an "expert" on discrimination (she has been discriminated against since she was a child), we can treat her statements and observations as facts.

Prewriting Strategies

NARROWING A TOPIC As students begin thinking about their own opinion statements, you might point out that Asfahani doesn't try to cover every issue related to discrimination. She narrows her focus and writes only about discrimination against Middle-Eastern immigrants. Before they begin their paragraphs, review with students the technique for narrowing their focus. See pupil page 167.

For more practice, see the **Prewriting and Writing** blackline master on page 238.

IV. WRITE

Set aside plenty of time for students to write their **articles**. Remind them to stay focused on the topic of fighting prejudice. Then, after they've finished writing, ask them to revise using the **Writers' Checklist.**

WRITING RUBRIC Use the writing rubric to help students focus on the assignment requirements and for help with a quick assessment of their writing.

Do students' articles

- begin with an opinion statement?

- contain at least three facts that support the opinion?

- end with a closing statement that "clinches" the argument?

Grammar, Usage, and Mechanics

You might take this opportunity to teach a mini-lesson on apostrophes. Remind the class that to create the possessive form of most singular nouns, you add an apostrophe and an *s*. To create the possessive form of most plural nouns that end in *s*, add only an apostrophe.

singular nouns	plural nouns	irregular nouns
brother/brother's	videos/videos'	child/children/children's
zebra/zebra's	girls/girls'	deer/deer/deer's

V. WRAP-UP

Check to be sure students have thoroughly **understood** what they've read. Let them explain to you what was difficult about the essay. Use their insights to help you plan strategies for the next lesson.

Assessment

For a comprehension check, ask students to complete the **Assessment** blackline master on page 239.

Name _____

VOCABULARY

Words from the Selection

DIRECTIONS On the blanks provided, write the letter of the best definition for each underlined word.

_____ 1. Immigrants to the United States sometimes face discrimination. (a) hunger and poverty; (b) difference in treatment because of their class or group; (c) unlawful use of force to make them do something.

_____ 2. Islam is a monotheistic religion. (a) believing in only one god; (b) religion practiced only in the Middle East; (c) believing in several gods.

_____ 3. Their different beliefs made the families incompatible. (a) not believable; (b) not capable of fitting together; (c) not able to be compared.

_____ 4. Sarita found that her ethnicity was the same as many others in her school. (a) racial or cultural background; (b) former education; (c) language and neighborhood.

_____ 5. The third-grade teacher thought her class was sometimes uncivilized. (a) without lunch money; (b) not aware of what was happening; (c) lacking in courtesy or manners.

Strategy Lesson: Greek Prefixes and Suffixes

DIRECTIONS Study the Greek prefixes and suffixes and their meanings in the left box. Then answer each question below by choosing the correct word from the right-hand column and writing it in the blank. You will not use one word.

mono-	=	single
poly-	=	much, many
theo-	=	god
-graph	=	write, draw, describe
-logy	=	study or science of

polytheism
theology
monotheism
monotone
monologue
polygraph

6. Which word means belief in only one God?

_____

7. Which word describes a manner of speaking or singing without a change of pitch?

_____

8. Which word means "the study of religion and religious belief"?

_____

9. Which word means "belief in more than one god"?

_____

10. What is another name for a lie detector?

_____

Name _____

COMPREHENSION
Brainstorming

DIRECTIONS With a writing partner, brainstorm a list of ideas of how to get rid of prejudice. Feel free to borrow ideas from Asfahani, but be sure to include some ideas of your own.

My brainstorming notes

Fact and Opinion

Now choose one of the ideas you and your partner came up with and explain it here:

My idea of how to get rid of prejudice: _____

_____

_____

_____

Why I think this idea is a good one: _____

_____

_____

_____

Any problems I see with the idea: _____

_____

_____

_____

Name _____

PREWRITING AND WRITING

DIRECTIONS Follow these steps to write an opinion paragraph.

STEP 1. WRITE AN ANECDOTE. An anecdote is a very brief story that helps you make a point. Write an anecdote about a time you saw someone being treated unfairly because of prejudice. Explain what happened in three sentences or less.

My anecdote about prejudice: _____

_____

_____

_____

STEP 2. WRITE AN OPINION STATEMENT. Next write your opinion statement. Use this formula:

A specific topic + a specific opinion = a good opinion statement.

my topic sentence: prejudice + (_____) =

STEP 3. GATHER FACTS. Now gather facts to support your opinion. These facts come from your own experiences and observations.

fact #1 _____

fact #2 _____

fact #3 _____

STEP 4. WRITE. Write your opinion paragraph. Open with your anecdote. Then give your opinion statement and support. End with a closing sentence that states your opinion statement in a slightly different way.

_____

_____

_____

_____

_____

_____

_____

_____

_____

_____

Name _____

ASSESSMENT

Multiple-Choice Test

DIRECTIONS On the blanks provided, write the letter of the best answer for each question.

_____ 1. When she is very young, how does Magdoline Asfahani feel about America?
- A. She is unhappy and wants to go home.
- B. She loves America.
- C. She is torn between like and dislike.
- D. She hasn't decided how she feels.

_____ 2. According to Asfahani, why do people discriminate against immigrants?
- A. Because they are jealous of them.
- B. Because they think immigrants are criminals.
- C. Because they are unlike the majority.
- D. none of the above

_____ 3. What is Asfahani's ethnic background?
- A. Latino
- B. Asian
- C. Middle Eastern
- D. African American

_____ 4. Why do Asfahani's classmates call her names after the TWA jet is hijacked?
- A. Her cousin was the hijacker.
- B. Her classmates think all Arabs are terrorists.
- C. She defended the hijacking in class.
- D. Her uncle was the pilot.

_____ 5. What do Asfahani's classmates say about Middle Easterners?
- A. They are uncivilized.
- B. They are anti-American.
- C. They are brutal.
- D. all of the above

_____ 6. What does Asfahani do after her classmates begin to tease her?
- A. She ignores them.
- B. She asks her mother for help.
- C. She tries to forget her heritage.
- D. She gets in fights after school.

_____ 7. When she is a teenager, how does Asfahani feel about her family heritage?
- A. ashamed
- B. excited
- C. proud
- D. curious

_____ 8. What causes Asfahani to become angry about the teasing and prejudice?
- A. Her mother explains what bigotry is.
- B. Her chemistry teacher makes a cruel joke.
- C. She meets another girl from the Middle East.
- D. none of the above

_____ 9. What does Asfahani's mother do when her son is teased?
- A. She yells at his classmates.
- B. She calls the principal.
- C. She tells him to ignore it.
- D. She visits his class to talk about her culture.

_____ 10. Now that she is an adult, how do you think Asfahani feels about America's treatment of immigrants?
- A. angry
- B. hopeful
- C. depressed
- D. scared

Short-Essay Test

What does Asfahani say we should do to end prejudice in the United States?

World War II—The Holocaust

Unit Background   **WORLD WAR II—THE HOLOCAUST** (pages 197–218)

The term *Holocaust* is used to describe the genocide of European Jews and others by the Nazis during World War II. The first concentration camps were instituted in the 1930s in Germany after the rise of Adolf Hitler, who wished to rid Germany of all Jews. The Allies liberated many concentration camps at the end of the war, and the first selection in this unit is a letter written from Austria by a United States soldier who witnessed the appalling conditions of the camp survivors.

The second selection is a poignant excerpt from an autobiography written by a Jewish woman who survived but whose family disappeared, presumably to be killed in a concentration camp.

Teaching the Introduction

The opening photographs depict the barbed wire that surrounded camps, people in camps, and camp survivors.

The Holocaust remains one of the darkest periods in recent history. Between 1933 and 1945 the Nazi government in Germany murdered millions of innocent people because of their race, religion, or beliefs. As the main targets of the Nazis, Jews suffered drastic losses. By the end of World War II in 1945, two out of every three European Jews had been killed.

1.

2.

1. Ask students what they know about the Holocaust in Europe and what questions they have.

2. Some students might have seen films depicting the Holocaust. If so, ask them to tell about these films.

Opening Activity

Some students might be interested in knowing about the efforts of people in Denmark, the Netherlands, and elsewhere to save Jews from destruction. If so, ask them to research this topic, either in books or on the Internet. Other students might research Anne Frank's diary and the play based on her diary. Alternatively, you might read parts of Anne's diary to the class.

A Soldier's Letter Home

STUDENT PAGES 198–205

Skills and Strategies Overview

THEME World War II—The Holocaust

READING LEVEL easy

VOCABULARY

◆ kilometers   ◆ pathetic   ◆ bawled   ◆ stunted   ◆ resistance

PREREADING K-W-L

RESPONSE mark, highlight, and question

COMPREHENSION directed reading

PREWRITING clustering

WRITING letter / subject-verb agreement

ASSESSMENT depth

BACKGROUND

The Nazis established concentration camps almost immediately after rising to power in 1933. By the early 1940s, twenty-two camps had been created, including the death camps Auschwitz-Birkenau, Lubin-Majdanek, Sobibór, Treblinka, and Semlin. All told, German Nazis imprisoned seven to eight million people in the camps, most of whom were European Jews.

In the spring of 1945, Allied troops invaded Germany and began the slow process of liberating the camps. The men and women who were a part of the liberation effort were horrified by what they found. Many of the twenty-two camps were littered with thousands of unburied dead. In other camps, there were mass grave sites that extended for miles. Camp survivors, like those described in "A Soldier's Letter Home," were for the most part severely debilitated by disease and hunger.

UNIT THEME The Holocaust is one of the world's most shameful memories. Reading about these horrors can help students understand why such bigotry and hatred must never occur again.

GRAPHIC ORGANIZER Students might construct a web that answers these five questions.

WHO?
Delbert Cooper
His wife, Joan
thousands of
concentration camp
prisoners

WHAT?
Delbert and fellow soldiers
liberate a concentration
camp

WHY?
The war ended; the
Nazi regime was
dismantled. Allied
troops moved in to help
prisoners.

"A Soldier's Letter Home"

WHEN?
5/6/45

WHERE?
Delbert writes from Austria; the
camp he liberated may have been
in Poland or Germany.

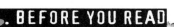

BEFORE YOU READ

Read the introduction to the theme on page 197 and the introduction to the lesson on page 198 with students. Explain that students will have a chance to record what they know about the Holocaust on a **K-W-L** chart.

Motivation Strategy

ENGAGING STUDENTS Tell students that the letter they are about to read was written by an American soldier two days before the Allies announced the surrender of German forces. Begin the lesson by asking students what they know about World War II and the Holocaust. Have students share "eyewitness stories" they've heard from relatives and friends. Students may also have seen television programs or movies about World War II or the Holocaust. These stories will help prepare students for the tone and subject matter of "A Soldier's Letter Home."

Vocabulary Building

Help students use **context clues** as they read to figure out the meanings of key vocabulary words for this lesson: *kilometers, pathetic, bawled, stunted,* and *resistance.* The footnotes define these words for students. Model using context and then checking your ideas against the footnote: "I don't know the word *bawled.* However, I can infer that the word must mean 'crying' because in a nearby sentence, it says that the inmates 'cry like a baby.' I can check the footnote to see if my guess is correct."

For additional practice, see the **Vocabulary** blackline master, page 246.

STRATEGY LESSON: ROOTS As students read, have them look for root words that are familiar. Knowing the meaning of the root can help them figure out the meaning of the word. For example, students might learn the root of these words: <u>terr</u>itory, and <u>prim</u>itive (terra = earth; prim = first).

For additional practice with this strategy, see the **Vocabulary** blackline master, page 246.

Prereading Strategies

Since Cooper's description of the concentration camp he helped liberate is so vivid and disturbing, you'll want to make sure that your students have a good working knowledge of what went on in the camps and why the Nazis built them. The **K-W-L** chart on page 198 can help you determine the breadth of students' knowledge. For the W column, direct the class to focus on what they want to learn about the liberation of the camps, as that is the topic of Cooper's letter.

Spanish-Speaking Students

Esta selección es la carta verdadera de un soldado norteamericano durante la Segunda Guerra Mundial. Acaba de liberar un campo de muerte donde miles de personas, la mayoría de las cuales son judías, fueron matadas o gravemente maltratadas por los Nazis. El soldado se siente muchas emociones al ver a las víctimas. Su carta expresa con claridad especial su simpatía e ira.

READ

As they are reading, students might think of **questions** they'd like to ask about the contents of the letter or events that Cooper alludes to briefly. Direct them to write their questions for Cooper, you, another classmate, or even themselves in the **Response Notes**. Explain how important it is to make note of their questions right away, so that they don't lose track of what they want to ask. When they've finished reading, ask for volunteers to read their questions aloud. Work as a class to find answers.

Response Strategy

REACT AND CONNECT You might also want to invite students to react and connect to the letter as they are reading. Many of your students will want to express their dismay at the scenes Cooper describes. Encourage them to jot down in the **Response Notes** whatever comes to mind. If they're angry, they should say so. If they're sad, they should make a note of that. These "first-pass" comments are often the most genuine reactions a reader can have to a text.

Comprehension Strategies

Directed reading can help reluctant or low-level readers better understand what they are reading. In a directed reading, the teacher or another student reads aloud while the class follows along in the book. The reader stops occasionally and poses questions meant to clarify the action. Even the simplest questions such as "What's happening here?" can help increase students' comprehension. Directed reading questions can also be used to gauge students' responses to the text. Questions such as "How does this passage make you feel?" will show students that their ideas and emotions are an important part of the reading process.

DOUBLE-ENTRY JOURNAL Since "A Soldier's Letter Home" is sure to prompt complex emotional responses, you might want to ask students to stop halfway through the reading in order to complete a double-entry journal. Quotations that will work well include these:

• "You could stand right in front of them & wave your arms for them to move over & they would just stand there, look right in your face and cry like a baby."

• "While we were standing outside the truck, any number of them came up & touched us, as if they couldn't believe we were actually there."

For additional practice, see the **Comprehension** blackline master on page 247.

Discussion Questions

COMPREHENSION 1. Why does Delbert Cooper go to the concentration camp? *(He is bringing food.)*

2. What do the prisoners do when they see Cooper and the other soldiers? *(They mob the soldiers and their truck.)*

3. Why does one inmate give Cooper his yellow star? *(because he is so grateful to Cooper for his kindness and humanity)*

CRITICAL THINKING 4. Why doesn't Cooper shoot the SS man? *(Answers will vary. Ask students to support what they say with quotations from the text.)*

5. Why does Cooper want to tell the world what he saw? *(Direct students to reread the final two paragraphs of Cooper's letter. This will help them focus on Cooper's "wish.")*

Literary Skill

CHRONOLOGICAL ORDER You might take a moment to discuss chronological order and its impact on a narrative. Help the class see the advantages of telling a story in chronological order. Explain that most writers of narratives use chronological order because it allows them to build naturally toward the climax that "opened their eyes" or changed their lives. If you like, ask students to skim the text, searching for transitional words, such as *yesterday, so, finally,* and *then,* or time-order phrases that Cooper uses as he retells the sequence of events.

III. GATHER YOUR THOUGHTS

Before they begin the prewriting activities, remind students to return to their **K-W-L** charts on page 198. Then have them create a set of **clusters** that explore Nazi concentration camps. Clustering is an excellent prewriting strategy because it can help students see connections between events and ideas. Students' clusters on page 203 might show a strong link between how the Allied soldiers were feeling and how the camp inmates were feeling. Both Allied soldiers and the inmates were horrified by what was happening. Both felt helpless in the face of so much agony. And yet, both groups of people were able to rise above their own anguish in order to unload the barrels and get food and supplies to the hungry.

Prewriting Strategies

TOPIC SENTENCES In Part IV, students are asked to write a letter to Cooper explaining their reaction to the story he tells. As an additional prewriting activity, you might want to spend some time helping students write topic sentences for their letters.

For more practice, see the **Prewriting and Writing** blackline master on page 248.

IV. WRITE

Remind students of the purpose for their letters. They will be writing to Cooper in order to say how his letter made them feel. After students have written a first draft, point out the **Writers' Checklist** and explain how it can help them during the revision process.

WRITING RUBRIC Use the writing rubric to help students focus on the assignment requirements and for help with a quick assessment of their writing.

In their letters to Cooper, do students

- open with a topic sentence that explains the purpose of the letter?
- respond to Cooper's wish that all Americans could be standing in his shoes?
- discuss their reaction to Cooper's experiences?
- stay focused on what Cooper discusses in *his* letter?

Grammar, Usage, and Mechanics

You might also take this opportunity to introduce the mini-lesson on subject-verb agreement. Help students "hear" problems with agreement. Read these sentences aloud. Ask for suggestions on how to fix them.

Incorrect: I sees a bunch of people standing around. They is hungry-looking and very weak. I hands out some food and motions for them to move away from the jeep.

Correct: I <u>see</u> a bunch of people standing around. They <u>are</u> hungry-looking and very weak. I <u>hand</u> out some food and <u>motion</u> for them to move away from the jeep.

V. WRAP-UP

To measure the **depth** of students' understanding, take a moment at the end of the lesson for students to reflect using the **Readers' Checklist**. Its intent is to help students decide how they feel about Cooper's writing. After they've looked at the checklist, students should be directed to respond to the question on page 205.

Assessment

For a comprehension check, ask students to complete the **Assessment** blackline master on page 249.

Name _____

VOCABULARY

Words from the Selection

DIRECTIONS Answer these questions that use words from the selection. Then write the meaning of the underlined words on the lines.

1. Is a <u>kilometer</u> longer or shorter than a mile?

_____

2. If I <u>bawled</u> at the sight of the children, does it mean that I laughed or cried?

_____

3. If her growth has been <u>stunted</u>, has it been slowed down or accelerated?

_____

4. If your dog shows <u>resistance</u> to going out, is he opposed to leaving or anxious to leave?

_____

5. If something is <u>pathetic</u>, is it sad or cheerful?

_____

Strategy Lesson: Prefixes and Roots

DIRECTIONS Study the Latin prefixes and the root word in the left–hand box. Then answer each question below by choosing the correct word from the right-hand box and writing it in the blank. You will not use one word.

terra = **earth** extra- = **outside, beyond** sub- = **under, beneath**	**subterranean** **extraterrestrial** **inter** **terrier** **terrace** **territory**

6. What is the word that means someone or something outside of earth?

_____

7. What word means "flat, raised land with sloping sides"?

_____

8. What word describes an underground place?

_____

9. What is the word for land or region?

_____

10. What word means "to bury"?

_____

Name _____

COMPREHENSION
Reciprocal Reading

DIRECTIONS With a partner, work through the answers to these questions.

CLARIFY How does Delbert Cooper feel as he looks at the prisoners? How do they feel as they look at him?

_____
_____
_____

PREDICT When Delbert Cooper returns home, do you think he will tell everyone about his experiences at the camp, or do you think he will keep quiet? Explain your prediction.

_____
_____
_____

QUESTION What question or questions are you left with when you hear about Nazi concentration camps?

_____
_____
_____

SUMMARIZE Tell what happens in "A Soldier's Letter Home." What makes Cooper's letter so moving?

_____
_____
_____
_____

Name _____

PREWRITING AND WRITING
Writing a Letter

DIRECTIONS **STEP 1.** **CHOOSE A RECIPIENT.** Your first step is to decide who will receive your letter; in this case you'll be writing to Delbert Cooper.

My recipient: _____

STEP 2. **KNOW YOUR PURPOSE.** Your next step is to be sure you know why you're writing the letter. Are you writing to ask a question? Are you writing to complain or give a compliment? Are you writing to react to something you heard or saw?

Purpose of my letter: _____

_____

STEP 3. **WRITE A TOPIC SENTENCE.** The topic sentence for a letter follows this same formula:

A specific topic + how you feel about the topic = your topic sentence.

My topic sentence: _____

_____

STEP 4. **LIST SUPPORT.** Plan how you will support your topic sentence. List three or four details here. Make sure each detail is clear and specific.

detail #1 _____

detail #2 _____

detail #3 _____

detail #4 _____

STEP 5. **WRITE A CONCLUSION.** Use your conclusion to say what you'd like the recipient to do. If you're writing to an author, for example, you might say that you want him or her to write a new book about a topic that interests you.

I'd like my recipient to _____ because _____

_____

STEP 6. **WRITE YOUR LETTER.** Use another piece of paper or the writing lines on page 204.

Name _____

ASSESSMENT

Multiple-Choice Test

DIRECTIONS On the blanks provided, write the letter of the best answer for each question.

_____ 1. Why does Delbert Cooper go to the concentration camp?
   A. to see what it is like   C. to take pictures for a newspaper
   B. to deliver food   D. to evacuate the prisoners

_____ 2. Who are the people in the camp?
   A. politicians   C. criminals
   B. captured soldiers   D. Jews

_____ 3. Where is Cooper writing from?
   A. Austria   C. Poland
   B. Germany   D. Russia

_____ 4. To whom is Delbert Cooper writing his letter?
   A. his commanding officer   C. his brother, John
   B. his wife, Joan   D. his mother

_____ 5. How does Delbert Cooper feel about what he sees?
   A. horrified   C. angry
   B. shocked   D. all of the above

_____ 6. What happens when Delbert Cooper arrives at the camp?
   A. The prisoners run away.   C. He is mobbed by prisoners.
   B. He fights with the guards.   D. none of the above

_____ 7. What do the prisoners want right away?
   A. to talk to the soldiers   C. food
   B. clothing   D. guns to fight the Germans

_____ 8. One prisoner gives Delbert Cooper a gift. What is it?
   A. his yellow star   C. jewelry
   B. an egg   D. a cigarette

_____ 9. What does Delbert Cooper do to make sure the prisoners will be okay?
   A. He sets up a camp hospital.   C. He gives them a trainload of supplies.
   B. He gives them money.   D. He gives them guns to fight with.

_____ 10. Why does Delbert Cooper consider killing the SS man he captured?
   A. for fun   C. He thought the SS man might escape.
   B. to get revenge for the prisoners D. He was ordered to kill the SS man.

Short-Essay Test

What are your feelings about Delbert Cooper?

STUDENT PAGES 206–218

Skills and Strategies Overview

THEME	World War II—The Holocaust
READING LEVEL	average
VOCABULARY	◇ embraced ◇ reluctantly ◇ security ◇ enclosure ◇ inscription
PREREADING	picture walk
RESPONSE	predict / clarify
COMPREHENSION	prediction
PREWRITING	brainstorm
WRITING	journal entry / confusing word pairs
ASSESSMENT	style

BACKGROUND

Although they lacked weapons and were weakened by disease and starvation, the Jews fiercely resisted the Nazis during World War II. More than sixty thousand joined underground resistance efforts. Those who did not go underground participated in huge ghetto uprisings that infuriated Hitler and his followers. Nevertheless, by the time the war ended in 1945, two-thirds of Europe's Jews had been murdered.

UNIT THEME Reading about the horrors of the Holocaust can help students understand how one group's bigotry and hatred can have a profound effect on the entire world.

GRAPHIC ORGANIZER Students might benefit by preparing an organizer showing a sequence of events.

Sequence of Events: "Good-bye"

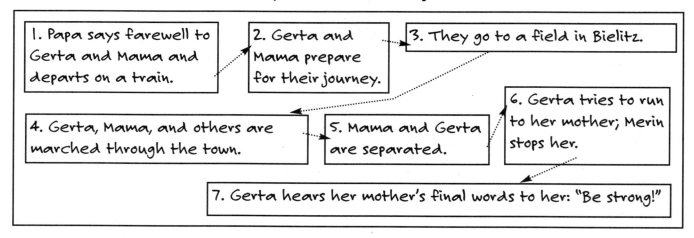

1. Papa says farewell to Gerta and Mama and departs on a train.
2. Gerta and Mama prepare for their journey.
3. They go to a field in Bielitz.
4. Gerta, Mama, and others are marched through the town.
5. Mama and Gerta are separated.
6. Gerta tries to run to her mother; Merin stops her.
7. Gerta hears her mother's final words to her: "Be strong!"

BIBLIOGRAPHY Students might want to read more about the Holocaust. Suggest they look at a combination of fiction and nonfiction. For example, you might have them read one or more of these books:

The Night Crossing by Karen Ackerman (easy—novel)
Anna Is Still Here by Ida Vos (average—memoir)
I Am a Star by Inge Aurerbacher (average—memoir)
The Diary of Anne Frank by Anne Frank (average—diary)
Explaining Hitler by Ron Rosenbaum (challenging—expository nonfiction)
A Mengele Experiment by Gene Church (challenging—memoir)

BEFORE YOU READ

Read the introduction to the lesson on page 206. Explain that "Good-bye" is an excerpt from Gerta Weismann Klein's memoir of the Holocaust, *All But My Life*. Then allow students plenty of time to do a **picture walk** of the selection. The comments they make in response to their picture walks may come in handy later during the lesson.

Motivation Strategy

Explain that "Good-bye" is the true story of a young Jewish girl who has to say good-bye forever to her father and mother. Ask students to imagine how she must have felt when she was saying farewell. What do they think would be a comfort to a person facing such an enormous amount of grief?

ENGAGING STUDENTS Ask whether anyone in the class has visited or heard about the Holocaust Memorial Museum in Washington D.C., which opened in 1993, or heard or read about the Holocaust victims fund established in Switzerland. If so, have them tell about what they know.

Vocabulary Building

Remind the class that learning the synonym of a word is sometimes quicker and easier than learning the full definition. Show students the five key vocabulary words for this lesson: *embraced, reluctantly, security, enclosure,* and *inscription*. Ask for volunteers to suggest synonyms for each word. If they need help, have them consult a dictionary or a thesaurus. For additional practice, see the **Vocabulary** blackline master on page 254.

STRATEGY LESSON: LATIN ROOTS Many words come from the Latin *ducem* (leader) or *ducere* (to lead, bring). For example, a *conductor* (page 208) is someone who leads or directs. Other words from the same roots include *deduct, induct, induction,* and *reduce*. Ask students to guess the purpose of a heating *duct*. Then ask what they would be doing if they were trying to *induce* (to lead or move by persuasion) a cat to come down from a tree.

For additional practice, see the **Vocabulary** blackline master, page 254.

Prereading Strategies

As a prereading warm-up, students are asked to do a **picture walk** through the selection. Remind students that during a picture walk, the reader looks at all art, photographs, and captions. These elements of a story can provide valuable clues about the topic of the piece. When they've finished their picture walks, students should make predictions about the selections. They should also note how the pictures made them feel. When they've finished Klein's memoir, students might return to the pictures and explain the connections they see between the photographs and the narrative.

ANTICIPATION GUIDE As an alternate or additional prereading strategy, you might have students complete an anticipation guide. Give students a series of statements about the topic and the memoir. (For example: Some people are too young to die.) Ask them whether or not they agree with the statements. After they've finished reading the selection, they can return to the statements and see if they'd like to change any of their answers. This reading strategy shows students that they are indeed affected by what they read. The articles and stories they read in school and at home can give them new ideas and help refine the ideas they already have.

Spanish-Speaking Students

Pocas personas han sobrevivido la pena que Gerta Weismann Klein ha experimentado. Ella describe su historia tumultuosa en "Adiós," una parte de su autobiografía, *All But My Life*. Viviendo en el ghetto judío durante la Segunda Guerra Mundial, Weismann Klein presenció y sufrió abusos e humillación por los Nazis. En uno de los momentos más conmovedores de la historia, describe el despido de su padre, que fue trasladado por los Nazis a un un campo de muerte. Describe también la inmensa dificultad que le costó en no desobedecer a los Nazis, que decidieron cada día si ella viviría o moriría.

II. READ

The directions on page 207 ask students to **clarify** elements of the memoir that seem confusing or important. Their comments can help them keep track of the sequence of events Klein describes. Encourage them to make a note each time the scene changes and each time Klein describes her many conflicting feelings.

Response Strategy

GRAPHIC ORGANIZER As an additional response strategy, ask students to make a graphic organizer like the one on the first page of this lesson.

Comprehension Strategies

At several points in the story, students are asked to **stop and predict** what they think will happen next. Making predictions can help readers feel more directly involved in a selection. Making predictions can also help readers make inferential-type responses to a text.

GRAPHIC ORGANIZER As an additional prewriting strategy, ask students to create a Venn diagram in which they compare Klein's World War II feelings and experiences to Delbert Cooper's feelings and experiences during the same war (pages 198–205). Remind students before they begin that Klein and Cooper both offer first-hand accounts of the atrocities of the Holocaust. What do the two writers have in common? Do they share the same views about the Holocaust? What differences do students see? Is one braver than the other? Is one more compassionate than the other?

For additional practice, see the **Comprehension** blackline master on page 255.

Discussion Questions

COMPREHENSION 1. Where is Gerta's father going on the train? *(to a concentration camp)*

2. Does Gerta's mother survive the war? *(no)*

3. Why does Merin throw Gerta back onto the truck? *(He says she is too young to die.)*

CRITICAL THINKING 4. Why does Gerta scream at Merin after he saves her life? *(Answers will vary. Encourage students to reread the passage on page 215 that ends with Gerta screaming in anguish for her mother. Then have them make inferences about Gerta's behavior.)*

5. What three words would you use to describe Gerta Weismann Klein? *(Encourage students to support what they say with evidence from the selection.)*

Literary Skill

INFERENCE Take this opportunity to discuss making inferences or drawing reasonable conclusions about an author or a happening. For example, ask students what they can infer about the title of the book from which this excerpt was taken (*All But My Life*). They might infer that everything was taken from the author except her life. They might also make inferences about the identity of Arthur and about the reason for sewing jewels into garments. Drawing reasonable conclusions can help students better understand and discuss the meaning of a literary work.

GATHER YOUR THOUGHTS

The activities on page 216 are designed to help students reflect on Gerta Weismann Klein: what she's like, how others feel about her, why she acts the way she does, and so on. In the first **graphic organizer**, students should list what they know and what they can infer about Gerta. Ask them to pay special attention to the box on the bottom left: "What Gerta thinks." They'll use their notes from this box to help them write a journal entry for Gerta in Part IV.

Prewriting Strategies

GRAPHIC ORGANIZER Gerta undergoes some profound changes over the course of the story. Have students complete the chart on page 216. Then have them work on a graphic organizer like the one at the beginning of this lesson.

For more practice, see the **Prewriting** blackline master on page 256.

IV. WRITE

Set aside plenty of time for students to write their **journal entries**. Most writers will benefit from feeling unpressured by time. When they've finished, ask students to review what they've written, keeping the items on the **Writers' Checklist** in mind as they revise.

WRITING RUBRIC Consider using the questions on the writing rubric to help you with a quick assessment of students' writing.

In their journal entries, do students

• explore Gerta's thoughts/feelings about the day she said her good-byes?

• write in the first person, as if they are Gerta?

• stay focused on the topic at hand?

Grammar, Usage, and Mechanics

You might also want to offer a brief mini-lesson on usage problems. Review with students when to use *they're/their* and *it's/its*. Remind them that a computer spell-check program will not catch these types of errors.

Incorrect: Its time to board they're train.

Correct: <u>It's</u> time to board <u>their</u> train.

V. WRAP-UP

Before you leave this lesson, ask students to comment on Klein's writing **style**. What strengths does she have as a writer? Does she have any weaknesses? Students will appreciate the chance to comment on a published writer's work.

Assessment

For a comprehension check, ask students to complete the **Assessment** blackline master on page 257.

Name _____

VOCABULARY

Words from the Selection

DIRECTIONS Read each word in column A. Find the word in Column B that most closely matches the word in A. Draw a line between the two.

Column A	Column B
1. enclosure	hugged
2. reluctantly	unwillingly
3. security	safety
4. inscription	letters or writing on something
5. embraced	fenced area

Strategy Lesson: Latin Roots

DIRECTIONS Study the Latin roots and their meanings. Then answer each question below by choosing the correct word from the right-hand box and writing it in the blank.

ducem = leader	introduced
ducere = to lead, bring	reproduce
	inducement
	produce
	conductor

6. Did everyone rise as the _____ walked to the front of the orchestra?

7. Were farmers able to _____ more corn this year than they did last year?

8. Can you _____ this photograph quickly?

9. Has the coach _____ all the players at the banquet?

10. Would a cup of cocoa be an _____ for you to stay?

Name _____

COMPREHENSION
Graphic Organizer

Directions Use this diagram to show how Gerta changes from the beginning of "Good-bye" to the end. Write words that describe her character at the beginning. Then write words that show how she has changed. List the events that brought about the change.

Write 3 events that cause her to change.

1. Gerta says good-bye to her father

2. _____

3. _____

confused _____ _____ _____   _____ _____ _____
BEGINNING OF "GOOD-BYE"   **END OF "GOOD-BYE"**

Write 3 or more descriptive words

Name _____

PREWRITING
Writing a Journal Entry

DIRECTIONS Before you can write a journal entry for a character, you need to know how that character feels.

STEP 1. CREATE A WEB. Use this web to show Gerta's many different emotions in "Good-bye." Write as many descriptive words as you can.

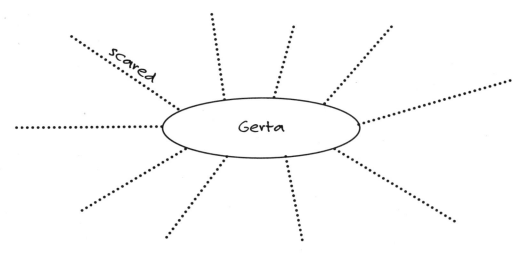

STEP 2. WRITE A TOPIC SENTENCE. Write a topic sentence for your journal entry.

Today I said good-bye to my father and mother. I feel so

_____

STEP 3. LIST DETAILS. Identify the events of the day that were particularly hard for Gerta.

detail #1 _____

detail #2 _____

detail #3 _____

Name _____

ASSESSMENT

Multiple-Choice Test

DIRECTIONS On the blanks provided, write the letter of the item that best completes each statement or answers each question.

_____ 1. Gerta's father helps save her life by telling her to . . .
   A. follow orders.
   B. sew jewels into her coat.
   C. stay close to her mother.
   D. wear her ski shoes.

_____ 2. What do you think Gerta's father means when he says "My child"?
   A. Be strong.
   B. Good-bye.
   C. Take care of your mother.
   D. all of the above

_____ 3. The yellow star means that the person wearing it is . . .
   A. a Russian.
   B. a prisoner.
   C. a Jew.
   D. a worker.

_____ 4. What does Gerta wish she had done on her last night at home?
   A. prayed
   B. seen her friends
   C. shown more love for her mother
   D. taken a final walk through town

_____ 5. What does Gerta's mother do every Monday?
   A. cleans
   B. cooks
   C. fasts
   D. shops

_____ 6. What do you think happens to the old and sick people who are put on the truck?
   A. They are murdered.
   B. They are taken to another ghetto.
   C. They are taken to a hospital.
   D. They are put to work.

_____ 7. What surprises Gerta on her final march through town?
   A. how ill she feels
   B. how upset the townspeople seem
   C. how normal life is for most people
   D. none of the above

_____ 8. What does Klein feel for Merin?
   A. respect
   B. pity
   C. hatred
   D. nothing

_____ 9. What do you think happens to Gerta's mother?
   A. She is killed.
   B. She retires.
   C. She remarries.
   D. She escapes.

_____ 10. How does Merin help save Gerta?
   A. He throws her back onto the truck.
   B. He lets her go to her mother.
   C. He shows her how to escape.
   D. He gives her some money.

Short-Essay Test

Klein asks why the Jews didn't resist and concludes that it was because of their faith in humanity. What does this mean?

Kurt Vonnegut

Unit Background **KURT VONNEGUT** (pages 219–238)

Born in Indianapolis, Indiana, in 1922, Kurt Vonnegut frequently writes about the influence of technology. He majored in biochemistry at Cornell University and enlisted in the army during World War II. In 1944 he was captured during the Battle of the Bulge and was a prisoner of war in Dresden. His many works, including *Cat's Cradle* (1963), *Welcome to the Monkey House* (1968), *Slaughterhouse Five: Or, The Children's Crusade* (1969), *Happy Birthday, Wanda June* (a 1970 play), *Breakfast of Champions* (1973), *Deadeye Dick* (1982), *Hocus Pocus* (1990), and others have earned him a devoted following.

In the two selections in this chapter, Vonnegut explores a future world in which all people are made equal by government decree and the life of a boy who has been rejected by almost everyone.

Teaching the Introduction

The introductory page depicts Adolph Hitler at upper-right (responsible in part for Vonnegut's World War II experiences), Vonnegut himself, and someone who just might be a product of a world in which people with extraordinary talents are made "average."

Kurt Vonnegut

1.

2.

Kurt Vonnegut (1922–) has written a variety of novels, plays, essays, and short stories. Many of his best-known works, including the novel *Slaughterhouse-Five* and the short stories in *Welcome to the Monkey House*, blend science fiction and fantasy and mix serious themes with humor.

KURT VONNEGUT WELCOME TO THE MONKEY HOUSE

219

1. Ask students how they would feel if the talents they possess were reduced in some way by the government so that others would not feel inferior. Ask them to suppose, for example, that if they had extraordinary athletic skills, they were forced to curtail them so that those with lesser skills would not feel bad.

2. Ask students to discuss what makes people feel hostile to the world around them. Is it because of past experience, such as rejection by family or friends, or something else?

Opening Activity

Ask students to draw a picture of themselves facing some aspect of today's world that they can't understand.

Harrison Bergeron

Skills and Strategies Overview

THEME	Kurt Vonnegut
READING LEVEL	challenging
VOCABULARY	◇ clammy ◇ ballerinas ◇ burdened ◇ winced ◇ envious
PREREADING	word web
RESPONSE	visualize / react and connect
COMPREHENSION	double-entry journal
PREWRITING	main idea and details
WRITING	three-paragraph essay / punctuating titles
ASSESSMENT	enjoyment

BACKGROUND

The story "Harrison Bergeron" first appeared in Kurt Vonnegut's 1961 book *Welcome to the Monkey House*. (For biographical information on Vonnegut, see page 258 of this book.) The selection students will read on pages 220–224 is an excerpt from this short story. Like many of his stories, "Harrison Bergeron" is darkly comic. In it, Vonnegut explores one of his favorite themes: dehumanization in a technological society.

If students like this excerpt from "Harrison Bergeron," encourage them to finish reading the story on their own. In the second half of the story, Hazel and George's son, Harrison, takes over the government television station and proclaims himself emperor of the world. He strips himself of his handicaps and encourages the most beautiful ballerina to do the same. For a brief while, they dance together, and the awe-inspiring sight overwhelms those who are watching. Eventually the Handicapper General appears on stage with Harrison and the ballerina and kills them both.

UNIT THEME Kurt Vonnegut explores the thematic question: What will happen to our society if we allow technology to dictate what we can and cannot do?

GRAPHIC ORGANIZER You might have students construct a plot line for this excerpt.

Plot Line: "Harrison Bergeron"

- Hazel suggests George remove his weighted handicap. (Rising Action)
- George insists that he and Hazel never want to see the "Dark Ages" again. (Climax)
- Hazel ponders George's view of society. (Falling Action)
- George and Hazel sit in front of the T.V. (Exposition)
- George and Hazel drop the subject. (Resolution)

BEFORE YOU READ

Read the lesson opener on page 219 with students. Then ask a volunteer to read aloud the introduction on page 220. Use the motivation strategies below to help students consider what they already know about the genre of science fiction. Then have students complete a **word web** for the word *equality*, which is thematically important to the story.

Motivation Strategy

To get your prereading discussion moving, have students think about stories they've read and movies they've seen in which technology "runs amuck." What happens and why?

ENGAGING STUDENTS To further engage students, ask what they would think about a society in which everyone is equal. Ask students to say what they think this world might be like.

Vocabulary Building

The vocabulary in "Harrison Bergeron" might be challenging for some students. Show a list of the key vocabulary words for the lesson: *clammy, ballerinas, burdened, winced,* and *envious*. Remind students that they should use **context clues** as they read so they don't have to constantly interrupt their reading to check definitions. Model using context clues by reading a passage aloud and talking your way through a difficult word. (For example, show students how to use context clues to define *vigilance* in paragraph 1.)

For additional practice, see the **Vocabulary** blackline master, page 264.

STRATEGY LESSON: PREFIXES As an additional vocabulary strategy, you might teach a lesson on prefixes. Remind students that prefixes are "word parts" that come before the root word. Show students a list of words from the selection that contain prefixes. (For example: *transmitter, unfair, unceasing, abnormal,* and *uncertainly*.) Explain what each of the prefixes means.

For additional practice with this strategy, see the **Vocabulary** blackline master on page 264.

Prereading Strategies

An excellent prereading strategy for a selection with challenging vocabulary is a **word web**. Have students list people, documents, ideas, examples, and images that come to mind when they hear the word and write them on page 220. With a word web, students learn to create their own definitions for a word that is important to the selection.

PICTURE WALK Students might enjoy doing a picture walk. Ask each student to predict what the story is about based on what they see in the art. List their predictions on the board. At a couple of points during their reading, interrupt them to ask: "Do you still think the story is about _____?" When they've finished reading, ask for volunteers to explain the mood that is created by the art and how it relates to the excerpt from "Harrison Bergeron."

Spanish-Speaking Students

Es el año 2081 y toda la gente de los Estados Unidos es igual. Los miembros de la sociedad son controlados psicológicamente y físicamente por los gobernadores, sin la habilidad de ejercer su individualidad, ni de hacer nada fuera de lo normal. Este es la imagen del futuro que autor Kurt Vonnegut crea en "Harrison Bergeron." El cuento corto se enfoca en las vidas de Hazel y George, una pareja que anhela deviar de las reglas y pensar por sí mismos.

READ

Vonnegut creates some fascinating word pictures in his story. Students should try to **visualize** the people and places he describes. Their mental pictures will help them better understand and enjoy the selection. Have students make quick sketches of what they "see" in the **Response Notes**. They might return to their sketches later, when it is time to write an essay about the selection.

Response Strategy

GRAPHIC ORGANIZER As an alternate response strategy, have students construct a plot line. See the first page of this lesson.

Comprehension Strategies

Double-entry journals give students the chance to share their opinions and reactions about a selection. Instead of asking students to react to an entire story (which can be difficult to do), a double-entry journal has students share their thoughts and feelings about a couple of important lines or quotations. Their reactions to individual quotes can give you an idea of how they feel about the selection as a whole, and whether they're having trouble understanding what the text means.

RETELLING As an alternate prereading strategy, ask students to retell a few different parts of the story. Whole-class retellings can benefit everyone, not just those in need of extra help. If a reader listens to a retelling, he or she might hear a word or phrase that provokes a whole new idea about the selection. Encourage students to take notes during the retelling just as they do when they are listening to a story read aloud.

For additional practice, see the **Comprehension** blackline master on page 265.

Discussion Questions

COMPREHENSION 1. Who is Harrison? *(He is Hazel and George's fourteen-year-old son.)*

2. What is the Handicapper General's job? *(She ensures the equality of all people in the year 2081.)*

3. Why does George wear a transmitter on his ear? *(He wears it to "handicap" him, so that he can't think too long about a particular subject or take "unfair advantage" of his brain.)*

CRITICAL THINKING 4. According to the story, what is the purpose of the 211th, 212th, and 213th Amendments to the Constitution? *(These amendments guarantee the equality of all people.)*

5. What does "equality" mean in the year 2081? *(No one is better than anyone else.)*

Literary Skills

SIMILE This excerpt from "Harrison Bergeron" presents an excellent opportunity to discuss simile. Vonnegut's similes bring a freshness and conciseness to his descriptions. For example, on page 221, Vonnegut says that George's thoughts "fled in panic, like bandits from a burglar alarm." Later, he compares the sound in George's head to a "twenty-one-gun salute." Notice the violence of these images. Vonnegut uses simile, metaphor, and other types of figurative language to give readers a strong sense of the violent nature of this society.

IRONY You might also point out to students that Vonnegut uses a great deal of irony in his story. In general, the irony is meant to mock our society's tendency to consider intelligence, beauty, and excellence elitist or unfair. For this reason, George, who is of superior intelligence, is handicapped so that he never has time to process a decent thought. Hazel, who is of average intelligence, wears no handicaps at all. She is, in fact, rewarded for her mediocrity.

III. GATHER YOUR THOUGHTS

Because this excerpt from "Harrison Bergeron" is somewhat complex, you might need to help students write their **main idea statements**. Remind students that the main idea is the point the author is making. Sometimes the author will state the main idea. More often, the author expects readers to make inferences about the main idea.

Prewriting Strategies

GATHERING DETAILS You might ask a series of questions that can lead students to examine the details in the writing. For example: "What is life like in the year 2081?" and "What type of people are 'handicapped' in this society? Why? What is the effect of this 'handicapping'?" Help students see that in the society Vonnegut depicts, there can be no creativity, new ideas, or true excellence. Society is, in effect, stagnant.

For more practice, see the **Prewriting and Writing** blackline master on page 266.

IV. WRITE

Some of your students might be intimidated at the thought of writing a **three-paragraph essay.** Show them, however, that a three-paragraph essay follows a specific and simple plan: paragraph 1: introduction; paragraph 2: supporting details; and paragraph 3: conclusion.

WRITING RUBRIC Use the writing rubric to keep students focused on the assignment and to help with a quick assessment of their writing.

Do students' essays

- contain an introduction, body, and conclusion?

- open with a topic sentence and close with a concluding sentence?

- stay focused on the topic of equality in "Harrison Bergeron"?

Grammar, Usage, and Mechanics

When students have finished writing, have them revise using the **Writers' Checklist** as a guide. At this point you might want to teach a brief mini-lesson on the proper form for titles of books, magazines, poems, and so on. Remind students that chapter titles and titles of short stories, poems, and articles all require quotation marks, while book, film, magazine, and newspaper titles are underlined or italicized. For example:

"Harrison Bergeron" is from the book *Welcome to the Monkey House.*

V. WRAP-UP

Take a moment to talk to students about whether or not they **enjoyed** the story. If they didn't like it, ask them to explain why. It's possible that they found it too difficult, and might benefit from a second reading done aloud. By the same token, ask students who did like the story to explain their opinions. Their comments will help you in planning future lessons.

Assessment

For a comprehension check, ask students to complete the **Assessment** blackline master on page 267.

Name _____

VOCABULARY

Words from the Selection

DIRECTIONS Answer these questions that use words from the selection. Explain your answers.

1. If a person is <u>burdened</u>, is he free or weighed down?

_____

2. If I've <u>winced</u>, am I reacting to pain or joy?

_____

3. When a person is <u>envious</u>, is he feeling disappointment or happiness?

_____

4. Is a <u>clammy</u> basement dry or wet?

_____

5. Do <u>ballerinas</u> dance or sing?

_____

Strategy Lesson: Prefixes and Roots

Read the definitions in the box. Then underline all the words in the sentence that have the roots *mittere* or *portare* or the prefix *trans-*.

mittere	=	**to send, let go**
portare	=	**to carry**
trans-	=	**across, over, through, or beyond**

(6) The transmitter was designed (7) to emit signals on the (8) transatlantic ship, which

usually (9) held exports or imports (10) being transferred to and from the harbor.

Name _____

COMPREHENSION

Double-entry Journal

DIRECTIONS Read these quotations from the story. Say how each makes you feel. What message is Vonnegut giving readers?

Double-entry Journal

QUOTATIONS	MY THOUGHTS AND FEELINGS
"Some things about living still weren't quite right, though."	
"Hazel had a perfectly average intelligence, which meant she couldn't think about anything except in short bursts. And George, while his intelligence was way above normal, had a little mental handicap radio in his ear."	
"'If I tried to get away with it . . . then other people'd get away with it—and pretty soon we'd be right back to the dark ages again, with everybody competing against everybody else.'"	

Directed Reading

DIRECTIONS Work with a partner to answer these questions about the story.

1. What handicaps does George have? Why does he have them?

_____

_____

2. What handicaps do the ballerinas have? Why do they have them?

_____

_____

3. Why is Hazel the only character without handicaps?

_____

_____

Name _____

PREWRITING AND WRITING

Writing a Topic Sentence and Details

DIRECTIONS Every paragraph you write must have a topic sentence. A topic sentence tells the topic of the paragraph and how you feel about the topic. (The topic sentence is a sentence that tells the main idea.) You can use this formula to help you write a topic sentence.

A specific topic + a specific feeling = a good topic sentence.

Now follow these steps to write a topic sentence and supporting details.

STEP 1. TOPIC SENTENCE. Write a topic sentence that tells about Vonnegut's view of equality in "Harrison Bergeron."

(Equality in 2081) + _____ = _____

(Vonnegut's view about equality) (your topic sentence)

STEP 2. GATHER DETAILS. Think of details or examples from the story that support your topic sentence. These details are "proof" that your topic sentence is correct.

detail #1 _____

_____

detail #2 _____

_____

detail #3 _____

_____

STEP 3. WRITE AN INTRODUCTION. Write the first paragraph of your essay here. Start by giving the story's title and the author's name. Then write your topic sentence.

_____

_____

_____

_____

_____

Name _____

ASSESSMENT

Multiple-Choice Test

DIRECTIONS On the blanks provided, write the letter of the item that best completes each statement or answers each question.

_____ 1. How are things different in the year 2081?
    A. There is no more government.
    B. Everyone is equal.
    C. No one follows the law.
    D. Everyone follows the law.

_____ 2. The 211th, 212th, and 213th Amendments state that no one will be . . .
    A. better looking than anyone else.
    B. stronger than anyone else.
    C. smarter than anyone else.
    D. all of the above

_____ 3. What is the job of the U.S. Handicapper General?
    A. She makes sure everyone is equal.
    B. She's in charge of the army.
    C. She provides advantages to women.
    D. all of the above

_____ 4. If you can think only in short bursts, Vonnegut says you have . . .
    A. average intelligence.
    B. above-average intelligence.
    C. below-average intelligence.
    D. genius capabilities.

_____ 5. Why does George wear a transmitter in his ear?
    A. It helps him get smarter.
    B. He listens to the ballet.
    C. He has above-average intelligence.
    D. He has below-average intelligence.

_____ 6. What kind of sounds does the radio transmitter send to George about every twenty seconds?
    A. classical music
    B. sharp noises
    C. sounds of the sea
    D. all of the above

_____ 7. How does Hazel feel about the sounds George gets to hear?
    A. She thinks they are bothersome.
    B. She thinks they are funny.
    C. She envies him a little.
    D. She is happy for him.

_____ 8. What noise would Hazel pick for the transmitter if she were Handicapper General?
    A. chimes
    B. car horns
    C. rain falling
    D. Harrison's voice

_____ 9. Why does George refuse to take off his handicap bag?
    A. It helps him to be smarter.
    B. He's proud to wear it.
    C. He doesn't trust Hazel.
    D. He fears he'll go to jail.

_____ 10. Why would competition be bad for Hazel?
    A. She might never win.
    B. She might never lose.
    C. She would learn from her mistakes.
    D. none of the above

Short-Essay Test

Why do you think George and Hazel's son, Harrison, was taken away?

The Kid Nobody Could Handle

Skills and Strategies Overview

THEME Kurt Vonnegut

READING LEVEL average

VOCABULARY ◆remorse ◆scar ◆expired ◆cadenza ◆blasphemy

PREREADING think-pair-and-share

RESPONSE question / predict

COMPREHENSION reciprocal reading

PREWRITING story map

WRITING story episode / end punctuation

ASSESSMENT ease

BACKGROUND

Kurt Vonnegut combines science fiction, social satire, and black comedy in his novels, which have been popular since the early 1960s. In much of his work, Vonnegut explores the horrors and ironies of 20th-century technology. His most famous novels, *Cat's Cradle* (1963) and *Slaughterhouse Five* (1969), earned him a huge reputation.

UNIT THEME Vonnegut explores the theme of human relationships when he describes a lonely foster boy who is in desperate need of a friend.

GRAPHIC ORGANIZER Students' story maps (page 236) might resemble this one.

TITLE: The Kid Nobody Could Handle

SETTING: place: small town   time: today

CHARACTERS: George Helmholtz—Music teacher   Bert Quinn—Jim's foster-father and
Jim Donnini—boy with a troubled past   Helmholtz's friend

PROBLEM: Jim cannot get along with others. He often lashes out and destroys other people's property.

MAJOR EVENTS: —Helmholtz gives Jim his trumpet as a trade for Jim's boots.
—Quinn makes Jim give it back and says he's going to send Jim away.
—Helmholtz destroys the trumpet.

OUTCOME: Jim joins Helmholtz's music class and learns to play the trumpet.

BIBLIOGRAPHY Other books by Kurt Vonnegut include *Mother Night,* 1961; *God Bless You, Mr. Rosewater,* 1965; *Bluebeard,* 1987; and *Fates Worse than Death* (autobiographical), 1991.

BEFORE YOU READ

Read through the introduction on page 228 with students. Ask the class to describe Kurt Vonnegut's writing style. What stylistic characteristics did students notice in "Harrison Bergeron"? When you feel they're ready to begin the lesson, have students complete the prereading activity—**a think-pair-and-share**—on page 228.

Motivation Strategy

Tell students that this story is about a boy who is totally out of control. Ask for suggestions on how to handle a child who lashes out at everyone and everything.

ENGAGING STUDENTS You might further engage students by telling them the story is about a child who has moved from foster home to foster home. Ask students to explain why this sort of life might be difficult.

Vocabulary Building

Help students use **context** as they read to figure out the meanings of difficult words. Remind them to pay particular attention to key vocabulary words for the lesson: *remorse, scar, expired, cadenza,* and *blasphemy.* The footnotes define some of these words for students, although you'll want to encourage them to try to define on their own before checking the footnote. Help them get into the habit of using their own "built-in" dictionaries. It's faster, easier, and makes reading more enjoyable.

For more practice defining in context, see the **Vocabulary** blackline master, page 272.

STRATEGY LESSON: SUFFIXES Write the following suffixes and words that have these suffixes on the board: *-er* (more), *-able* (that can be, inclined to), and *–ful* (full of, showing). You might write *fast + -er* (more fast), *use + -able* (that can be used), and *faith + -ful* (full of faith). Since the suffix *-able* forms adjectives from verbs or nouns, students should be able to come up with additional words with this suffix. If not, write these words on the board: *enjoyable, answerable, perishable,* and *fashionable.* Emphasize that these words might look difficult, but they may not be when they are divided into their separate parts.

For additional practice with this strategy, see the **Vocabulary** blackline master, page 272.

Prereading Strategies

Students are asked to complete a **think-pair-and-share** before they begin reading "The Kid Nobody Could Handle." A think-pair-and-share can help students become actively involved in a selection even before they begin reading. In addition, this activity can help refine students' ability to work cooperatively in a group. During the "pair" exercise, students should build upon others' ideas to answer the questions.

QUICKWRITE As an alternate prereading strategy, ask students to do a **quickwrite**. Read the first paragraph of the story aloud while students follow along in their books. Then have them do a one-minute quickwrite about a topic you assign. For example, you might have them write about "kids at risk" or "teacher-student relationships." Remind them that a quickwrite can't be "right" or "wrong." Quickwrites are meant to help readers begin connecting their own thoughts and ideas to a story or article.

Spanish-Speaking Students

"El chico que nadie podía aguantar" se trata de los empeños fútiles de un maestro de música en ayudar a uno de sus estudiantes penosos. Jim es un adolescente que se siente abandonado y aislado. Como resultado de su frustración y desilusión, intenta destruir el colegio a que asiste. El maestro le da su trompeta preciosa, esperando que pueda aliviar el espíritu del chico. Los dos aprenden, sin embargo, que antes de que uno puede amar a otra cosa, primero hay que amar a sí mismo.

READ

Encourage students to list their **questions** as they read. Their during-reading questions can help keep students involved in the story and perhaps provide interesting subject matter for an after-reading discussion. Model the kinds of questions that might occur to students as they read, such as "Why does Jim act this way?" and "Why does Helmholtz care about Jim?"

Response Strategy

PREDICTION As an alternate or additional strategy, have students stop at one or two different points in the reading and make predictions about outcomes. Have them pause at the bottom of page 229 and say what they think Jim will do with the trumpet. Ask them to stop again at the bottom of page 232 and predict whether or not Quinn really will send Jim away. Their predictions will help hold their interest until the end of the story.

Comprehension Strategies

In a **reciprocal reading**, pairs of students alternate reading aloud to each other. Occasionally the reader will interrupt in order to ask questions designed to elicit factual and inferential responses. There are four types of questions used in a reciprocal reading: 1. questions that ask students to clarify the problem, characters, and setting; 2. questions that ask students to predict outcomes; 3. questions that ask readers to summarize the events; and 4. questions about the literature, author's message, and main idea.

DOUBLE-ENTRY JOURNAL A double-entry journal can also encourage active response to a text. For a double-entry journal, students find statements, quotations, ideas, or events in the selection, record them, and then note their thoughts and feelings. To help students get started, you might ask them to respond to these two quotations:

• "Isn't there anything you care about but ripping, hacking, bending, rending, smashing, bashing?"

• "You're somebody, Jim. You're the boy with John Philip Sousa's trumpet!"

For additional practice, see the **Comprehension** blackline master on page 273.

Discussion Questions

COMPREHENSION 1. What is the setting of this story? (present-day; small town)

2. Why does Jim behave so badly? (He is angry about his life. He feels neglected and unloved.)

3. Who is Quinn, and what is his relationship to Jim? (He is Jim's foster-father. He owns a restaurant in town.)

CRITICAL THINKING 4. Why does Helmholtz give the trumpet to Jim? (Answers will vary. Possible: He hoped that the trumpet "would buy a soul" for him.)

5. Why does Jim make a "small cry of despair" at the end? (Answers will vary. Perhaps he feels self-doubt.)

Literary Skill

CHARACTERIZATION You might use "The Kid Nobody Could Handle" to initiate a discussion of characterization. Explain to students that writers have several different methods of establishing character. The first is to describe the character—how he or she looks, talks, acts, and so on. Another way an author can establish character is to show the person through the eyes of someone else in the story. In "The Kid Nobody Could Handle," for example, we get almost all of our information about Jim from Helmholtz and Quinn. They talk to him and about him. From their dialogue, we can find many clues about Jim's personality.

III. GATHER YOUR THOUGHTS

The goal of these prewriting activities is first to help students collect what they learned, and then to help them build a topic to write about. On the first half of page 236, students will complete a **story map** that shows them how to organize setting, characters, problem, major events, and outcome. Work with students to be sure they understand the major conflict of the story. Questions such as "What's Jim problem?" and "Why does he act the way he does?" can move students toward the main idea of the selection.

Prewriting Strategies

QUICKWRITE The second part of page 236 asks students to complete a quickwrite about the selection. Since the writing assignment is to write a new episode for "The Kid Nobody Could Handle," you might post these topics on the board and ask students to keep one in mind as they are writing:

- Band C's first spring concert
- Helmholtz and his wife invite Jim over for Sunday dinner.
- Quinn lays down the law with Jim and gives him a new set of rules to live by.
- A fire breaks out in Quinn's diner; Jim saves the day.
- A group of kids tease Jim about his trumpet; the "new" Jim responds without fighting.

For more practice, see the **Prewriting and Writing** blackline master on page 274.

IV. WRITE

Allow plenty of time for students to plan, write, and revise their **story episodes**. You might assign writing partners who can keep an eye on each other's writing throughout the process. When they've finished their rough drafts, ask students to revise using the **Writers' Checklist** as a guide.

Consider using this writing rubric for a quick assessment of students' writing.

WRITING RUBRIC Do students' stories

- describe and develop a new episode about Jim?
- include detailed descriptions of events and characters?
- stay consistent with the framework of Vonnegut's story?

Grammar, Usage, and Mechanics

You also might take this opportunity to teach a mini-lesson on punctuation. If necessary, remind students about the rules for end punctuation. A statement ends with a period; a question ends with a question mark; an exclamation ends with an exclamation point; and a command ends with either a period or an exclamation point.

Incorrect: Isn't Jim a mess. He can't find his way out of a paper bag?

Correct: Isn't Jim a mess? He can't find his way out of a paper bag!

V. WRAP-UP

Encourage students to look carefully at the **Readers' Checklist** on page 238. Tell them that you're interested in their responses to the story. Ask them to explain what was difficult or **easy** about Vonnegut's writing style.

Assessment

For a comprehension check, ask students to complete the **Assessment** blackline master on page 275.

Name _____

VOCABULARY

Words from the Selection

DIRECTIONS Answer these questions that use words from the selection. Then write the meaning of the underlined words on the lines.

1. If you feel <u>remorse</u>, do you feel sorry or angry?

_____

2. Would you have a <u>scar</u> on your skin or in your hair?

_____

3. If a person has <u>expired</u>, is she still alive?

_____

4. Is <u>blasphemy</u> an insult or a compliment?

_____

5. Is a <u>cadenza</u> a part of a musical work or a move in gymnastics?

_____

Strategy Lesson: Suffixes

DIRECTIONS Add one of the three suffixes in the box to each of the words below. Then use each new word in a sentence of your own.

```
-er   =   more
-able =   that can be, liable to be
-ful  =   full of, showing
```

6. slow   + _____

_____

7. great   + _____

_____

8. break   + _____

_____

9. harm   + _____

_____

10. care   + _____

_____

Name _____

COMPREHENSION
Storyboard

DIRECTIONS Before you can write a continuation or a new episode, you need to be sure you understand the original story.

Use this storyboard to record the events of "The Kid Nobody Could Handle." Draw pictures of story events in the boxes. Then write a short caption underneath each picture.

Storyboard: "The Kid Nobody Could Handle"

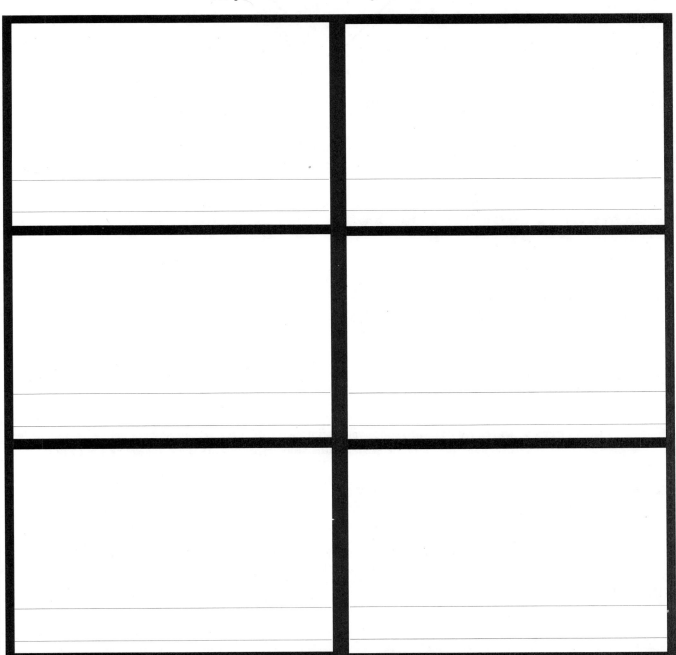

Name _____

PREWRITING AND WRITING
Writing a Story

DIRECTIONS **STEP 1.** **PLAN.** Use this story pie to plan your story. Fill in as much information as you can and give as many details as you like.

Story Pie: A New Episode for "The Kid Nobody Could Handle"

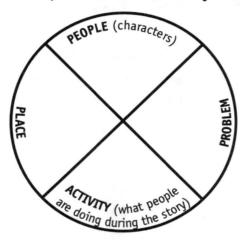

STEP 2. **WRITE.** Most writers will tell you to write the middle of your story before you write the beginning or the end. This is because it's easier to describe the action than it is to describe the characters or setting.

the middle of my story
_____
_____
_____
_____
_____

STEP 3. **WRITE AN OPENING.** Once you've finished writing the action, go back and write an opening paragraph that sets the scene for the story. Explain who's there and where the story takes place.

my opening
_____
_____

STEP 4. **WRITE A CLOSING.** Finish by writing the closing paragraph. Tie up any loose ends. Leave your readers wanting to hear a little bit more.

My closing
_____
_____

Name _____

ASSESSMENT

Multiple-Choice Test

DIRECTIONS On the blanks provided, write the letter of the best answer for each question.

_____ 1. What does Jim get in trouble for at the beginning of the story?
   A. being disrespectful   C. destroying property
   B. skipping class   D. smoking at school

_____ 2. What musical instrument does Helmholtz give to Jim?
   A. a saxophone   C. a guitar
   B. a trumpet   D. a keyboard

_____ 3. What does Helmholtz ask Jim to do with the musical instrument?
   A. smash it   C. take good care of it
   B. hide it   D. clean it up

_____ 4. What is so special about the musical instrument?
   A. It is brand new.   C. It is autographed by Jim's father.
   B. It was owned by John Philip Sousa.   D. It was Helmholtz's childhood instrument.

_____ 5. What kind of shoes is Jim wearing at the restaurant?
   A. sneakers   C. his old boots
   B. Oxfords   D. a brand new pair of boots

_____ 6. What does Quinn say he is going to do with Jim?
   A. give him another chance C. send him to another foster home
   B. let him live with Helmholtz D. none of the above

_____ 7. How does Helmholtz react to Quinn's idea of sending Jim away?
   A. He sadly agrees.   C. He decides to have Jim live with him.
   B. He begs him not to.   D. all of the above

_____ 8. Why does Helmholtz smash the trumpet?
   A. It was broken anyway.   C. He realizes it means nothing to Jim.
   B. He is angry with Jim.   D. none of the above

_____ 9. How does Jim feel when he sees the smashed trumpet?
   A. pity   C. that someone really cares about him
   B. fear   D. all of the above

_____ 10. How does Helmholtz feel at the end of the story?
   A. angry   C. sad
   B. desperate   D. hopeful

Short-Essay Test

Why do you think Jim decides to play in the band?

THE GOOD DAUGHTER

II. Read

How did the dry cleaner's words affect Caroline?
(They upset Caroline.)

What 2–3 things have you learned so far about Caroline?
(Caroline does not speak Korean as easily as she does English. Caroline is unsure of her identity. Caroline grew up feeling more American than Korean.)

Why did Caroline feel like she let down her parents?
(Caroline's parents sacrificed a lot so Caroline could enjoy a privileged and comfortable life in America. By not becoming a lawyer and by dropping out of graduate school, she feels she took unfair advantage of her parents' sacrifices.)

What does Caroline consider "the rocks in the path" of her life?
(Caroline sees her cultural dilemma—her confusion about her identity and her struggle to please herself and her parents—as "the rocks in the path" of her life.)

Vocabulary

1 queries
2 flippant
3 mirthless
4 flinched
5 abyss
6 im + possible = not possible
7 mis + pronounce = pronounce incorrectly
8 un + satisfied = not satisfied
9 dis + obey = not obey
10 dis + integrating = not integrating, falling apart

III. Gather Your Thoughts

CAROLINE WANTS TO BE...	THE HUANGS WANT CAROLINE TO BE...
1. a writer	1. a lawyer
2. able to speak Korean	2. fully assimilated into America
3. free to study, behave, and marry as she pleases	3. predictable—to study, behave, and marry as they see fit.

Topic: Finding an Identity — growing up, making decisions, understanding what you want

1–3. Students' answers will vary.

Assessment

1 A   6 C
2 B   7 B
3 C   8 A
4 C   9 B
5 D   10 D

BRIDGES

II. Read

What I've learned about Mr. Dean:
(Mr. Dean died in 1986. Mr. Dean worked hard his entire life. Mr. Dean got into trouble with the law for refusing to compromise his personal dignity.)

What I know about Mrs. Dean:
(Mrs. Dean was good looking. Mrs. Dean was poor, but driven to succeed. Mrs. Dean worked hard both outside and inside the home.)

What I know about the narrator:
(The narrator loved to read and write. The narrator gradually distanced himself from his less educated parents. The narrator immersed himself into rough street life when he discovered he couldn't afford to go to college. The narrator's relations with his parents, and especially with his father cooled over the years. As his father neared death, the narrator realized how much he needed his father's approval.)

What I know about the Dean family:
(Mr. Dean needed help with reading, but told wonderful stories. Mr. and Mrs. Dean raised the narrator to be imaginative and to appreciate hard work. The Dean family provided the narrator with the tools to build a better life for himself.)

Vocabulary

1 tenets
2 voraciously
3 refrained
4 angst
5 juvenile
6 persuaded
7 easily angered
8 important
9 money; pay
10 judgment

Assessment

1 A   6 C
2 C   7 B
3 B   8 A
4 D   9 A
5 C   10 D

PILOTS' REFLECTIONS

I. Before You Read

How long ago was World War I?
(World War I began in 1914 and ended in 1918.)
How did countries use planes during the war?
(At first, planes were used to drop bombs and to explore areas below from high above. Later they were used in battle.)
What did W. S. Douglas do when he saw an enemy plane?
(W. S. Douglas waved at the enemy.)

Vocabulary
1–5 Students' sentences will vary.
6 a three-wheeled vehicle
7 plane having two wings on each side
8 plane having three wings on each side
9 able to speak three languages
10 able to speak two languages

II. Read

Summarize what just happened.
(The narrator described his first encounter with an enemy German pilot during World War I. Unarmed and unprepared for battle, he was in the air only to take pictures of a trench system. The German pilot was carrying out a project of his own. Despite the fact they were at war, neither pilot fired at the other.)
Summarize the problem von Richthofen faces.
(Von Richthofen has battled an enemy English pilot for nearly 15 minutes. He is determined to shoot him down. When he is in the right position, von Richthofen fires his machine guns only to discover he is out of ammunition.)

III. Gather Your Thoughts
Students' answers will vary.

detail
W.S. Douglas encountered an enemy pilot while taking pictures from his plane.

detail
W. S. Douglas and the German pilot did not fire at each other because of a code of sympathy they shared.

The writer wants to say Battles in the air were unpredictable

detail
Von Richthofen was surprised by how long he had been battling the English pilot.

detail
Von Richthofen discovered he had run out of ammunition just as he prepared to shoot the enemy.

Assessment
1 A
2 A
3 C
4 B
5 D
6 B
7 C
8 B
9 D
10 A

ADVENTURES OF THE U-202

II. Read

Will the captain still torpedo the ship after seeing the horses? Why?
(Yes, the captain will still torpedo the ship because that is his mission.)

Vocabulary
1 nephew
2 starboard
3 rudder
4 hare
5 insane
6 thing that steams
7 having to do with murder
8 full of desire
9 without a point
10 thing that fries

III. Gather Your Thoughts

A. FIND A TOPIC
"Adventures of the U-202" is about an English sailor who helped track and sink an enemy steamer during World War I.
B. LIST DETAILS (Students' answers will vary.)
(4–5 possible details include: Baron Speigel carefully and silently observes an enemy steamer from a submarine. Through calculation and the plotting of points, the sailor determines the exact moment at which to strike the steamer. When he has located the steamer's position in the water, Baron Spiegel looks through his periscope and sees the people and animals he is about to destroy. He fires the torpedo that sinks the steamer, and secures victory for the English.)

Assessment
1 D   6 C
2 C   7 C
3 D   8 A
4 A   9 B
5 C   10 A

YOU'RE BEING SO GOOD, SO KIND

III. Gather Your Thoughts

A. UNDERSTAND CHARACTERS

Students' answers will vary.

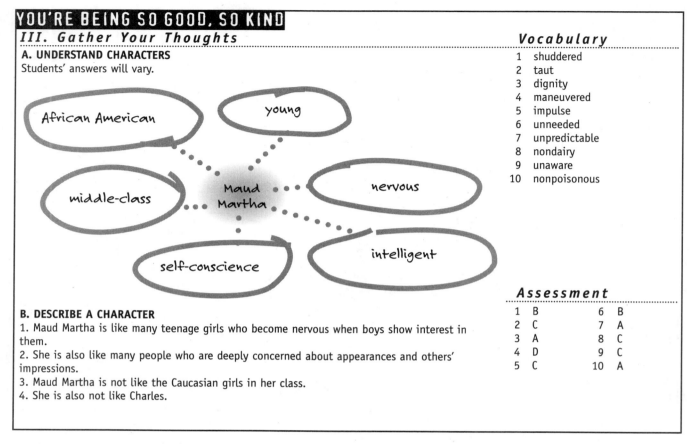

B. DESCRIBE A CHARACTER

1. Maud Martha is like many teenage girls who become nervous when boys show interest in them.
2. She is also like many people who are deeply concerned about appearances and others' impressions.
3. Maud Martha is not like the Caucasian girls in her class.
4. She is also not like Charles.

Vocabulary

1 shuddered
2 taut
3 dignity
4 maneuvered
5 impulse
6 unneeded
7 unpredictable
8 nondairy
9 unaware
10 nonpoisonous

Assessment

1	B	6	B
2	C	7	A
3	A	8	C
4	D	9	C
5	C	10	A

MAUD MARTHA AND NEW YORK

II. Read

What does Maud Martha like most about New York?
(Maud Martha like the stylish way of life in New York—the fancy clothes, the lavish furniture, the gourmet food.)

Finish these sentences.
1. For Maud Martha, New York means the essence of what life should be like.
2. Maud Martha wants to be a part of the New York life style she has dreamed about.
3. She doesn't want to be stuck in the same town and life she has always known.

Write 6 or more adjectives about Maud Martha and New York.
1. ambitious
2. imaginative
3. determined
4. worldly
5. idealistic
6. open-minded

Vocabulary

1 antique
2 figurines
3 plush
4 caviar
5 pore
6 harsh
7 flickering or wavering
8 decorative plants
9 hazy
10 distant or far away

Assessment

1	D	6	C
2	C	7	D
3	A	8	A
4	D	9	B
5	A	10	B

LEGAL ALIEN AND IMMIGRANTS

III. Gather Your Thoughts

A. BRAINSTORM

Red, white, and blue

apple pie

Bombarded by symbols

blonde hair, blue eyes

typical names

Vocabulary

1 A paneled office might have wood panels or boards on the walls.
2 yes. *Exotic* means "strangely beautiful."
3 around the edges. *Fringe* means "outer edges."
4 no. *Discomfort* means "uneasiness" or "lack of comfort."
5 yes. *Bilateral* means "having two sides."
6 making or writing a rough copy
7 speaking easily and rapidly
8 written or printed with a hyphen

Assessment

1	B	6	B
2	D	7	C
3	A	8	A
4	D	9	C
5	D	10	B

A SIMPLE PROPOSITION

II. Read

SETTING
The story takes place in Boston during the narrator's last year of high school.

PROBLEM
The problem that the narrator wants to solve is her insecurity about being so smart in math and being viewed as an outsider at school.

GOAL
The narrator wants to be asked to the prom.

PLOT CHART List in order 3 things that have happened so far. (Students' answers will vary.)

1. Emma goes to her math class.

2 Emma and her rival, Arthur, find an error in a solution to a math problem.

3 It is announced that Arthur and Emma have won the Sterns Mathematics prize and made it to the finals.

CHARACTER DEVELOPMENT

EMMA
ARTHUR

at the beginning Emma is insecure about how other people view her and wants desperately to fit in. Arthur is arrogant and proud.

at the end Emma doesn't care what other people think about her and decides to be true to herself. Arthur is arrogant, proud, and conniving.

CLIMAX
The high point of the story is when Emma decides not to accept Arthur's proposition.

RESOLUTION
Emma's goal to go to the prom is not realized.

Vocabulary

1–5 Students' sentences will vary
6 cannot be measured
7 partly final
8 not personal
9 lack of courage
10 not attractive

Assessment

1	B	6	A
2	A	7	B
3	A	8	C
4	D	9	D
5	D	10	C

THE CYCLOPS' CAVE

I. Before You Read

PREVIEW CARD

Who are the Cyclopes?

(The Cyclopes are one-eyed, beastly giants who live on a far-away island.)

Why might Ulysses feel sorry for the Cyclopes?

(Ulysses might feel sorry for the Cyclopes because they were expelled from Mount Olympus, where they once made thunderbolts for Zeus, and sent to live miserable lives on an island.)

How will the Cyclopes feel about Ulysses coming onto their island?

(They will want to kill him and his crew.)

II. Read

Story Frame

1 Ulysses and his crew disembark on the island of the Cyclopes, hoping to find food and shelter. Polyphemus traps Ulysses and his men in his cave, where he plans to kill and eat them all.

2 Ulysses organizes their escape by getting the Cyclops drunk, calling himself Nobody, and then blinding the Cyclops.

3 Ulysses and his men hide under the bellies of the Cyclops' goats and wander out of the cave.

III. Gather Your Thoughts

The sequence should be as follows:
1. Ulysses and his men arrive on the island of the Cyclopes.
2. Polyphemus traps them in his cave and eats a few of the men.
3. Ulysses organizes a plan of escape. He gets Polyphemus drunk, tells him his name is Nobody, and pokes his eye out with his sword.
4. Ulysses and his men hide under the bellies of goats and wander out of the cave.
5. Polyphemus realizes the men have escaped but his inability to see, and the fact that his fellow Cyclopes think "Nobody" has hurt him, make him powerless to capture them.
6. On board his ship, Ulysses foolishly shouts out his real name to Polyphemus. The Cyclops then prays to Poseidon to curse the rest of Ulysses's journey home.

Vocabulary
1 savage
2 vigil
3 heed
4 niche
5 aghast
6 go ashore from or get off a ship
7 not watered or pure
8 took off or unfastened
9 not conscious or not awake
10 not wanted or not desired

Assessment
1	D	6	B
2	C	7	D
3	A	8	A
4	C	9	A
5	C	10	B

HERCULES

I. Before You Read

1. "This was the first time he dealt a fatal blow without intending it."
2. "Then his sanity returned. He found himself in his bloodstained hall, the dead bodies of his sons and his wife beside him."
3. "So I will die."
4. "The eleventh labor was the most difficult of all so far."
5. "He was never tranquil and at ease."

II. Read

What 3 words would you use to describe Hercules?

(Students' answers will vary.)
1. strong
2. remorseful
3. heroic

Why did Hercules kill his family?

(The jealous Hera made him mad and sent him into a murderous rage.)

Why does Hercules agree to perform the twelve labors?

(Hercules wants to pay for his crime and bring himself peace.)

What are the labors up to this point in the story?
1. the killing of the lion of Nemea
2. the killing of the Hydra
3. the capture of a stag with horns of gold
4. the capture of a great boar
5. the cleaning of the Augean stables
6. the driving away of the Stymphalian birds
7. the capture of a savage bull in Crete
8. the capture of man-eating mares

Character Analysis (Students' answers will vary.)

How the character acts and feels: Hercules is brave and fierce, but emotional as well.
How the character looks: Hercules is strong, tall, and heroic-looking.
How others feel about the character: Hercules has allies like Theseus and enemies like Hera.

Vocabulary
1 comes all of a sudden. *Impulse* means "sudden wish."
2 confused. *Bewilderment* means "confusion."
3 yes. *Defiled* means "made dirty or polluted."
4 hate. *Loathing* means "hatred."
5 yes. *Immortal* means "unable to die."
6 predict
7 chronology
8 capture
9 sympathy
10 captive

Assessment
1	B	6	B
2	D	7	A
3	C	8	C
4	A	9	C
5	A	10	D

III. Gather Your Thoughts

1. Wears lion skin; looks full-grown and strong. 2. Kills his family; shows courage.
3. Like an animal; like a god or hero.

THE RICHER, THE POORER

II. Read

What have you learned about Lottie up to this point?
(Lottie is stingy with her money, bent upon working in order to earn more and more.)
What have you learned about her sister Bess?
(Bess is not concerned about money, preferring to spend rather than save.)

Vocabulary

1–5 Students' paragraphs will vary.
6 tender
7 growing
8 meagerly
9 boyfriend
10 partly
11 meet
12 delicious

III. Gather Your Thoughts

A. ORGANIZE DETAILS

Assessment

1	A	6	A
2	C	7	B
3	C	8	A
4	C	9	B
5	D	10	A

LOTTIE

1. Lottie is stingy and obsessed with saving money.
2. Lottie has worked hard her entire life so she won't have to worry about not having enough money.
3. Lottie becomes greedy in her older age, not wanting to share her home or earnings with anyone—not even her sister.

BESS

1. Bess is free spirited and financially unstable.
2. Bess has traveled all over the world, living hand-to-mouth and enjoying time with her husband.
3. Bess feels sad about the life Lottie has chosen to lead.

THE RICHER, THE POORER continued

III. Gather Your Thoughts

(Students' answers will vary.)
A. FIND THE THEME
(Life is too short to be taken for granted.)
B. FIND SUPPORTING DETAILS
What does Bess say or do that supports this theme?
(Bess tells Lottie fascinating stories of her travels to distant places, speaking with great emotion and knowledge drawn from her first-hand experiences.)
What does Lottie say or do that explains this theme?
(Lottie is most happy after she cleans and decorates her house to make it look nice for her sister.)
How have the characters changed? What changes in them help support his theme?
(Lottie admits that she has not made good use of her life. She realizes she has wasted the years saving for the future and denying herself personal pleasures. Bess's outlook on life hasn't changed but her situation has changed. With the death of her husband, she is not able to roam the world with him anymore. She now needs her sister's support.)

Vocabulary

1 no. A *parlor* is a room set aside for the entertainment of visitors
2 no. *Gleaming* means "shining."
3 no. *Clarity* means "clearness."
4 in the kitchen. *Basting* means "moistening with liquid."
5 no. *Finery* means "fine things."
6 bright
7 ignoring
8 happiness
9 smooth
10 flexible
11 serious
12 bearable
13 ugly
14 unhappy

Assessment

1	B	6	A
2	B	7	D
3	C	8	A
4	A	9	A
5	D	10	D

ANIMALS UNITE!

II. Read

What is the main point Major is making? Is he serious?
(Major says the lives of animals are miserable because they are controlled by humans. Yes, he is serious.)

III. Gather Your Thoughts

| A. ORGANIZE IDEAS |

Major's Speech

PROBLEM	SOLUTION
Poor living conditions for animals	→ Remove man from the scene
Victims of overwork, slaughter, and a lack of individual freedom	→ → → Work hard to overthrow the human race. Focus on rebellion and never lose sight of the goal.

B. DESCRIPTIVE WORDS
(Possibilities include: stout, majestic-looking, wise, benevolent.)

Vocabulary

1 killed
2 done away with
3 comfortably settled
4 young offspring of a horse
5 braided
6 E
7 H
8 C
9 A
10 J

Assessment

1	D	6	C
2	B	7	A
3	C	8	B
4	C	9	D
5	D	10	C

THE FAST

II. Read

What effect did Gandhi's fast have on others? Explain.
(The laborers were shocked and amazed by Gandhi's determination and loyalty to the cause. They wanted to fast. The mill-owners were angered by Gandhi's position, but equally dedicated to their cause.)

STORY FRAME

1. THIS STORY TAKES PLACE IN
India.

2. Gandhi IS THE MAIN CHARACTER IN THIS STORY

3. WHO IS
a leader of
India's poor.

4. A PROBLEM OCCURS WHEN
an escalating dispute between laborers and mill-owners leads Gandhi to get involved on behalf of the laborers.

5. AFTER THAT, HE
decides to fast in order to bring about a peaceful solution.

6. THE PROBLEM IS SOLVED WHEN
Gandhi's fast creates an atmosphere of goodwill among the laborers and mill-owners.

7. THE STORY ENDS WITH
the two groups deciding to end the dispute by appointing an arbitrator and ending the strike.

Vocabulary

1 a
2 a
3 c
4 c
5 b
6 bare
7 great
8 die/break
9 right
10 bear

Assessment

1	C	6	D
2	C	7	B
3	C	8	A
4	B	9	B
5	A	10	C

A SEA OF DUNES

I. Before You Read

What part of the world does this article describe?
(The Namib Desert)
(Students' answers will vary.)
The photo of the oryx tells me that animals inhabit the Namib Desert.
The photo of camels tells me that they are an essential part of people's lives in the Namib Desert.

II. READ

oryx
The oryx adapts to the desert by getting food and water from the sweet grass. Because its body temperature is so high, the blood that goes to the brain is first cooled.
palmetto gecko
The palmetto gecko adapts to the desert by licking the moisture from its lidless eyes.

beetles
Beetles adapt to the desert by standing nearly upside down and allowing water to accumulate on their bodies. They then drink the water when it trickles down.
sidewinding adder
The sidewinding adder adapts to the desert heat by finding coolness in the sand. It captures prey by burying itself in the sand and leaving its eyes exposed.
grouse
The sand grouse adapts to the dryness of the desert by flying miles away to a water hole, where it collects moisture in its feathers. It then flies back so its chicks can sip the moisture from the wet feathers.

Vocabulary

1 cascading=falling in a series of stages, like a waterfall
2 precipitation=water antifreeze or moisture
3 adaptation=change in an animal that allows it to fit in with and live longer in its environment
4 capillaries=tiny blood vessels
5 oryx=an African antelope

III. Gather Your Thoughts

A. FIND THE MAIN IDEA
Main Idea
In order to survive, animals in the Namib Desert adapt to their surroundings.
B. ADD SUPPORTING DETAILS
(Students' answers will vary.)
What desert is like
"For part of the year a hot, dry wind blows from the east bringing food—a scattering of organic particles from which desert plants draw nourishment."
Example of Survival
"The palmetto gecko, for instance, licks moisture from its lidless eyes."

Another Example
"The sidewinding adder finds not only coolness in the sand but also camouflage."
The author's point was to show the many ways animals adapt to their surroundings.

Assessment

1	D	6	B
2	D	7	D
3	A	8	B
4	B	9	C
5	D	10	D

THE WIDOWS OF THE RESERVES

I. Before You Read

Which sentence appears first in the story? Which one appears last?
a. appears first, b. appears last.
What can you learn about the "widows" from these sentences? (Student's answers will vary.)
(The widows lead lonely, difficult lives of labor and poverty.)

II. Read

What makes farming difficult for the women?
(They have poor ploughing tools, and must farm either by themselves or with the help of their young children.)
Are methods of farming to blame for their problems?

Explain why or why not.
(Students' answers will vary.)
(The methods of farming are partially to blame because they require a great deal of physical labor. The widows' problems are also due to their having to labor by themselves.)
How do they hope to free themselves of poverty?
(They hope their children's education will eventually free them from poverty.)

Vocabulary

1 bewildered
2 starvation
3 strenuous
4 scraggy
5 emaciated
6 neighborhood
7 brotherhood
8 kingdom
9 filmdom
10 parenthood

III. Gather Your Thoughts

A. REFLECT
What might it mean for the family when a woman gets a letter form her husband?
(A letter could be either good or bad, promising money or word of work, or bringing news of illness or incarceration.)

B. COMPARE AND CONTRAST

MEN: live in work centers / work wherever they can / work with other men

(overlap) lonely / poor / work hard

WOMEN: live in the Reserves / work in their land / work alone or with their children

Assessment

1	C	6	C
2	A	7	B
3	D	8	D
4	C	9	C
5	C	10	A

RAMIRO

I. Before You Read

Ramiro's father used to be in a gang.

set in Chicago

Ramiro

Ramiro's family is Hispanic.

Ramiro is in danger of entering gang life.

Ramiro is a teenager.

II. Read

Why is Ramiro in danger? Why is his father worried?
(Ramiro is in danger because he's been in trouble at school for fighting with students, and has bad relations with gang members. His father is worried because Ramiro continues to fight and disobey the law.)

III. Gather Your Thoughts

A. ORGANIZE

1. The Rodriguez family moves to a house in Humboldt Park, where close living quarters and the inherent danger of the neighborhood make life tense.

2. Ramiro's behavior worsens, as he's been suspended from school for getting involved in a gang fight.

3. One of the gangs has placed an S.O.S. contract on Ramiro, and he is sent to another school.

4. Ramiro is kicked out of the new school, sent to jail for fighting, and given stitches to heal a wound above his eye.

5. Rodriguez admits he too was in a gang as a teenager and barely survived the experience.

6. Rodriguez is determined that Ramiro not fall victim to street life and violence.

Vocabulary

1 dirty. *Scum* means "dirty or worthless matter."
2 It will occur. *Imminent* means "about to occur."
3 leave her alone. *Beleaguered* means "harassed" or "filled with trouble."
4 people. *Personnel* means "people employed by an organization."
5 winter. An *icicle* is formed by freezing water
6 not tolerable
7 not expected
8 placed apart or away from
9 not likely
10 the reverse of obedience

Assessment

1	B	6	D
2	C	7	B
3	C	8	D
4	B	9	D
5	D	10	C

RAMIRO continued

II. Read

Whom or what is Ramiro running from?
(Ramiro is running from his father and family.)
What do you predict Rodriguez will say to his son?
(Students' answers will vary.)
What do you think Rodriguez means when he says that his voice cracked "open the winter sky"?
(Rodriguez means that he saw and heard his former self in Ramiro, whose harsh words were loud and fierce enough to crack "open the winter sky."

III. Gather Your Thoughts

A. SUMMARIZE

1. How does Rodriguez know that gang life is dangerous?
(Rodriguez used to be in a gang, and he has witnessed the violence and harsh realities of street life.)
2. What kind of life does Rodriguez want for Ramiro?
(Rodriguez wants Ramiro to lead a safe and productive life.)
3. What is his relationship with his son in this excerpt from *Always Running*?
(Rodriguez has a tense and confrontational relationship with Ramiro, whom he sees declining into a dark and dangerous existence.)

B. ORGANIZE

How Ramiro feels
Ramiro feels annoyed by his family's pressure to be a good kid.

What Ramiro does
Ramiro continues to disobey his family and the law.

Ramiro

How I feel about him
(Students' answers will vary.)

How his father feels about him
His father is very worried and desperate to help him.

Vocabulary

1 *Ultimatum* means "final statement."
2 *Scurried* means "ran off."
3 *Dissipating* means "disappearing."
4 *Hysteria* means "uncontrollable emotion."
5 *Frigid* means "extremely cold."
6 vastness
7 election
8 prediction
9 shyness
10 Illness

Assessment

1	D	6	A
2	C	7	D
3	C	8	D
4	C	9	B
5	C	10	C

REFUSING SERVICE

II. Read

The story takes place (in a barber shop).
(Banks, the barber, and a prospective Negro customer) **are characters in the story.**
A problem happens when (Banks refuses to cut the Negro's hair).
After the problem develops, this happens next:
(Banks and the other customers in the shop throw the Negro out.)
How does the incident end?
(The Negro is thrown out and everyone goes about their business, secure in the knowledge that no harm was done to their jobs or livelihoods.)
Why do you think Hurston tells this story?
(She probably tells the story to show the tremendous risks and difficulties associated with the fight for civil rights.)

Vocabulary

1 belligerently
2 snarled
3 sanction
4 militant
5 crusader
6 pedometer
7 pedicure
8 manuscript
9 curator
10 scribble

III. Gather Your Thoughts

(Students' answers will vary.)
B. SUPPORT AN OPINION

Self-interest is often more important than any other loyalties.

FACT | "Don't argue with him. Throw him out of here!" And in a minute, barbers, customers all lathered and hair half cut, and porters, were all helping to throw the Negro out."

FACT | "I did not participate in the mêlée, but I wanted him thrown out too. My business was threatened."

FACT | "But here were ten Negro barbers, three porters, and two manicurists all stirred up at the threat of our living through loss of patronage."

Assessment

1	A	6	C
2	B	7	B
3	D	8	B
4	B	9	C
5	D	10	D

TIME TO LOOK AND LISTEN

I. Before You Read

Skimming

PLACES
America, Athens, Beirut, Lebanon, Israel, Middle East, Oklahoma City

PEOPLE
Arabs, Americans, Muslims, Jews, Christians

KEY WORDS AND PHRASES (Students' answers will vary)
"Discrimination is not unique to America." "As I grew older and began to form my own opinions, my embarrassment lessened and my anger grew." "Education is the key to understanding. As Americans we need to take a little time to listen carefully to what is around us and not rush to judgment without knowing all the facts."

Vocabulary

1 b
2 a
3 b
4 a
5 c
6 monotheism
7 monotone
8 theology
9 polytheism
10 polygraph

II. Read

(Students' answers will vary.)
PROBLEM
Asfahani is the only Arab in her class at school at a time when discrimination against Arabs is high.

ISSUE: Asfahani feels she has to lie to others about where her parents are from and actually tries to forget how to speak Arabic.
ISSUE: Asfahani is overwhelmed and burdened by the stereotypes of Arabs, feeling she always has to explain herself to others.
SOLUTION
Asfahani says it is essential that Americans respect other people's differences and not make rash assumptions about their lives.

III. Gather Your Thoughts

A. LOOK CLOSELY
1. "My classmates told me I came from an uncivilized, brutal place, that Arabs were by nature anti-American, and I believed them." "I tried to forget the Arabic I knew, because if I didn't I'd be forever linked to murderers." "The Arab world is a medley of people of different religions; not every Arab is a Muslim, and vice versa."

Assessment

1	B	6	C
2	C	7	A
3	C	8	B
4	B	9	D
5	D	10	B

A SOLDIER'S LETTER HOME

II. Read

Why are the prisoners crying?
(They are crying because they feel relieved and incredulous at the same time, unable to control the emotion of being liberated from the Nazis.)

Why do they refuse to move away from the truck?
(They refuse to move away form the truck because they can't believe that the liberators have enough food for everyone.)

How does the soldier feel as he looks at the prisoners?
(The soldier feels shocked and saddened by the prisoners' condition and wants to help them any way he can.)

Why does the soldier wish that "130 million American people" had seen what he saw?
(He wishes people could have seen what he saw so they could more keenly understand the tragedy of the Holocaust and know never to allow it to happen again.)

Why does he want to shoot the SS man? What stops him?
He wants to shoot the SS man to punish him for the horrible crimes he committed against the Holocaust victims. He doesn't shoot him because he would only be stooping to his level of a cold-blooded killer.

Vocabulary

1 shorter. A *kilometer* is about two-thirds of a mile.
2 cried. *Bawled* means "wept loudly."
3 slowed down. *Stunted* means "hindered; slowed down from normal growth."
4 He is opposed to leaving. *Resistance* means "opposition; attempt to fight back."
5 sad. *Pathetic* means "pitiful."
6 extraterrestrial
7 terrace
8 subterranean
9 territory
10 inter

III. Gather Your Thoughts

B. CLUSTER
How soldiers felt: shocked, saddened, sickened, angry, needed
concentration camps: prisons, crowded, places of death, places of labor, dirty
people who were in them: enslaved, overworked, abused, starved, desperate

C. UNDERSTAND
1. What date is the letter written? (May 6, 1945)
2. What is the name of the person being sent the letter? (Joan)
3. What 2 or 3 things did Cooper want to tell about in his letter? (Students' answers will vary.)
(He wanted to describe the condition of the Holocaust victims when they were liberated, his feelings upon seeing them, and his decision not to kill the SS man.)

Assessment

1	B	6	C
2	D	7	C
3	A	8	A
4	B	9	C
5	D	10	B

GOOD-BYE

III. Gather Your Thoughts

A. COLLECT INFORMATION

> **HOW GERTA ACTS**
> Gerta acts bravely.

> **WHAT GERTA THINKS**
> Gerta thinks she will never see her parents again.
> Gerta thinks that humanity will triumph in the end.

> **HOW OTHERS FEEL ABOUT GERTA**
> Her parents love her deeply.
> Merin feels she is too young to die.

Vocabulary

1 enclosure=fenced area
2 reluctantly=unwillingly
3 security=safety
4 inscription=letters or writing on something
5 embraced=hugged
6 conductor
7 produce
8 reproduce
9 introduced
10 inducement

B. LOOK AT A CHARACTER

	BEGINNING	MIDDLE	END
1. WHAT HAPPENS?	Gerta's father is taken away.	Gerta and her mother are taken away. They watch the Nazis abuse the Jews of the Ghetto.	Gerta is separated from her mother.
2. GERTA'S REACTION	Gerta weeps and wishes to grieve alone.	Gerta is strong, clinging to her mother for support, but becomes more and more afraid.	Gerta struggles not to look for her mother, then cries out for her.

Assessment

1	D	6	A
2	D	7	C
3	C	8	C
4	C	9	A
5	C	10	A

HARRISON BERGERON

III. Gather Your Thoughts

(Students' answers will vary.)

A. STATE THE MAIN IDEA
The story "Harrison Bergeron" shows that equality is manufactured and imposed on people.

B. SUPPORT THE MAIN IDEA
1. George is required to wear a handicap radio in his ear.
2. The ballerinas are burdened with sash weights and birdshot.
3. George has forty-seven pounds of birdshot padlocked around his neck.
4. Hazel has no mental handicap; she is already average.

Vocabulary

1 weighed down. *Burdened* means "weighed down."
2 to pain. *Winced* means "to draw back out of pain."
3 disappointment. *Envious* means "showing disappointment because someone else has what you want"
4 wet. *Clammy* means "damp and cold."
5 dance. A *ballerina* is a woman who dances in a ballet
6 transmitter
7 emit
8 transatlantic
9 exports, imports
10 transferred

Assessment

1	B	6	B
2	D	7	C
3	A	8	A
4	A	9	D
5	C	10	A

THE KID NOBODY COULD HANDLE

I. Before You Read

2. Who are some of the characters in the story?
(Jim Donnini, Quinn, Hemholtz)

II. Read

How has Hemholtz tried to help Jim?
(Hemholtz gives Jim his valuable trumpet to prove to him he has value, too. He also invites Jim to stay with him.)

Think about what happened. If this trumpet is important to Hemholtz, why did he break it?
(Hemholtz breaks the trumpet to prove that no material gift or personal treasure can change another person's behavior or feelings.)

SUMMARIZE (Students' answers will vary.)

How would you explain in your own words what Jim is feeling at the end?
(Jim has felt alone and frustrated all his life. When Hemholtz laments that "Life is no damn good," Jim feels he can finally relate to someone. He feels more hopeful about the future, knowing he is not as isolated as he once believed and can play an important role in making life better for himself and others.)

III. Gather Your Thoughts

A. USE A STORY MAP
TITLE
("The Kid Nobody Could Handle")
SETTING
(high school, diner)
CHARACTERS
(Hemholtz, Jim Donnini, Quinn)

PROBLEM
(Hemholtz struggles to help a troubled teen, Jim, whom everyone else seems to have given up on.)
MAJOR EVENTS
(Hemholtz gives Jim his precious trumpet in exchange for Jim's boots. Jim does not

respond to Hemholtz's attempts to help. Hemholtz breaks the trumpet in frustration.)
OUTCOME
(Jim feels akin to Hemholtz and takes up the trumpet. He feels less desperate about life in general.)

Vocabulary

1 sorry. *Remorse* means "deep, painful regret."
2 on your skin. *Scar* means "mark left by a healed cut or wound."
3 no. *Expired* means "died."
4 an insult. *Blasphemy* means "abuse or hatred of God or sacred things."
5 a part of a musical work. *Cadenza* means "showy part or flourish in a musical work."
6 slow+er
7 great+er
8 break+able
9 harm+ful
10 care+ful

Assessment

1	C	6	C
2	B	7	B
3	A	8	C
4	B	9	D
5	C	10	D

Index

PE signals a pupil's edition page number.

TG signals a teacher's edition page number.